The Variety of
Dream Experience

Books by Montague Ullman

Dream Telepathy
(with Stanley Krippner
and Alan Vaughan)

Working With Dreams
(with Nan Zimmerman)

The Variety of
DREAM EXPERIENCE
Expanding Our Ways
of Working With Dreams

Edited by Montague Ullman, M.D.
and Claire Limmer, M.S.

CONTINUUM • NEW YORK

ACKNOWLEDGMENTS

The authors wish to express their deepest appreciation
to Eleanor Friede for her support and encouragement,
and to Barbara Bowen for keeping us on track from the very beginning.

1987
The Continuum Publishing Company
370 Lexington Avenue, New York, N.Y. 10017

Printed in the United States of America

An Eleanor Friede Book

Library of Congress Cataloging-in-Publication Data

The Variety of dream experience.

Bibliography: p.
1. Dreams. I. Ullman, Montague. II. Limmer, Claire.
BF1078.V36 1987   154.6'3   87-584
ISBN 0-8264-0381-6

Contents

III · APPLICATIONS IN PSYCHOLOGY AND PSYCHIATRY

Introduction

In *Working With Dreams*, a book Nan Zimmerman and I wrote a number of years ago, we posed the question: Can dream work be extended safely and effectively beyond the confines of the psychotherapist's consulting room? We felt that it could, and we described a group approach to working with dreams that could meet the standards of responsible dream work and could also be entrusted to an interested public.

Since that time I have been involved in exploring and extending the small group process we developed in two directions, one toward the furthering of dream work in the community and the other in the training of psychotherapists. I have pursued these goals through workshops and training sessions held in the United States and Scandinavia and through various writings. In the training of therapists my approach was intended to give the beginning therapist a "hands-on" feeling about dreams and the healing value of dream work. In the community, as dream groups were organized in homes, churches, and schools, I became convinced that group work, as we developed it, could be placed in the hands of the general public.

To say I was gratified with the results would be an understatement. It was more a feeling of elation at witnessing the positive response from both the public and psychotherapists who were exposed to the process. What delighted me was the way that dream work touched on and opened up dormant areas of interest, liberated creative energies, and, in some instances, found new directions for those energies. My own understanding of dreams has been greatly enriched and revised because of this experience.

The past several decades have seen the emergence of many new ideas about dreams and the critical examination of old ones. The public is beginning to take a more active interest in its dream life, and a number of guides have appeared on the scene to further this endeavor. I am more and more convinced that by going beyond the privacy of the self, by sharing and working on dreams with others, we can have a most satisfying experience, one that meets a universal need to unload personal secrets in a safe environment and to meet others at deeper levels than in ordinary social intercourse.

This need is largely unmet in what we somewhat euphemistically regard as civilized society. When a supportive and stimulating structure is offered, it is amazing how responsive people are to dream work and how rapidly they acquire the skills needed to help the dreamer. Much more useful work can be done with dreams than we now are doing. We have failed to appreciate the resources in each of us that can be developed to achieve this goal. We have treated dream work as too specialized a task and have assigned it exclusively to the province of the psychoanalyst, or else we trivialize it by sweeping it under the rug, leaving people on their own to find some way of dealing with their dreams.

In short, we have the ability to be a healing influence for one another through dream work. In order for this to happen we must understand and respond to the two basic needs of the dreamer—first, to feel safe as he or she moves along this private path back into the intimate domain of the psyche, and second, to be helped to see what the dream images may be revealing that are difficult for the dreamer to see alone. I refer to the first as the Safety Factor and to the second as the Discovery Factor. For dream work to be effective, it has to meet both these needs. Anyone who is motivated enough can learn the necessary skills to accomplish this. It makes available a natural pathway toward emotional healing, toward becoming more whole, toward becoming more of what we are capable of becoming. Every therapist is aware of how powerful a tool a dream is in the therapeutic process. The point is that dream work can also provide the basis for a healing experience outside the consulting room without the formal trappings of a therapeutic arrangement. It can be therapeutic without being therapy.

The path is not easy. There are booby traps all along the way. Those who wish to pursue dream work will have to disengage from certain widespread but false notions about the nature of our dream life. These have become so deeply entrenched that they have reached the status of prevailing myths which are not recognized as such. They include the belief that the necessary skills for dream work can come only from professional training and experience and that dream work therefore should remain exclusively in the hands of the expert, that it otherwise carries a certain danger and, finally, that dream work carried on by nonprofessionals is apt to remain at a superficial level.

My experience in group dream work points in a different direction. I am convinced that it need not remain a specialized tool in the hands of the expert but that it can develop into a culturally sanctioned, generally available approach to a deeper understanding of the emotional side of our lives. The skills involved can be identified, learned, and applied by anyone interested enough to do so. They are not the exclusive result of training in psychotherapy, although one object of such training should be to develop such skills.

Is dream work dangerous? There is the possibility of danger, but it is not intrinsic to the dream or to what the dream says to the dreamer. The danger does not come from that source. It can come from a wrong approach to the dreamer. By a wrong approach I mean one that is intrusive, one that does not respect the limits set by the dreamer, one that is conducted from an authoritarian stance, one that superimposes interpretations.

A dreamer who awakens with a dream is potentially ready to be confronted by the information in that dream. However, the dreamer awake is not prepared to be quite as honest with himself as he was while dreaming. He views himself more cautiously. In dream work outside a clinical setting he is not seeking professional help but is testing his own ability to allow himself to relate to all the information embedded in the dream imagery instead of screening out whatever might not feel comfortable for his waking ego. He is there to learn to use the dream itself as a healing instrument. The ability to do this depends on how secure he is made to feel by the way the group process is structured; this, in turn, depends on how respectful the group is of the dreamer's right to manage his own defenses. In practice the factor of safety in combination with the natural curiosity of the dreamer and the support and stimulation from the group all have the effect of minimizing defensive operations and, in turn, allow meanings in the dream to come into clearer focus.

Many years as a practicing analyst have left me with some idea of what can and what cannot be achieved with dream work in individual therapy. It is true that defensive operations come into play during dream work and therapy does address that question. It is also true, however, that those operations are not immutable and that, as people experience trust in the dream group process, they also change in relation to the importance they place on maintaining their defenses. I have seen remarkable and sometimes rapid changes in this respect. In many instances they occur sooner than they might in individual therapy, where the very situation both creates as well as makes it possible to analyze resistances. The result is that profound conflicts and the deep levels of one's psyche are exposed, experienced and worked upon. As I extend my efforts to do dream work with a broader population, I find the notion of superficiality simply does not hold. Criticism on that basis is without merit.

Certain real problems are encountered when an effort is made to extend serious dream work beyond the arena of therapy. Questions of safety do arise. Any process, regardless of how intrinsically safe it may be, can be misused. It seems to me that the rewards gained by educating the public to the significance of dreams and the way to work with them in a supportive social context far exceed the risk involved. People who start at the same level of experience and are aware of the precautionary measures to be observed will do productive work. There will always be some who overestimate their capacity and present themselves as leaders without a sound grounding in leadership skills. In other words, when groups are organized at a peer level the problems that arise can generally be handled by the group. If, on the other hand, one organizes dream groups on a professional basis, taking on all comers, so to speak, it is incumbent upon that person to have had sufficient leadership training. It is then no longer a peer group but one that looks to the leader for help in gaining mastery over the process.

I do feel that mental health professionals have an important role in the extension of dream work into the community. Sweden offers a model in this respect. Since working intensively with such professionals there for over ten years, I have reached many more than I do in this country. If dream work is to extend into the community, it will depend in large measure on the attitude and willingness of therapists to appreciate the need and to lend their skills to the task of educating and training others in the skills necessary to do dream work. I stress the fact that they are skills that can be shared, and a start has to be made somewhere. Since Sweden is a small country it proved to be an ideal testing ground. Psychoanalysis came late to Sweden, and there is less of an entrenched notion that the only approach to dreams is via the analytic couch. The myth of the expert was not so strongly entrenched, particularly in relation to dreams. Professionals have been more open to participating in dream groups. In most instances they have remained involved in leadership training to the point of feeling confident of their own mastery of the dream group process. Included among these are psychiatrists, psychologists and social workers, nurses, priests engaged in pastoral counseling, and teachers interested in counseling or guidance. As a result, dream groups have been organized in hospital settings, training centers, churches, schools (gymnasia or junior college level), and in addition, in the community with partial funding from the government. In a small country the fallout from this activity is quite visible. Interest in dreams is increasing, and dream groups have been formed in almost every major city. All this offers a glimpse of what might be possible in extending safe and effective dream work to within the reach of all who are curious about their own dream life. And that includes just about everyone.

In *Working With Dreams* Nan Zimmerman and I wrote:

> Nan and I have tried to pass on the message that more can be done with our dreams than most of us are doing. Our hope is that the process developed in this book will make its

way into the systems that shape so many of our choices—
into industry and institutions, into school programs at all
educational levels. For parents and teachers who agonize
over the distance between themselves and their children
dreams offer a warm and honest connection. Dream work
could find its place in halfway houses or prisons. It could
open up something new for senior citizens at a time when
society tends to disregard or discard them. Dream appreciation can become accessible to everyone in any setting where
understanding and compassion are valued. (p.319)

The present volume is a step in the direction of the fulfillment of these expectations. All the contributors have had exposure to the group process I use, and all have linked it to their
own special areas of interest, areas as divergent as literature,
the ministry, art, political science, computer science, anthropology, and the training of psychotherapists.

This book is addressed to both the interested layman and to
the therapist who uses dreams in his practice. There has been
no attempt to cover ground dealt with elsewhere, such as the experimental studies on dreaming. We have tried rather to pull together a number of threads to weave a pattern that reflects not
only the growing interest in dreams but also the seminal effect
that dream work can have in diverse fields. The contributors to
this volume are trying to extend dream work in their own way
into their specialized fields of interest. They cut across a number of disciplines and represent a number of emerging trends.
Their range illustrates the diverse ramifications that dream
work can take. What is unique is that the work presented is
rooted in an experiential process that enriches the more abstract and theoretical levels of discourse. As it taps into the
creative source in each of us, dream work spills over and opens
other channels for creative expression. The ensuing chapters
offer only a small sample of the possibilities we are tapping into.
Our hope is that they will stimulate further exploration of the
many constructive ramifications that dream work can have in
our lives.

Claire Limmer has participated in dream workshops with me
since the very first one I held in this country in 1976. She is a
skilled dream worker. Because of a unique set of personal cir-

cumstances, she has also come to a deeply felt sense of what it means to link the notion of healing to dream work. Aspects of this are touched on in the chapter she contributed to this volume. As coeditor, she has helped shape the form and content of the book as well as taken over many of the more onerous tasks of an editor. I am profoundly grateful for her help and for the very generous way it was offered.

If we have succeeded in a small way in the rather formidable task of transforming oneirophobia (fear of dreams) into oneirophilia (love of dreams), we will have felt our efforts have been rewarded.

Montague Ullman
Ardsley, New York, 1987

The Variety of
Dream Experience

·1·

The Experiential Dream Group

MONTAGUE ULLMAN, M.D.

This chapter outlines the rationale and structure of the experiential dream group process. All the contributors to this volume have at one time or another participated in this process. For those who had considerable prior experience with dreams it added a useful dimension to their knowledge and way of practicing and teaching dream work. For some it served as an introduction to dream work and provided them with a basis for moving into it on their own and exploring its usefulness in their own lives and/or in their own disciplines. The pursuit of dreams is a serious undertaking that requires a degree of both new learning and skill mastery. The point to be emphasized is that the knowledge and skills necessary can and should be available to everyone.*

My goal in this chapter is to describe a group approach to dream work oriented to connecting the dreamer to the dream in a way that is different from the way dreams are used in a formal therapeutic situation.

In working with dream groups I find it helpful to offer some preliminary orientation to the nature of the dream and the value of dream work. The first session is devoted to a description of the phenomenology of dreaming. For those who are new to dream work a clear distinction is drawn between dreaming and the dream. Although one is derivative of the other, they occur in two profoundly different states of being. Dreaming is a function

---

* When the first person is used in any of the introductory remarks, it refers to M.U.

of the sleeping organism and occurs in repetitive cycles during the night, irrespective of recall. Its purposes are still under investigation and are by no means clearly understood despite the many theories that have been proposed. Psychoanalytic theories have ranged from the Freudian notion of the release of instinctual impulses to Jung's emphasis on communication and compensation. The experimental work on sleep and dreams over the past thirty years has ushered in a number of new approaches, such as dreams serving a sentinel function (Snyder), a vigilance function (Ullman), an information processing function (Palumbo), and a learning function (Greenberg).

The dream is something quite different. It is a memory in the waking state of some aspect of the dreaming experience. Although clearly related to dreaming it lacks the involuntary and spontaneous quality of the dreaming experience.

Dreaming consciousness differs from ordinary waking consciousness in both form and content. Dreaming consciousness is experienced in a predominantly sensory mode. While dreaming we are involuntary witnesses to a symbolic display of some aspect of our life, usually in the form of visual imagery but not exclusively so. Although borrowed from the world about us, the elements in the dream are not photographic reproductions of that world. Instead they come at us transformed into metaphorically expressive symbols that portray facets of a current life predicament in a highly specific and selective way. Everything in this form of consciousness is pressed into metaphorical usage —words, color, numbers, and other sensory impressions in addition to the visual.

Here are some examples of a "visual metaphor":

> A young man still in the throes of a difficult divorce has become seriously involved with another woman, and the issue of marriage has been raised. In his dream he sees himself leaving one hotel and walking in the street toward another hotel. While in the street he tries to put on his tie but discovers he is already wearing one.

> A woman who has just been through a difficult period is looking forward to the future in a free and more expansive way. She dreams of a boat that succeeds in moving through a very narrow channel into the open sea.

A young woman, rather shy about her initial presentation in a dream group, dreams of sitting on the toilet. To her surprise people keep opening the door to the bathroom, going in and out. What has heretofore been a most private experience is now exposed to public viewing.

So much for the form that dreaming consciousness takes. What about the content? There are vulnerable areas in each of us, vestiges from the past that have not been mastered, or aspects of our personality and resources about which we are ignorant. Encounters that touch on these set up tensions that we cannot resolve at the time. It is this tension that surfaces when we dream. The feeling residues associated with the recent encounter shape the ensuing images. These feelings point to some issue of current significance connected with our past but not yet set to rest. They serve as a guide into the past as we go in search of earlier experiences that, in a feeling way, are related to and can shed some light on the present encounter. We transcend temporal relationships to bring together these emotionally related bits and pieces from our past. In effect, we have embedded a current challenging context into its historical past. We dream about selected aspects of our lives because the issues involved have historical ramifications that are not clear to us at the moment. Our dreams thus have relevance to our present situation, enabling us to bring together information about the particular issue at hand in a way that is not easy to do when we are awake.

There is another feature of dreaming consciousness that makes the remembered dream so useful an instrument for getting to know who we really are and what we really feel. I refer to the intrinsic honesty with which events are registered in the imagery we create. We are completely alone while dreaming. With no one looking over our shoulder it is as if we risk taking an honest look at ourselves and allow ourselves to see just where our unique life history has brought us in relation to the issue we are dreaming about. I am not referring to seeing ourselves in a state of angelic bliss; rather, whatever deceits we are capable of are honestly displayed for us. The relevance of the dream to a still active issue in our life, the mobilization of pertinent information from our past, and the ability of the dream to bring us closer to the truth are the three features of our dreaming experience that give value to the dream and render it a potentially healing source in our everyday life.

The scenario of a dream often follows the structure of a three-act drama. The first act depicts the impact of an intrusive novel experience on a preexisting emotional state, the second develops the background of the tension from a historical perspective, and the final act is devoted to an effort at resolution. Awakening occurs when there are accompanying feelings that are too intense or too disturbing to be resolved.

The dreamer, of course, has a problem. The remarkable images he has crafted defy his understanding. He is not at ease with either the language of the dream or what it might be saying. No one has taught him much about the former, and the latter touches on aspects of his psyche that have not yet clearly emerged in consciousness. He needs help, and to get that help he must share the dream.

A small group (eight to ten people) can provide a most effective way of getting that help. Once the needs of the dreamer are understood, a process can be structured to meet those needs in a safe and effective way. What I am saying is that the task of helping a dreamer can be placed in the hands of anyone who is willing to take the trouble to learn what those needs are and how to work within a process designed to meet them.

To understand the needs of the dreamer let us look at his predicament more closely. In sharing his dream he is doing two things neither of which is familiar or easy. He is exposing a most personal and vulnerable side of himself. He is jumping into water the depth of which is not known to him. None of us knows in advance where dream work will take us. This double jeopardy defines the first and basic need of the dreamer, the need for safety. He has to be assured that the dream work he is to engage in will take place in a way that will provide the degree of safety he needs. In a general way this means that every stage of the process control will remain in the hands of the dreamer, that the process will evolve in a nonintrusive way that respects the privacy of the dreamer and his authority over the dream. Concern with the Safety Factor then, is the first major determinant of the structure of the process within which the dream work will take place.

The group has to respond to another overriding need of the dreamer, namely, to be helped to make discoveries about himself that are difficult to make alone. I refer to this as the Discovery Factor and this, too, has to be built into the structure of the process.

The process Nan Zimmerman and I have evolved for group dream work has been described in considerable detail elsewhere (Ullman and Zimmerman). Here I will simply outline it, presenting briefly both the rationale and the way that each stage of the process meets both the Safety Factor and the Discovery Factor.

Stage I

A. A dreamer *volunteers* a dream.
B. The group may ask questions to clarify the dream and to grasp it as clearly and as completely as possible. Any real characters in the dream are briefly identified.

The Safety Factor: The emphasis is on a dreamer volunteering to share a dream. This is a decision left completely in the hands of the dreamer.

The Discovery Factor: On occasion the simple act of relating a dream to others results in a sudden insight. The decision to share a dream is based on a readiness to lower one's defensive operations. Any lowering of defenses paves the way to greater insight.

Rationale: The presentation to the group is limited to the dream itself. The dreamer is asked to refrain from giving any associations or any ideas about the meaning of any element in the dream. This is important in relation to the next stage, where the group makes the dream their own. Were the dreamer to give associations or offer meanings, he would track the response of the group along the lines he is setting down for them and in that way limit the free play of their imagination.

Stage II

This is a game or exercise that the group plays by making the dream their own. They will speak of it as their own dream, and what they offer to each other (they do not address the dreamer) will be their own projections. The dreamer is asked to listen without actively participating. He is free to accept or reject anything that comes from the group.

A. Group members share with one another any feelings or moods that the imagery conveys.

B. Next, the imagery is addressed and explored in its metaphorical potential. The task of the group is to use their imagination and attempt to link the images in the dream to possible life situations or concerns suggested by the imagery. This is a random process offered in the hope that some of the group's responses will have meaning for the dreamer.

The Safety Factor: As members of the group address each other, they leave a clear space around the dreamer who then feels free to accept or reject anything coming from the group. He also remains in control of his thoughts and reactions to the input of the group and is under no obligation at a later stage to share more than he wishes.

The Discovery Factor: Despite the fact that, at this stage, the group is unaware of the events in the dreamer's life that shaped the dream, many of their projections do succeed in bringing the dreamer closer to his dream. Several factors are at work aside from images the group comes up with that feel right to the dreamer. The dreamer responds to the group's interest in his dream, the sharing of themselves through their own projections, and the commonality of experiences as revealed by these projections. All have the effect of helping the dreamer move closer to the dream.

Rationale: At first glance it might seem unlikely that a group working on someone else's dream without knowing the dreamer's associations would come up with anything relevant to the plight of the dreamer. The fact is that they do. Even when the dreamer is a stranger, there are spontaneous and intuitive responses from the group members that touch the dreamer. In an ongoing group where there has been much sharing of dreams the projections offered by the group often get closer to the mark. Another factor, of course, is that there are a limited number of basic human issues (for example, issues around identity, authority, individuation, and so on) that touch us deeply enough to dream about. We may well relate to the metaphorical images of a dream the same way the dreamer did.

Stage III

The dream is returned to the dreamer who is then invited to respond to and share to the extent he wishes how far he has come in understanding the dream. He is free to shape his responses in any manner he wishes and is given as much time as he needs without interruption.

If further work is necessary, it proceeds in the form of a dialogue between the dreamer and the group. The purpose of the dialogue is to contextualize the dream. We do this by helping the dreamer explore his life context, beginning with recent events, until there is a felt sense of connection between dream image and waking reality. It is as if we are attempting to bring the two terms of the metaphor together to the point where a spark of understanding jumps the gap between them. Questions are put to the dreamer in an open-ended fashion. Their only purpose is to help the dreamer to focus on a particular aspect of the dream. These are information-eliciting, not information-demanding questions. The dreamer can deal with the questions as he wishes, including the right not to answer.

Our first goal is to clarify the immediate life context that shaped the dream and defined the issue being dreamt about. What can the dreamer recall about happenings in his life the day before the dream that will help him come upon the events that shaped the dream? After we have gone as far as we can in eliciting the immediate context, we can then further explore the context by referring back to the dream somewhat differently. We take an image or a scene that is still obscure and ask the dreamer if there is anything more he can say about it. He is now in a position to play the dream against the amplified context that has been elicited. He has more to work with in his search for connections between image and reality.

When we have elicited as much of the context as can be recalled by direct questions, we introduce another level of questioning. The relationship between one or more images in the dream and the life context that has been shared by the dreamer may still elude the dreamer. If a member of the group, however, thinks he sees a possible connection between an image and an aspect of the shared context, it can be offered to the dreamer as a question. It must be made clear to the dreamer that this is offered as the group member's projection. The final arbiter of the fit is the dreamer.

When what the dreamer has shared is worked out in relation to all the images in the dream in proper sequence, it is referred to as an orchestrating projection. An attempt is made to bring together all the dreamer has shared but to organize it now in its possible relation to the meaning expressed by the sequential arrangement of the imagery of the dream. Although one tries to base it only on what the dreamer has shared and what is in the dream, it is still considered a projection of the person offering it until, and if, it is subsequently validated by the dreamer.

The Safety Factor: In the dreamer's response the control remains in the dreamer's hands. He alone decides on the level of self-disclosure with which he is comfortable.

In the dialogue the dreamer remains in control by having the right to answer, or not answer, any questions put to him.

In the orchestration the dreamer is free to accept or reject any part of the orchestrating projection that has been offered.

The Discovery Factor: As he begins to respond, the dreamer will often come upon new ideas about the meaning of some of the imagery. When questioning is pursued in a nonintrusive way the dreamer is able to develop more of the waking life context of the dream. With it comes a greater ease in seeing the way an image connects to a life situation. Often the dreamer is helped by an orchestration that highlights relationships not seen before.

Rationale: As a rule the dreamer has been able to come closer to the dream through the work done by the group. However, the dreamer may have difficulty in fully contextualizing the dream. By that I mean he may not know how to clarify the immediate relevant life events and he may have difficulty in accounting for various elements in the dream. Some elements may pose problems because they touch on sensitive areas. Others may simply have escaped the dreamer's attention. In either case he is in need of help from others who, with no ax to grind, can call attention to whatever elements in the dream have not adequately been developed and who can, when necessary, pose the kind of questions that can elucidate the precipitating emotional context. As long as the dreamer retains his sense of controlling the exploration and experiences the questions in a nonintrusive way, there is a natural tendency to come forth with relevant data and to move farther into the dream.

Stage IV

A. The dreamer reviews the dream between the time the dream was presented and the next meeting of the group.
B. The dreamer is invited to share any additional thoughts about the dream at the next meeting of the group.

With the completion of Stage IV the dream work is ended.

The Discovery Factor: Reviewing the dream alone in the light of the work done in the group, the dreamer sometimes is freer to see more than he could at the time he first shared the dream.

Rationale: While in the group the dreamer is often exposed to more input than he can handle at the time, input that may have touched him at many levels of his psyche without providing the time or opportunity to work through and clarify the feelings that have been set in motion. Furthermore, his position vis-à-vis the group, where he is constantly faced with the decision of how much to share, may limit to some extent his self-exploration. Reviewing the dream on his own, after the group's work, frees him from that constraint and provides him with the opportunity to examine some of the felt reactions set in motion by the group work.

Skills

We have referred to the fact that certain skills are needed. Since one of the basic skills is the art of knowing how to listen to the dreamer, therapists who come to group dream work may have this skill developed to a high degree. In that sense they may have an advantage. The point is that it is not a skill that is theirs exclusively; others who are interested enough can also master it. Let us look more closely at the skills involved.

There are two active ways in which the group offers help to the dreamer. Distinct skills can be identified with each of these ways.

1. In the second stage the group makes the dream its own and works with projected feelings and meanings. The skills involved are easily learned. There is no particular difficulty in picking up the mood and feeling tones evoked by the imagery. There is a good deal of freedom to proceed in any way one likes and to read whatever feelings one wishes into the individual pictures and the story they seem to be telling. To some extent one approaches the role of the dreamer as an actor or actress might, bringing to that role the feelings he or she deems appropriate.

The transformation of the imagery of the dream into possible life contexts is a bit more difficult at first but, once the idea takes hold, there is generally no further difficulty. Here, again, the fact that one can give one's imagination free rein and that nothing offered is wrong as long as it is based on the dream, allows for plenty of room for experimenting with and learning how to find possible life contexts that might be suggested by the images. The group members do have to divest themselves of waking prejudices about what might or might not be important to the dreamer. They need to address every element in the dream, every detail that has been given by the dreamer, for the possible reality reference that may be encoded in it.

2. Conducting the dialogue in a way that helps the dreamer come upon the information necessary to contextualize the dream is difficult, but it can be taught and mastered with experience. It is difficult because one must bear in mind not only what to look for but also how to put questions to the dreamer while, at the same time, respecting his privacy and the limits he sets.

The prerequisite skill for conducting the dialogue successfully is learning how to listen to the dreamer during his response at the beginning of the third stage. As any therapist knows, the art of listening is not as simple as it appears. It involves, first of all, the ability to set aside our own ideas about the dream, regardless of how convinced we may be that the dreamer will benefit from our view of the dream. Secondly, it involves listening without pre-judging to everything the dreamer has to say. Thirdly, it involves listening not only to what the dreamer says but also to what the dreamer does not say. While listening, we have to make a mental note of the extent to which the dreamer has clarified the current context. Has he done so to the point where the connection to the dream is obvious and where he now understands why he had the dream on that particular night and on no other? To what extent have all the elements in the dream been addressed and their con-nection to the life context, past and present, been noted? In short, the listener must listen attentively while keeping track of the extent to which the dream, in all its elements, has been con-textualized.

This is by way of preparing for the dialogue and the two main goals connected to it, namely, to discover the immediate context, if the dreamer has not done so, and to address those images that have not yet been contextualized or contextualized adequately.

The group has to learn the kind of questions that can help the dreamer recapture the current context. If the goal is kept clearly in mind, the questions will follow more easily. That goal is to learn as much as possible about the emotional forces that im-pinged on the dreamer as he went to sleep on the night of the dream. It involves a systematic exploration through the use of open-ended questions about the thoughts and feelings that emerged from the previous day's activities. What situations was he exposed to that left him with residual or lingering feelings? What was on his mind just prior to falling asleep? In dream work, where ideas about what the image may mean crowd in on the mind of the questioner, he has to learn how not to ask a lead-ing question. By a leading question I mean one based on an idea the questioner has of the possible meaning of the image, and where the question is asked in order to validate that idea. It is very tempting to ask leading or information-giving questions rather than information-eliciting ones. Put in an open-ended way, the latter stimulates the dreamer to identify more of the context. When we do succeed in eliciting the relevant data, the dreamer himself, in most instances, can see the connection to the dream image. Asking leading questions or offering interpretive comments tends to complicate the search for context by puzzling the dreamer and possibly raising his anxiety level. He is deflected from the internal search to the task of evaluating connections someone else is making.

Initially, the questions should be put in the most open and general form possible. The questioner must learn how to be guided by the dreamer's response. The following issues arise at this point:

1. Judging by the dreamer's response we need to ask ourselves if the dreamer seems interested in exploring the question further, or if it is obvious that he prefers not to? In other words, is he inviting us in or inviting us out?

2. If the latter is the case, we don't pursue the matter.

3. If he seems interested in going further, then we have to form a judgment as to whether and to what extent the dreamer's response sheds any light on the imagery of the dream.

4. If there is insufficient clarification, then questioning proceeds in the same open-ended way and, with the dreamer's cooperation, moves from the general to the specific, always measuring the answer against the dream, being sensitive to whether the dreamer wants to go further, and continuing until some aspect of the relationship to the dream has been clarified.

5. The group has to learn to help the dreamer address every detail in the dream, not just the most striking ones.

Up to this point the group has been asking information-eliciting questions (not information-demanding ones). The questioning has been persistent without being insistent. Helping the dreamer externalize the information relevant to the dream can be all that is needed for the dreamer to see the connections of the dream to his life. In some instances, however, more is needed. This happens when all the relevant information has been brought out but in such a random fashion that the essence of the dream still eludes the dreamer. One has to learn to recognize that this is so and that further questioning will simply result in repetition of answers already given. The mode of questioning must now shift to what I call an integrating or orchestrating mode. On the basis of what the dreamer has shared with the group both in his initial response and in his answers to the questions in the dialogue, someone in the group may have an idea how some of the material fits the metaphorical meaning of an image. Possible relationships are raised and addressed to the dreamer as questions. It is made clear that this is to be considered as the questioner's own projection unless it has meaning for the dreamer. When this type of projection is made in connection with the entire dream, that is, when there is an attempt to match the dreamer's responses to all the images of the dream in their sequential relationships, it is referred to as orchestration. This, too, is offered to the dreamer as the questioner's own projection in the hope that it may be of help to the dreamer. Although the general idea can be grasped easily, the art of orchestrating is a skill that can come only with experience. It is contingent in large measure on the group's learning to listen to all the dreamer's responses during the dialogue, to sense where the dreamer is emotionally as he responds, and to give these responses a higher priority than one's own ideas about the dream. One must always keep in mind the basic reality of dream life. The images spring from the individual and unique life experiences of the dreamer, not the listener.

The basic skills to be learned in orchestrating are:

1. listening to everything the dreamer says, not only in his initial response but in all that he says during the dialogue;

2. while listening, looking for relationships between what the dreamer is saying and the metaphorical possibilities of the images of the dream;

3. learning how to stay with what has emerged from the dreamer and to avoid what may be sheer projection on the part of the one offering the orchestration;

4. learning how to pick up more in the way of significant relationships between image and context by examining the serial relationship of the images;

5. learning how to organize the material so that relationships emerge more clearly as the sequences in the dream are played back against the context that has been elucidated.

Problem Areas

There are a number of problem areas connected with group dream work.

In the second stage, when the group is working with the dream as its own, there is a tendency to lose sight of this fact and to discuss the dream in a way that leaves the impression that the group is offering interpretive comments and not really talking about the dream as its own.

The dialogue is the most difficult part of the process. It is not easy to contain what I refer to as the "interpretive impulse," namely, the compulsion on the part of the listener to offer immediately an interpretive comment. We have to disavow any conviction we may have as to where the dreamer should go with the dream. It is difficult at times to restrain the tendency to validate through our questions our own impression of what the dream means. To do so is a breach of the basic rule that we follow rather than lead the dreamer. We have to rely on the dreamer's ability to make discoveries on his own to the extent he feels ready to after we have elucidated the context, and we need to base the questioning only on what is obvious to the dreamer, that is, on what is in the dream or on what the dreamer has shared. Any question that is not obvious to the dreamer and not referred to in the dream, but that is derived from something in the interrogator's mind, is apt to raise the anxiety level of the dreamer (what does the questioner know about my dream that I don't?) and is apt to be self-defeating.

The sole purpose of a question is to help the dreamer retrieve a bit more of the life context. Simple and direct questions can accomplish this most easily. Their aim is to elicit information from the dreamer in an unbiased way. If one is trying to clarify the current life context, a typical question might be: "Do you recall what feelings the day (prior to the dream) left you with?" If one is trying to help a dreamer do more with a particular image in the dream it suffices to ask: "Why do you think such and such an image appeared in your dream that night rather than some other night?" Instead of staying with this simple information-eliciting approach there is an almost irresistible urge to test one's hunches about an image before the dreamer has provided a context that would bring a possible relationship out into the open. An inexperienced group will have trouble staying with a line of questioning, moving from the general to the specific, until a clear relation between context and image is established.

Sensing the proper point of closure can be difficult for beginners, who often probe more deeply than is either possible or appropriate in the group setting as it is structured.

A newcomer to the process who presents a dream for the first time may have difficulty seeing the imagery metaphorically and will tend to be unaware of the role that recent life events play in shaping the dream. It takes some experience before a dreamer feels at ease with the visual metaphorical language of the dream and what that language is expressing about present and past aspects of his life. There is a tendency to expect some sudden, spontaneous, exotic revelation from the dream. The dream yields its secret only after the slower but more rewarding work of gradually contextualizing the images.

Most people come to a dream group because they have a serious interest in learning more about their dreams. On rare occasions someone finds his way into the group with an agenda of his own, one that has nothing to do with dreams. The dream is simply a pretext for fulfilling some other compelling personal need, such as exhibitionism, dependency, or the like. Whatever the motive, unless checked, there will be an attempt to manipulate the group into fulfilling this need.

More common is the person who, having had a great deal of experience with other kinds of groups, has difficulty accepting the constraint that comes from the fact that the emphasis here is not on the interpersonal processes going on but is exclusively on the group's ability to be of help to the dreamer. The dreamer's needs come before those of any other group member. There may be attempts to transform the dream work into group therapy or an encounter type of situation where there is more freedom to confront. With time most catch on to the basic difference between the experiential dream group and other groups. It takes time to get used to the idea of a group that is solely a support system, offering stimulation to the dreamer to the extent that the dreamer seeks and can use it. It is not there to satisfy the needs of other members of the group.

This approach stresses the importance of helping the dreamer recapture the emotional residues of the period immediately preceding the dream. This, of course, is done more easily with a fresh dream. In the case of a dream that is days or weeks old or older, if the dream is important to the dreamer, the group can often help the dreamer bring back enough of the context to make the effort worthwhile.

In the examples given below some aspects of the process will be highlighted. In the actual workshop situation there is a sense of drama and tension as image and context gradually come together.

In this first example a young female social worker presented a dream that had occurred the night before the session.

The Dream

"I was a kindergarten teacher in a classroom with little children. Things were going smoothly. We were all getting along. Then there was some kind of change. Some of the children began to get unruly. I couldn't control them. I was pointing my finger at them and scolding them. A little black child, her hair in braids, said: 'No, I don't have to do what you want.' She started to walk to the door. I grabbed her arm and said: 'No, you can't leave.' At that point an obese black woman came in. She seemed perplexed by all the confusion. Then she became a music teacher. She handed tambourines to all the children. I relaxed and felt that I didn't have to do anything anymore. The children were happy with her and started to sing a Beatles's song, 'Back in the USSR.' I turned to see my daughter in the group. I tried to make eye contact and said excitedly: 'That's the Beatles song.' Another little boy said: 'Yeah, that's the Beatles.'"

The Response of the Group: The group worked with the dream as their own and shared the feelings and moods evoked by the imagery. What follows is a foreshortened rendering of the group's response over a fifteen-minute period.

I've lost control and feel helpless and frustrated.
I feel the soothing quality of the music.
I feel confused. Something has happened, and I don't understand it.
What a relief it would be to have someone come in who knew how to control the situation.
I feel inadequate that I can't do it by myself.
That black woman conveys a very motherly feeling.
I feel anger at the child who won't obey me.
The reference to the USSR gives me a dictatorial feeling. I am the teacher and am acting like a dictator and feel guilty at trying to control the kids.
I have a nostalgic feeling about the Beatles song. It brings back to me a freer time.

The group then worked with the metaphorical possibilities of the imagery. What follows captures only part of what evolved over a twenty-minute period.

The control comes with the singing. Then there is a fuller and freer expression of feeling.
The song is symbolic of defiance. It is a cynical statement defying authority.
I saw a family at the clinic where a small child was involved. Things were going well, and then something happened.
The music teacher is experienced and competent as an authority.
The child wants to separate, and I have difficulty letting that happen. I want to pull her back.
I had a strong feeling of the importance of making eye contact. It was like maintaining a connection.
I'm struck by the contrasting images of the bad black girl and the good little white girl.

The Dreamer's Response: "Everything you said evoked very strong feelings. I was troubled about what went wrong. My daughter has just turned two. She has just changed. She is not the same person. I keep wondering what I have done wrong. I was feeling inadequate. I can't do what I'd like to do sometimes, which is just—leave. I wonder if maybe some part of me does want to leave her.

"I had a strong reaction to the image of the black woman. She is my version of a mother.

"About the song—I like the Beatles' songs. I often play the White Album as my daughter likes it. It makes me feel happily connected when I can give something to her.

"Last night she was having a fit. She absolutely wouldn't let me put on her pajamas, and the situation was getting out of control. I looked at her and then suddenly began singing a song from Mary Poppins and started dancing around the room like a nut. She started to laugh, and after that things went smoothly.

"Someone mentioned a client's child. Actually, I was in a situation where a child was involved. On the first visit it went well, but then they stopped coming.

"The eye contact was important for me. What was said and what I hadn't thought of was that I was trying to hold part of her and was not wanting to let her go.

"I now realize the black child was my daughter. I had fixed her hair in braids."

At this point the dreamer invited the dialogue.

What were your last thoughts on falling asleep last night?

"Actually, I thought about wanting to have a dream tonight. I was also reading a cook book in anticipation of a party we are going to have."

Were there any other thoughts about having a dream in connection with coming into a dream group the next day?

"Nothing specific about last night, but in general I felt both interested in sharing and also nervous about it."

Did anything else happen recently that touched you emotionally?

"Nothing that I feel is related to the dream. After my daughter went to sleep I had a conversation with my brother-in-law. He is recently separated. He also had a sick baby that died. My husband is away. He suggested making a date to go to a movie. I had a sad feeling about his situation and excited feelings about going out on a date."

The dream opens with you as a teacher. Can you say anything about that?

"It's not a comfortable role for me. It's a controlling role."

And about the black child?

"Do I see black as bad? Rebelling as bad? What struck home

was to see the child as one of my impulses getting out of control. I do have angry impulses in me and can get very angry."

Can you say any more about the song in the dream?

"I don't think it had to do with the specific song. The title wasn't important. What was important was the bouncy excited feeling."

The above are the highlights of an interchange that extended over a twenty-minute period. An orchestrating projection was then offered as a question to the dreamer:

"The problems you face as a mother and as a professional woman were highlighted the night you had the dream. During the day your self-esteem was ruffled by the family you had as a client not returning. At night you faced the challenge of a rebellious child. The incident with your brother-in-law may have triggered a fantasy of how nice it would be to be free of family responsibilities. Looking for a quick and easy way to control the situation you become the stern, controlling parent. This doesn't work. Your own innate capacity to be a truly responsive mother comes to your rescue. A mothering figure replaces the authoritarian one. The verbal scolding approach is replaced by a nonverbal musical one. The situation is resolved. The dream used a pictorial language to depict what you yourself went through last night in the incident with your daughter."

The dreamer nodded her agreement.

In the following example the dream presented was a month old. The dreamer, a forty-two-year-old woman could date it only approximately. Under these circumstances the initial strategy of the dialogue, namely, the attempt by direct questioning to help the dreamer reconstruct events in her life immediately preceding the dream was, of course, quite limited and in no way comparable to what one can do with a recent dream. Nevertheless, the two remaining strategies, namely, helping the dreamer play each image back against whatever context she was able to recall, and then offering her an integrative projection proved to be very helpful.

The Dream

"I'm saying good-by to my mother because I have to go to jail. The reason has to do with some form of embezzlement. Three other people seem to have been involved. I know I am innocent, but I have to go to jail anyway because somehow I am connected with it.

On the way to the jail, or perhaps in jail, I have to go to the ladies' room. The restroom is filthy. I can't find a clean stall. The floor is wet. My feet are bare. I remember standing on the commode to urinate. I couldn't stand anywhere else.

Then I find myself in a cafeteria in the jail. It's almost time for me to be released. I'm carrying a tray with food. I also have my dog on a leash around my wrist. The dog pulls on the leash, and the tray leaves my hand, spilling food all over. I know that because of this I will be punished and will have to stay in jail longer."

The Response of the Group: What follows are some of the feelings shared by the group.

> I feel like a victim, as if I've been duped by someone.
> I usually don't mind saying good-by to my mother, but this time I'm the one being left.
> I have an underlying sense of guilt . . . it's ongoing. When the tray spills the punishment is kept going.
> It's disgusting to be in that filthy ladies' room. It makes me feel hopeless about my life.
> It's a miserable feeling being barefoot on the dirty floor of the ladies' room.
> I'm happy the dog is with me. It's the only consoling creature in the dream.
> Things are totally out of control.
> I have a feeling of guilt by association.
> Things happen beyond my ability to face them.
> I feel deprived—no money, no food.

The group then went on to work on the possible metaphorical reference of the images.

> It strikes me as significant that it's my mother and not my husband or children in the dream.
> I'm saying good-by, but I feel connected to her in some important way.

I seem to be imitating a man urinating.

I'm leaving home and becoming an adult, but I'm paying a heavy price.

I'm relieving myself but not in comfort.

I'm getting my feet wet, a necessary part of growing up.

The dog on the leash is trying to be released.

Losing the food is connected to my mother and her poor nurturance.

Embezzlement is something sneaky done by very respectable people.

The bare feet make me feel very vulnerable.

I don't belong in jail.

The dog is an animal part of me. It's a protest against what a child would do.

I associate the cafeteria with freedom of choice. Strange that it should be in jail.

I'm a prisoner of my own emotions.

The rest room is an opportunity to relieve myself.

I'm trapped in a domestic situation.

Some authority has power over me.

Ordinarily there wouldn't be the freedom to have a dog in jail.

The Dreamer's Response: "When I had the dream I felt it was connected to what I was going through with my mother. There have always been difficulties in my parents' marriage, but it has become much worse. My mother and father haven't spoken to each other for the past six months. My mother is becoming increasingly depressed over this to the point where I'm worried about her. It has always been my job to make things better between them.

"A month or so ago I was convinced I would have to tell my mother to go for therapy. My sister-in-law called, urging me to do something. Two other members of my family also called for the same reason. The three calls made me angry. I have been the one always to take responsibility for my mother. I felt like I wanted to say good-by to my responsibility for her and leave it up to my three brothers to take care of her. But I don't see how that fits in with the question of embezzlement. Family members were phoning and asking how we were going to handle Christmas with the situation between our parents being so bad. Perhaps the guilt and embezzlement are connected with our talking about them without their knowing about it. I did want to let go of my responsibility, but I also had a strong sense of guilt. I have always been there for her as her listening ear. How would it be if I sent her off to therapy?

"The bathroom scene did connect with what you said about relieving myself of this burden, getting my feet wet, letting go, separating from this role. I was aware around this time of beginning to avoid my mother. I stopped calling so often. She was giving me indirect messages that she was aware of this and making me feel guilty.

"About feeling depressed. I know I didn't get the nurturance I needed as a child. I was always the nurturing one.

"This situation with my parents happens over and over again. It keeps me locked up. But in the dream letting go is what got me more into jail. I've often dreamt of bathroom scenes and wanting to relieve myself and never being able to do it. Here I am being jailed in the process.

"The dog—I don't know why it's with me. In the dream I had the feeling I had to do everything right and perfect, and I couldn't with the dog tied to my wrist. Maybe the dog represents my anger at having to deal with the whole situation."

The dreamer ended her response at this point and invited the dialogue. She had provided the general context of the dream, namely, the tension in connection with her mother. The only way now to be of further help in amplifying the context was to help her play back the imagery of the dream in the light of the context she had provided. Her attention was called to the first scene, involving saying good-by to her mother, going to jail for embezzlement, and feeling innocent but connected to the three other people involved. The dreamer was asked to consider this opening scene and to play it back against the context she had shared with us to see if there was anything else she could say. She then responded:

"I have a feeling the other three are my brothers. I know I did everything I can do with regard to my mother, and they haven't. In that respect I would feel innocent. Still there was a sense I was somehow connected to the embezzlement. I'm accepting blame even though I know I'm innocent."

What can you say about going to jail?

"The idea of personal confinement is frightening. I like my independence. It would make me feel helpless and like a child, having no control over what happens. If I'm breaking away in the dream, I should feel free. I was accepting what was happening to me. I was not fighting it." (At this point the dreamer recalled that, in the dream, she was crying when she said good-by to her mother.)

The dreamer's attention was then called to the scene in the ladies' room, and she was asked if there was more she could say.

"It's as if I had to go through the humiliating scene in the ladies' room to be worthy of release. My standing on the commode was not like a man urinating. It was just that I was very tall and removed from the mess. It was my way of getting away from what was beneath me. Could it be my unconscious? Past repressions? At the same time I was relieving myself of more mess."

The questions brought her back to being on her way to jail or being in jail.

"It forces me to deal with the mess. I have to stay put long enough to deal with the mess. I picture the dog trying to pull me away. He wants to run and be free. His need for freedom stops me from being free."

She was asked if there was more she could say about that.

"It's my wanting to run from the situation but knowing that wouldn't help. It would just make for more trouble. Running from her, avoiding her, made it worse. Then she thought I didn't care either. I had to stay still to stop the running. I finally stayed put, and that's what happened. What someone said about the dog seeking release brought it all together. It wanted to run."

Why the dog in the dream?

"It was being held on to. I was restraining some animal feeling."

Why use the image of embezzlement in the context you have described?

"For me it means taking something that doesn't belong to me. Could it be taking on the responsibility for my mother when it didn't belong to me?"

How would that fit in with the idea of embezzlement which usually has a negative connotation?

The dreamer was having difficulty developing the dream further on her own and was still not clear about the imagery of embezzlement and jail.

The following was offered to the dreamer as an orchestrating projection. Although not put as a question, it was intended as such. In developing it there is a conscious effort to base it on the imagery in the dream and the related context shared by the dreamer.

"People go to jail if they are guilty of something. In the dream you are puzzled by this. You feel you are innocent, yet you feel connected to whatever the crime is. In the dream, with great sadness, you are saying good-by to your mother. In waking life you felt upset at the realization you were pulling away from her and you felt guilty that, in bringing up the question of her seeing a therapist, she would feel you were experiencing her as a burden to be turned over to someone else. You have three brothers, and they have reneged in their responsibility to her. In our culture daughters are generally closer to their mothers and more apt to carry this responsibility. Despite the unfairness of it part of you still does feel a sense of your personal responsibility toward her. Coming back to the image of embezzlement, what was it that you were guilty of embezzling and had to be punished for? The only guilt-provoking act you spoke about had to do with your withdrawal from her and beginning to actually avoid contact with her. Might it not be that, in doing that, you were acting like your three brothers in stealing from your mother what was rightfully hers, namely, your concern and ability to help her in this hour of need? Then comes the toilet scene. What kind of messy stuff did you have to avoid? You said you had three calls from various members of your family in one way or other presuming to call your attention to your responsibility. The calls made you furious. They opened up the emotional mess you felt you were in and that you had to deal with. Could it be that, standing on the commode, you tried to find relief by rising above a mess that was not of your making? Although their calls were presumptuous, they nevertheless touched on the guilt you felt in being tempted to turn away from your mother. The struggle to be free seems to be further developed in the next scene. The very effort to pull yourself free entraps you more."

The dreamer found the above formulation helpful. She felt that the development of the imagery around the commode, and later around the dog tugging on the leash, pulled the dream together for her.

She added as a footnote that, even though she had not worked on the dream at the time she had it, she felt it somehow influenced her subsequently to handle the situation with her mother. "I did manage to get her into treatment in a loving way. I felt good at how I dealt with it."

Afterthoughts: At the next meeting of the group one week later the dreamer had more to say about the dream. The "embezzlement" image continued to puzzle her. The notion of guilt and punishment didn't quite seem to fit. Her continuing work on the dream led her to further clarity.

"The feeling in the dream was more one of conspiracy rather than of committing a crime. It seemed to connect with those three telephone calls (urging her to do something about her mother) I got. It left me with the feeling of talking behind her back, of being in cahoots with others. They made me aware of how trapped I felt by the problem. I did feel guilty about my inability to do anything about it. The calls made me aware that, up to that time, I had been ignoring it. They helped get me going toward a resolution."

The work in the group gave the dreamer the start she needed so that she could then go farther on her own. She managed to do this with the two images that were still puzzling, namely, getting closer to the embezzlement image as feeling more like a conspiracy, and the jail image, which signified her feeling of being trapped.

In a mystery story the plot unfolds bit by bit. So it is in group work with a dream. The search for context is often difficult and laborious. It takes the combined efforts of dreamer and group to dislodge psychological blocks in order to examine the life that has been hidden from view. If the dreamer wants to unravel it and if he is made to feel safe as he struggles with it, then the group can provide enough leverage to do it. The end result is the product of an equation with many different contributory factors. When they work harmoniously there is movement into the dream, a feeling of relief, and a sense of doors being opened. That good feeling may be the result of encountering something new or feeling something more deeply and more truly than one has in the past.

In summary, a small group process has been described, designed to be of help to the dreamer in a safe and nonintrusive way. The structure is protective of the privacy and authority of the dreamer while, at the same time, allowing for the free play of the imagination of the various group members as they work with the dream as their own. This serves to open up possibilities for the dreamer. More specific connections are then made as the questions from the group help to bring out more and more of the relevant context. The dreamer is, in effect, using the group as an instrument as he explores the dream's metaphorical references to his life.

References

Greenberg, R., and Pearlman, C. "Cutting the REM Nerve: An Approach to the Adaptive Role of REM Sleep." *Perspectives in Biology and Medicine* 17:4, 513–521, 1974.

Palumbo, S. R. *Dreaming and Memory*. New York: Basic Books, 1978.

Snyder, F. "Toward an Evolutionary Theory of Dreaming." *American Journal of Psychiatry* 123:2, 121–136, 1966.

Ullman, M. "Hypotheses on Biological Roots of the Dream." *Journal of Clinical and Experimental Psychopathology* and *Quarterly Review of Psychiatry and Neurology* 19:2, 128–133, 1958.

Ullman, M., and Zimmerman, N. *Working With Dreams*. Los Angeles: Jeremy Tarcher, Inc., 1979.

Part One

Aspects of Group Dream Work

·2·

A Mothers' Dream Group

JENNY DODD

For dream work to move into the public domain in an effective way it will require people like Jenny Dodd, possessed of a passionate enough interest to learn the basic facts about dreams, to undertake the training that sharpens their skills in group dream work, and then to organize and develop their own groups.

Jenny Dodd comes to the task with a unique endowment. She is the youngest of three generations of dream workers. Her grandmother, Dr. Winifred Rushforth, one of the earliest physicians in Britain to turn to psychoanalysis, began to develop dream groups after her retirement from practice. When I saw her last in Edinburgh she was ninety-six, had just written a book, and was leading seven dream groups a week. Her daughter and Jenny's mother, Dr. Diana Bates, also leads dream groups. Soon after her arrival in this country Jenny sought out instruction and training with me.

The group described in this chapter is unique in a number of ways. The members are all women, adapting to life in this country, coming from abroad, most with young children. With the exception of Jenny they were all new to dream work. I have had the pleasure of working with them on two occasions a year apart. The skill and sophistication they have developed is impressive.

Experiences like those described in this chapter have convinced me of the feasibility of extending dream work beyond the confines of the therapeutic consulting room and entrusting dreams to the care of those who dream them.

Our Friday morning dream group was started in January 1981 and has continued to meet every week without interruption. Originally it numbered seven women with ten children in tow, all under five years of age; now, four years later, we are nine women with only one or two children remaining, the rest now in school. A factor of some significance to our long survival, but by no means the only one, may have been our similar backgrounds; we were from England, South Africa, and Canada. There was only one American among us. Whether this was by accident or design is a matter of conjecture, but the fact remains that rather quickly we formed a cohesive group. We rotated meetings at one another's houses. Those with swimming pools or access to beaches were favored in the summer, those with warm basements, in the winter, for we soon found it necessary to organize child care efficiently. Each week one of us would take on the responsibility of providing snacks and entertainment for the children during the two hours or so of the meeting.

The Friday morning dream group is indeed a very special event in each of our lives. It is a time to which we voluntarily commit ourselves to the search for deeper understanding of both ourselves and others. We believe that at the very least a dream is some sort of a communication. None of us is a professional, but each of us brings an intelligent mind, a wealth of life experience, and a warm sensitivity to the world of feelings and intuition—all of which have served to deepen our sharing and helped to form quite a special dream group. We hesitate to make any great claims for ourselves as dream experts, but there is no doubt in any of our minds that being a member of this group and sharing dreams is now quite central to our lives.

One member begins to notice a significant effect on her writing, saying that sharing a dream can sometimes release greater creativity and freedom; another member, aware of conflicts in her professional artistic life, is finding that sharing her dreams and isolating particular areas of conflict is helping her make the right decisions for her future development; a third woman values most the sharing of feelings at a more meaningful level than she finds in her daily life; yet another, older woman, feels enriched by meeting regularly with people who are engaged in a similar task of searching for a deeper significance in life and relationship, and by the sense of shared experience and struggle. As for myself, I value the continuously renewed experience of perceiving someone close to me grappling with issues honestly and bravely, coming away with a sense of having touched or re-owned a part of herself for which she is now the richer.

Recently this dream was shared:

*"I am at a summer school. I am sitting in a group. Two of my children, covered in mud, rush in, and roll on the floor. I watch dismayed but unresponsive. They run out laughing. As my anger rises, I rush out after them, determined to punish them for their behavior.

"I run down to the bottom of the garden and find them hidden in the showers. Their clothes are scattered everywhere. A German au pair girl appears to give me a hand. I find a large white towel with which to dry them, and as I wrap it around L. we notice a large worm has become enfolded in the towel. I am repulsed, but L. is intrigued and tries to unwrap it. The worm turns out to have nipping claws, and L. withdraws.

"We go back to the house. I feel as if I still have to punish the children and have difficulty in finding clothes for them.

"Then a woman appears displaying two beautiful dresses which she has made. One is finished; she is wearing the second. It is gray and white, a beautifully tailored dress with a panier-type underskirt. I am impressed by the detailed work she had done, particularly on the paniers. I watch her walking away with the underskirt showing, but unfinished. I feel challenged by her, invited to do the same."

After the dream was presented, the following feelings were expressed as each member made the dream her own. There is a peaceful feeling at the beginning which is disturbed by the chil-

---

*Dreams are given in the dreamer's exact words; only small points of detail are omitted for brevity's sake. The dreamer's response is paraphrased and includes only those parts relevant to the overall theme of mothers. Sometimes this will give an incomplete impression of the dream work. Initials of people are used for confidentiality's sake.

dren; things are happening too fast, there is confusion; I feel annoyed that I have to leave the group; I am resentful of the demands the children make on me; it's hard to reconcile these demands with my own needs and interests; I feel frustrated and impatient; there's a feeling of conflict; there is a feeling that I need help with the children; I am not being treated with consideration.

Working with the dream imagery, the group offered the following ideas: the group is the dream group, the work I do; the gardens are ordered and beautiful, but also a place for mud; the showers are cleansing; the children are natural, free, and admirable; the worm seems to be part of that naturalness, the way things are, but it's a part of me snapping; the beautiful dresses are also a part of me, what I can and want to be. There is a contradiction between the freedom of the children and the discipline of dressmaking.

The dreamer then responded. She had a sure sense of where this dream had come from. The day before, her two children had gone out to play just as the family was leaving for an ice-skating expedition. In a matter of minutes they had become muddy, too muddy in fact for the dreamer to contemplate putting them into the car. Both she and her husband responded with anger, sending them upstairs, and the family expedition was canceled. Secondly, the dreamer had hoped that over the weekend she would find time to start making her sister-in-law an exciting new outfit, but she had not been able to do anything at all. The main feeling for the dreamer was the anger she felt toward her children and the frustration she felt at not being able to start her dressmaking. The dream put her closely in touch with the anger felt toward the children the day before and her need to discipline them, reactions that created some conflict. The dried-up worm in the towel seemed to suggest the conflict. The snakelike creature was harmless, representing instinctual life, but also something repulsive, even dangerous. Perhaps this part of the dream was expressing the dilemma she experienced in having to discipline her children. It was necessary, but what harm might it do to a young child's naturalness? The intensity of the dreamer's anger and the frustration she felt had made her feel guilty. The woman in the dream who appeared with the beautiful dresses felt like the dreamer's self a few years earlier when she had no children and spent blissful uninterrupted hours creating handsome outfits for herself and others. There was a taunting quality about this dream figure which the dreamer felt strongly. In reality the fabric she was hoping to sew into an outfit was lying in a bag; it beckoned and challenged her, and she was frustrated not to have been able to work on it.

As a mother, one is continually interrupted in thought, conversation, and work. I can remember clearly, as we started meeting on Friday mornings, how many of us appreciated the luxury of having two hours every week to work with dreams. We were not seeking advice or solutions, but just the opportunity to air our worries or joys and accept the conflicts and apparent contradictions in our lives. I am convinced that by now, after four years, most other voluntary peer groups would have petered out. It impresses me deeply that we are still functioning and growing, committed to the task of sharing our dreams in the knowledge that they do contain some valuable information for us. Not only is this information helpful to the dreamer, but we find it is frequently relevant to each of us. There is universality in most dreams.

An example springs to mind:

"I can see a pyramid of fine, beautiful, shiny red apples on a table top. I am lying on my side looking at these apples. Shafts of light are coming down and around me from several different directions. These shafts of light are perpendicular, clear, almost like sheets of glass.

"As I am watching, the hand of a child stretches out to take the top apple. I say to myself, 'She's going to bite it, and it's rotten.' "

In her feedback the dreamer shared much that touched us all deeply. She felt that the apples were magical and "core things"; in fact, the whole dream had a magical, enlightening quality for her. It felt like a core experience. The light was layered, and the dream's message came through to her in layers. Her eldest daughter, the top of her pyramid of five children, had given up the magic that she, the mother, had tried to maintain and give her. She had in fact "turned rotten," left home, leaving no address, and remaining out of touch for many months at a time. All her life the dreamer had been affected by light; she could lie and look at it for hours. She had wondered as a child who was delivering the light, the sun or herself? She had been reading an article that evening about light and the connection between lack of sunlight and depression in certain people. She had said that her daughter experienced depression most often in the winter. She repeated that apples were for her "core" things and that, approaching middle age, she now felt she was discarding the frills, discarding doing what she'd always been told to do, was coming to the core of herself. The dream was speaking of something creative emerging, to do with light. She concluded poignantly by saying that she'd had to get rid of the most beautiful part of her family, her oldest daughter, in order to preserve the whole.

The striking simplicity and beauty of the dream image, the subtle weaving together of incidents from the dreamer's childhood and motherhood, the dispassionate observation of the removal of the top apple (as paralleling the painful experience of relinquishing any mother/daughter relationship with her eldest for the time being at least), and the sense of something creative emerging for herself were all shared simply, yet sincerely, without self-consciousness or shame or pride. The dream work drew us closer together as human beings, leaving us all enriched.

Another dream is offered for the way in which it produced a sense of healing in the dreamer:

"I am visiting a man who was once very dear to me. He was living in a beautiful apartment. The rooms were huge, and his paintings were hung on every wall. He was dressed in a dressing gown, and I had the feeling that the woman who lived there with him was not there.

"His son was calling him from down a long hall, but he was quite involved with discussing his paintings with me. The ones that I was most impressed with were of horses. He had done a lot of paintings with horses, in fine detail, almost living/breathing horses. Then his son came into the room, and he too seemed very proud of his father's paintings. I did feel that the paintings lacked spontaneity or originality.

"It was night, and the lights were very bright."

The dream took the dreamer back to a period of her life thirty years ago. It was triggered by coming across, earlier in the day, a silver coin which the man in the dream had given her, and also by a violent political row with her husband the evening before the dream (it was the time of the recent political election). The argument took her back to the McCarthy era and the time when she had been romantically involved with another man and was on the verge of divorce. The dream was revealing the relationship to this man in its true light. In the thinly disguised sexual overtones (the dressing gown and the horses), in the theatrical air, in the distant relationship between the man and his son, the dreamer saw and understood why she had decided to stay with her husband rather than go with her lover. She had sensed then the nature of her husband's loyalty and could now perceive the shallowness and superficiality of her relationship with the other man despite the lure of his wealth and extravagant tastes. The dream was confirming of her actions, reassuring her that her instincts at the time had been right.

The dreamer proceeded to talk about the impossibility of achieving the fulfillment we seek in any one relationship, the desire to escape the conflicts of daily living, the question of loyalties and making choices, the woman's drive for maternity, and her acute awareness of her children's needs. In the dream the man had ignored his son's calling, which distressed her. She was reminded of how distressed she had been many years ago when her lover stated that her children could visit "from time to time" after the divorce. As she viewed current issues against the background of her dream, the dreamer gained a sense of peace and reconciliation and a greater understanding of herself and her past. We were all touched by her candid sharing and evident triumph.

Not all of us have the kind of glowing, healing experience which this dreamer experienced in the dream work. Indeed, for some it can be a painful, if ultimately rewarding, experience. For those of us with unhappy childhood memories a dream can often touch so directly on our pain and suffering that it takes some courage to face it honestly, to accept it as having been, and with the distance of maturity, perhaps to forgive.

In this dream:

"I was sitting in a bar/restaurant, weeping quietly. A rather ghostly-type man sitting at the bar said to me, 'You used to have class, but you don't anymore.' Whereupon I looked around at him and at everybody in the bar. They were all wearing Pacific Northwest Coast Indian motifs on them. When I saw that I wept and wept."

The dream followed a particularly tense Thanksgiving celebration in which for the first time the dreamer had managed to prepare herself a vegetarian dinner while providing the traditional fare for the rest of the family. This had taken some not inconsiderable resolve. The dream was also directly triggered by the dreamer having viewed *Kramer Vs. Kramer*. She had been struck by the character portrayed by Streep, who seemed natural with her feeling and suffering; she had strength yet could also show feeling. The weeping in the dream was directly related to the movie. The dream brought the dreamer in touch with how much of her life she had spent doing and being what she was told to do and be. Her mother, described as "the perfect mother," had been extremely rigid. Everything had been done to absolute perfection, which denied her any fulfillment of the artistic potential with which she was endowed. The dreamer perceived her mother as being false, and of living up to false ideals. In the dream, triggered by the anxiety the dreamer had felt at following her own dictates, not those of her family or society, the dreamer was confronted with her true, sad feelings. The man in the dream would have admired the old role as she played it. He rejects her now as she is visibly weeping, being herself. The Indian sweaters bring back unhappy memories from childhood, of being regimented, unsympathetically handled, and overdressed by a rigid nanny. In the dream the dreamer is discarding parental images and contacting the childhood pain. "Something is changing and it's painful," she was able to say. A week later the dreamer reported that she had experienced a freeing-up from a lot of stuff, especially related to her mother.

Dream work can be just as meaningful if positive or happy childhood memories are recalled. What seems to happen is that the dreamer discovers hidden strengths and resources within herself which, when consciously mobilized by dream work, can serve her in whatever predicament she may currently be facing. The following dream did such a thing for one of our members.

"I'm with R., and the countryside seems wild, dusty, and lovely. I'm on a road, near her house, standing in front of a lovely big tree. All the other dream group people have gone on ahead in their cars. It feels frivolous, lighthearted, and carefree. I see the dust in the air in front of us. I feel as if we're on top of a cliff. . . .

"They're heading toward the water straight ahead. R. tells me how to follow. I'm on foot, barefooted. I feel excited; something is happening.

"I chase after them; I reach a point after fifty yards where the road goes straight ahead down to the beach, over a cliff. A middle road curves along the cliff top. A third road goes off to the right beside a solid stone cottage with beautiful roses all over it. I know that the cars have not gone down to the beach, and I think, 'What a pity,' because I know it is the perfect place to be at that moment.

"There is another big tree where I'm standing. Resting against it are three rectangular boxes with three different types of citrus fruit. The fruit is dusty but beautiful, larger than life. The right-hand box had only one orange left; the others are full.

"I take the orange, but as I take it something gets triggered, and I think, 'No, how could you take the last one?' and I drop it quickly. It rolls away. Eventually I take a beautiful tangerine from the left-hand box and go on to the cottage.

"A woman comes out, speaking German; she tells me that the wonderful fruit is from South Africa. She gets out a very old book with German prose set in the middle with a border round it on each page. I'm understanding it, and it does tell about South Africa. She tells me that the cars have gone down the road past the cottage."

This was a long, rich dream, and the dreamer's feedback was very personal, full of feeling yet increasingly tranquil. The dream was full of sensual experiences—barefoot, heat, space, luscious fruit, heavenly scented roses, quantities of them—all of which reminded the dreamer of her childhood spent in South Africa. That afternoon she had spoken to her mother in South

Africa who had just returned there after a two-week visit to the States. The dream also appeared to stem from a viewing of Alice in Wonderland, which played into the feeling of things being bigger than life, unreal and slightly puzzling. But the overriding feeling for the dreamer was of standing in one spot. Her outer personal life was in such turmoil, full of uncertainty and conflict.

> *I feel as if I am at a standstill with no direction, but this dream gives me something I can draw on, something out of my life; in particular my free, sensual childhood. The only thing I can pull out now is being in touch with my different senses; there is no other growth or movement right now. I'm staying in one spot. I really wasn't able to show my mother how much I had enjoyed her stay, what a good time we had had together. It was rather like not being able to catch up with the dream group (which is a very positive thing for me). Seeing the fruit takes me back to a time when I was young and things did seem bigger and better, nothing could mar it, a quality only a child can see. It's showing me that I don't really experience these feelings anymore, but they are there. In my upbringing I was taught to care for the other person first and myself last, but it hasn't worked out for me now to care for someone else above my own feelings; it hasn't proved to be healthy. I want something very sensuous in my life, the part that was nourished in me as a child, which now feels so denied. I feel that the dream is showing me that I have a rich place to stand still in and take my own time and find my own direction guided by the wealth and wisdom of my background.

In dream work we are learning to be guided by our feelings. It is not always possible to arrive at an "interpretation"; what we are guided by is how the dreamer *feels* about her own dream. In the above case, the peaceful way in which the dreamer could conclude a long and thorough response was sufficient for all of us to feel satisfied that we had served our purpose as a group and helped the dreamer to get in touch with her own inner strength, which she needed at that time in her life.

---

*This dreamer's feedback was so eloquent, I've quoted it verbatim.

Our own mothers and our own ageing have appeared as themes running through our dreams. Two of our members had recently lost their mothers. Here a third dreamer shares her dream:

"I was walking in a rocky place, almost mountainous. Out of the blue I met a girl from school (she had never been a close friend) called L.L. (very slim, bony prominent nose, attractive, dark-eyed, thin hair). She was carrying a body under her arm. She had a machine round her neck, like a box on her chest, and tubes went into the body, connected in, like a life-support system.

"I asked, 'Why are you carrying this person?' She replied, 'Oh, it's my mother, I must keep her going.' I said, 'If you go on the rocks, the mountains will support her.' The body was naked, but there was no hair; it was a clothlike body, but I knew it was alive and female."

The dreamer was anticipating the arrival of her ageing parents for their annual holiday. She was wondering how she would be affected by the frailty in her mother who had been unwell, someone who had always been "such a strong person." She had been looking at photographs of the mountains and had been watching *The Return of the Jedi;* she had been thinking about space where a portable life-support system was essential. She had been impressed by how other dream-group members had coped with the death of a mother. The dreamer had always felt how important she was to her mother's survival after an earlier family tragedy. She felt a responsibility for her parents which was frustrated by the distance that usually separated them. The mountains gave her a feeling of support and solidity. The appearance of L.L. from her early school years put her in touch with the miracle of a sensitive person who had survived the tortuous atmosphere of boarding school, cut off from all family support. She was reassured by this and, in the dream, by L.L.'s strength and loyalty. In sharing anxious feelings, the dreamer was able to come to terms with the unease she was feeling with her parents' imminent arrival. In the dream image of L.L. she would identify with those aspects of herself that were resourceful and strong.

Some of us are artists working in the community. Dream work has proved valuable in helping us understand more clearly the nature of interpersonal relationships and in making decisions vital to the future of careers. Here is a recent example:

"I'm at Hawnes (boarding school in England), but the time is now, and I am me, now. The school is being run by D.W. (current head of a department where I work). It is being run totally differently. There are computers everywhere. At one point I am invited to join a class. At the end of each row there is a Rainbow System by Digital. The kids in school are able to wear their own clothes, with no restrictions.

"Something has changed about the layout of the school. The long drive is the same, and the fields and woods are all there, and the front facade is the same, but at the back it opens out onto a street in an old town, with narrow winding streets.

"A lot of people from where I work are in the school. I stop to talk to D.W. as an equal, as a visiting colleague. We walk around the school together, talking. I'm telling him about what it was like when I was there, and how much I hated the headmistress, Miss Twist (an archetypal English headmistress; graduate in English from Cambridge, unmarried with a little dog called Ricky and very heavy on discipline)."

As the dreamer worked on the dream a crucial feeling link was made between Miss Twist and her present boss, H., a link which the dreamer experienced as releasing. The dreamer had been having conflict in her work situation for some time, and the dream was triggered by a four-hour harangue from her boss in which the dreamer had been humiliated and embarrassed to the point of breaking down. The resentful feelings caused by this event were linked in the dream to a time of similar emotions at boarding school. It was an environment from which she had begged to leave every week in letters to her father for the two years she had spent there. The feelings of powerlessness, helplessness, and revenge were paralleled. The links thus made freed the dreamer from responding on an infantile level. They enabled her to remain clear and levelheaded in the present situation and not to allow herself to be further manipulated or humiliated. But perhaps more importantly, the dream also helped to confirm her growing ambition to set up her own studio, having at last found supportive and influential people in her own field (as represented by D.W. in the dream).

The last dream I would like to share is an illustration of one of the times when the dreamer felt released into creativity as a result of sharing the dream. It runs as follows:

"I am in Oxford with my husband. I said, 'Let's go and see A' (an old flame). So we went to Balliol College.

"On the tower, inside the door, was a big, gaudy notice, a wooden plaque with red and green writing. It said, 'In Memoriam Prof. G.S.' (the same A.) I said, 'It shouldn't say that; it should say A.H.' and I realized that A. was dead.

"Inside the college there was an exhibit about A. We were ushered in; a secretary was sitting behind the desk. Above the desk was a portrait of A., as a king or chief, dressed in Peruvian/Aztec costume with feathers and bright colors. I kept looking at the portrait to try to see his face clearly, but I couldn't. Also in the exhibit were photograph albums of A. as a child, with his sisters, in a Greek play.

"I said, 'What happened to him?' She said, 'Oh, they made him a king and then they murdered him.'

"So then I said to my husband something about A. 'Oh, you're one of the people who called him A,' said the secretary, and everyone started being very deferential toward me. I decided to go to A.'s room, which is now a cross between an office and a museum. There's a reception desk at the front, and I see on it, in A.'s handwriting, pieces of paper asking for money for lectures/work he had done—sort of like I.O.U.'s.

"I think it is sad that they did not pay for the ordinary things he did. I say, 'I want to see D.' They say, 'Oh yes, D.'s a junior professor and is is doing some of A.'s teaching for him.'

The dream was triggered by having spent some time the day before looking for a letter from A., distinctly remembering his handwriting but failing to find the letter. It was placed in the general context of writing a story about this period in her life, as well as having recently been home, having looked up A.'s address without contacting him. The main thing that emerged for the dreamer was that the dream highlighted two conflicting images of the same person: one, the mythic godlike figure; the other, the very ordinary, day-to-day person. In reality A. was a manic-depressive personality, a powerful, wonderful person who was fatally flawed. The figure of A. was a prominent person in the dreamer's imagination and in her writing about him.

What the group helped the dreamer to see clearly reflected in the dream was what she was trying to do with A. in her short story. The direction of the story could now take off. A week later the dreamer described the release she felt that affected her writing positively. In a strange way, she stated, as a result of the dream story, she no longer felt quite so obsessed by the memory of A. How marvelous that a death in the psyche can be experienced as a release into a new stage of life!

And thus, with these examples from our dream work over the years I hope that some of the benefits can be felt. There is much that comes up that cannot be shared and much that is separate from specifically mothering experiences. I have offered a sampling with deep indebtedness to the members of the group for giving this material freely and so movingly.

It never ceases to amaze me that despite sick children, vacations, business trips, and difficult family times, we have always met. Whatever the weather, whatever the problems, at least three of us are there, though the number is usually seven or eight. On only one occasion do I remember there being no dream to share. I think that dream work of this kind is a unifying experience that satisfies in a unique way both social and personal needs. We have built up an arena in which we all feel safe, where there is an atmosphere of trust and sharing that all of us value supremely.

We all want to know more about ourselves and believe that the dream is an important phenomenon, serving this end precisely if we are given an effective tool with which to work. We are all discovering lost and forgotten things about ourselves, maybe even unlikable things some times. We must surely be growing in tolerance if nothing else.

There is a deep feeling of satisfaction at the end of working with a dream, whether it be one's own or someone else's. We have been in touch with something meaningful, truthful, revelationary, creative, or painful, and all of us are enriched. The undivided attention and concentration we give are refreshing in themselves in the context of our often harried and fragmented lives with young children. We are touched and healed by the process of sharing a dream, fearing no censure or criticism or unwanted advice. We are not so isolated after all. To share our feelings and use our intuitive imagination is both consoling and stimulating. We are all equals whatever the perceived differences. Our dreams show us this truth. We each have a lot to give and to share, and we have quite unique gifts valued by everyone. Dream work assists us in the difficult task of facing ourselves honestly and coping with the troubled society in which we find ourselves. It is unifying and personally enriching. Dream work will continue to play a vital part in all our lives for as long as we wish and dream.

·3·

After the Dream Is Over

NAN ZIMMERMAN

Nan Zimmerman is the coauthor of our book, Working With Dreams. *Poet, writer of children's stories, music teacher, homemaker, and mother, she has an unerring sense of metaphor. Her natural feel for the essence of the dream allows her access to its unique perspective. A dream presents us with an opportunity to realign our lives so that we can become more of what it is in our nature to be and less of what we are made to feel we have to be.*

Since our early work together Nan has continued to be involved in the world of dreams, leading dream groups and workshops. In this chapter she is looking beyond the actual dream work experience and raises an important question concerning the nature of follow-up to dream work. What resources might be helpful to the dreamer once an emotionally vulnerable area has been exposed? In this instance the issue is death and the feelings of loss that ensue.

In dream appreciation we work to make clear the current stress point in our lives. The problem remains, how do we deal creatively with this stress?

Dreams have been called moving metaphors (Ullman and Zimmerman); that is, they are animated expressions of our true emotions. A difficulty may arise, however, when we attempt to use this identifying material for the purpose of changing our behavior and relieving stress. If we work alone, we may correctly identify an emotion, but incorrectly interpret how it relates to our life as it is being lived. We may use it to further entrench destructive ways of seeing ourselves. This is one reason that working with others is of value. Fellow dreamers give us a broader perspective. Letting the dream go public helps us see where we may be using a dream to confirm an old way of seeing a problem rather than to affirm the new possibilities. Viewed within the confines of our individual perspectives, dreams may seem to make us both worse and better than we are. Our dreams are honest. Unfortunately our waking selves do not always bring spontaneous honesty to work on the dream.

"I dream of walking down a dark path. I see a storybook cottage with warm light flowing from the windows. A light snow falls. I peek into a window and see my family as it was when I was eight. Two children and their parents sit around a large oak table having supper. They laugh and eat, the epitome of 'family.' I am sad and long to be inside."

When I awake sadness engulfs me. I want my life now to be as it was. I feel justified in my dissatisfaction in what my life is now.

I share my dream with friends, and they tell me how they feel when they pretend the dream is theirs. Through their projections I see the truth, which I was cleverly avoiding. I am sinking into sentimentalism. My early home life was never idyllic. I am using a storybook version of my past to keep me a child, locked out of my own home. I am not a child looking into what was. I am an adult, wanting to be free of adult responsibilities. If my path is dark, I must find ways to light the path. By peering woefully into a sentimentalized past I remain outside in the cold.

This debunking of my dream came as I talked to others. Nevertheless, I am left at the end with: What is the light I need?

The primary purpose of a dream-appreciation group is educational, learning the skills to help us tap into the great resource of understanding that our dreams provide. But as our groups work together we become more and more concerned for each other. We become sensitive to each other's pain, more desirous of finding ways of helping each other move through the crises with courage and hope. Our sense of interconnectedness increases.

We could no more disregard our concern for a member's pain than we could neglect our responsibility to follow through on the truths made evident in our own dreams.

As I have worked with dream groups and friends, we have often reached out to each other with suggested readings in the area causing the dreamer uncertainty or pain. Frequently a dreamer mentions these readings the next time we are together, incorporating the expanded view of the reading into help given by other dreamers.

Folk and literary knowledge found in books, periodicals, and to some extent community services, such as self-help groups, have often provided the needed encouragement in finding our paths. These resources did not solve our problems, but rather gave us choices. They helped illuminate the darkness and increased our ability to make our own way. We broadened our thinking by accepting, discarding, or holding for further reference material we would not have seen otherwise.

Through my own inner development I have come to appreciate the variety of spiritual expressions. I understand the world to be bound together by a consistent reality so immense that viewing it at different times from different places gives it the appearance of staggering complexity. I am indebted to Warren Weaver, for many years director for science of the Rockefeller Foundation, through whose writing I have come to appreciate the quantum theory of complementarity. No matter how contradictory two ways of looking at reality may appear, they can often be viewed as complementary, and thus, equally valid. The truth of it depends on the perspective of the one who holds the idea. By combining two apparently contradictory descriptions or opinions, and letting each exist under certain circumstances, our concept of reality is enriched. This is the essence of a holistic approach to healing, creative expression, and acts of compassion.

In our work with dreams we come to understand all dream content as purposeful, and all comments on our dreams as helpful in sorting out the dream's meaning. In literature, also, we look through many eyes at the reality that binds various views together. We take dreams and writings and come upon our own view, our own action, our own healing.

The greatest value of a dream metaphor is its pointing beyond itself to the emotional tone of our waking lives, pointing not to emotions as disembodied spirits: Guilt, Panic, Frustration, and so on, but emotions embodied in the immediate events of our days. So, too, the symbols of words often stimulate us to pass beyond the words themselves to inner direction. The words gesture toward truth that we have dimly known, but may not have been ready to trust or act upon. Words, if they are to have any genuine effect, are never accepted as static statements; rather, they lubricate the flow of our thoughts, and we sense the result as original and freeing.

The combined symbolism of the dream, pointing to our honest emotions, and words, both spoken and written, pointing toward honest response to the emotions, releases within us a rumbling of excitement. We move from resignation to acceptance, to recognition of our own power to generate change.

After the dream is over, the living of the dream begins, again.

As dreamers we are making an effort to understand what emotional forces within are affecting the way we live out our days. But we are urged on to a higher effort, to appreciate the resources we each have, many of which are already in our dreams. Our resources need to be appreciated and released, as does the source of our discomfort. Sharing what we read is a way of releasing possibilities to each other. I have come to believe that the artist within that created our dreams is reaching out to the artists beyond ourselves, the great writers, thinkers, engagers in life who can urge us through the pain, into the mystery, the grandeur surrounding us.

Certainly there are those of us who at times need professional help, but more often what is needed is others who care about us, and words that will help us discover our own wisdom, releasing the courage to accept our personal responsibility for taking steps toward change.

To be specific about how dream work may support our coping purposefully with life crises, let us look at several dreams that have metaphors related to the common theme of death. We will see how the dreamer identifies the emotions in the dream, relating them to his or her waking consciousness. Next I suggest you consider whether death is a theme in your dreams. Work on your dream and add it to the ones presented here. The dreams will be followed by a short bibliography of books pertaining to death. These selections are a small reservoir of writings on death in which you may dip and perhaps retrieve something that fits your experience, that touches your dreams, something that leads you beyond your conscious understanding, setting in motion the stirrings of new possibilities. I have also included a brief list of support groups available to people suffering from losses associated with death experiences.

Of the great mysteries the one to which we are all ultimately heir is death. In some fashion we learn to live with its inevitability and survive the loss of those we love. How we absorb the reality of death and the weight of grief has much to do with the quality of all our days.

In our dreams death wears many faces and looks on life from many angles. Most typically "death dreams" deal not with the loss of life but the loss of a way of life or change not yet fully absorbed. A young man dreams he is flying in a powerful 747 to a foreign country. There is a bomb threat aboard the plane. Before it can be checked out by the flight attendant the plane explodes, and the young man is plunging to the ground. He awakens in a sweat, knowing death is imminent. The dreamer wonders if this is a precognitive dream. Should he cancel a planned trip? Possibly, but first the dream is talked over with a friend. She associates the bomb with sexual frustration and fear. Although the dreamer considers this logical, it does not resonate to his feelings, nor does it touch his fear that the dream is a proclaimer of an actual impending disaster. The dreamer shares his day residue. He has been selected for a significant promotion. Outwardly he expresses delight. Inwardly he wonders if this will move him into a job so high-powered that he will "bomb out." Is he capable of handling the new responsibility? Does he really want the pressure? Is he being propelled by the assumption that "upward mobility" is the obvious vocational choice of direction?

As the emotions in the dream are identified with his waking circumstance, the fear of physical death fades, and the impending death of his familiar life-style is recognized.

Another way death enters our dreams is through the appearance of a deceased family member or close friend. An unresolved relationship takes on a new dimension through a dream encounter. Whether or not the personality of the dead person is actually communicating with us in our dreams, or whether our projection of that person accounts for the presence, is not the issue here. The dead person appears so convincingly alive that a change can take place in the dreamer through the encounter.

When my father died I had just been graduated from college, struggling to dislodge myself from the dependency of childhood. My father had believed in me with such completeness that I had spent most of my early years living up to his high regard, grossly aware of unexpressed weaknesses that depressed and frightened me. Secretly I felt that if my father knew the anger I felt toward his benign trust, it would either destroy him or I would be cast outside the family walls forever. When he died, I was filled with sorrow, guilt, and anger. It was several years later that I had a short dream which transformed his death into a simpler grief and a great appreciation of his love for me.

"I was furious with my father. He had placed himself at a distance, slightly amused when I tried to talk to him. Suddenly I lost control. I screamed and screeched all my pent-up grievances. At last I stopped, ready to step back in self-defense, but half frozen with fear. My father looked at me and smiled. It was a smile of complete acceptance. There was no defensiveness, no condemnation, no hurt. An avalanche of relief rushed over me. And I awoke."

While alive, my father would not have had the maturity to accept my barrage of emotion, but when I awoke from my dream I was absolutely certain that he could now accept me without being diminished in any way. Several years after his death we had accomplished a level of relationship, and I a freedom, impossible while he was alive.

The death of a child is a crushing reminder that death is to be part of all our lives. But death of a child by suicide is perhaps of all loss the most devastating. Sylvia was a member of some of my earliest workshops. She brought great perception to her dreams and offered projections to others that often led them into a more precise meaning of their dreams.

I had taught piano to her son, Paul, when he was in high

school, and knew him as an attractive, shy young man, gracious and gifted. Sylvia and her husband, Bill, were well aware of Paul's struggle with depression. They had given him loving support. Paul was under the care of a psychiatrist but dropped out when he was moved from individual to group therapy. The psychiatrist had advised Bill and Sylvia to leave him alone and let him work out his own dependency needs. Six months later, at age twenty-five, Paul shot himself.

The year after Paul's death Sylvia and one of her daughters, Margaret, drove across the United States. In Sylvia's words, "One of the goals of this trip for me was to visit the relatives along the way and really sort of wrap up Paul's suicide." Sylvia felt some relatives had been too shocked by the suicide to react openly on the phone. Their trip released much talk about other tragedies in the family. Some had been unknown to Sylvia before their visit. One night after an intense conversation with her relatives she had the following dream:

"Bill and I were dragging a coffin into our living room. I looked in. There was Sammy [their dog, now dead]. His dog form known to me. I was a bit shocked because I was sure it would be Paul. I ran my eyes over him, the ears, the spots, the flank, the tail, the paws. Dear Sammy. I turned away, and when I looked again, the body was no longer Sammy, but Paul as we found him. It was the whole suicide scene, just exactly as he was lying there, except he was in the coffin. Black blood caked on his face. As before, I ran my eyes over the beloved body. The body was clothed, and I paused at the hips, wondering if the lipoma from his childhood was still there. I looked for a while at the body as though from a distance of time. And it wasn't nightmare horrible, as at the time of death. When I awoke I immediately knew the meaning of the dream. We have brought the death into the living room. And we can live with it. I awoke satisfied that the dream reflected the truth."

When Sylvia returned home from her trip she told her husband her dream. They talked about how, for so long, it seemed Paul's death would never be put to rest. Now they had shared openly with their relatives and had faced the horrible loss. Paul was dead. Memories and desires remained, but their son was dead. The distance Sylvia felt as she looked at the blood-caked face and beloved body was not one of avoidance; it was distance from the immediacy of grief and an awareness that Paul must be released—a natural distance, a moving on. Sylvia was saying: I am here. I am alive, but Paul is dead. However I rage, or yearn, his death remains a death.

Sylvia's family knew before Paul's death that their dog, Sammy, had cancer and would soon die. But the cancer went into remission, and the dog lived on a year after the suicide. Sammy sensed the family's grief and would go from bedroom to bedroom after Paul's death. Sylvia called him "a minister to us." In the dream it was as if Sammy's death enabled Sylvia to get closer to Paul's death. In waking reality the visit to her relatives was the agent for laying her son's death out in the open, and by so doing, aided Sylvia in accepting her horrible loss.

The day Sylvia shared this dream with me she said, "Someone once asked me if I had known I would have a child who would die of suicide, would I have wanted to have the child. And I said, 'Yes, I really think I would.' Because those times, all those good experiences of having him and living with him and growing up with him, they were pretty terrific. Some people have none of that. If he had lived, we would have had other times. But what we've had, we've had. I remember sometimes at night Bill and I would talk and put the kids to bed. We'd say what a good day this was for them, and then we'd say, 'Well, it's one day under the belt, ' in a contented voice, and think of all the good it will do, this one day. It was a good feeling. I have asked now: What about those days? Where are they? But I guess they are complete in themselves."

Later that day Sylvia read to me from James Hillman's *Suicide and the Soul,* a book that helped her through the darkest times.

Gram Shriver was 94 when she died, leaving sadly empty the corner seat, second row, in the Episcopal Church she had attended longer than other members could remember. She had lived for years with her daughter, Lil, a widow of remarkable versatility. Lil loved her mother deeply.

Some months before her death Gram remembered two dreams that she shared with me and with Karen Anderson.

Karen is the mother in "The Family That Dreams Together," whose story is told in *Working With Dreams* (Ullman and Zimmerman, Chapter 9).

Dream 1: "I saw two feet. They were surrounded in light. I knew they were the feet of Jesus. I tried to look up and see his face, but I couldn't. I wanted so much to see Jesus, but it wasn't possible. I was sad. I felt I had more to do."

Dream 2: "I was in a plane. Then I was outside the plane. It was glorious. I was flying through the sky, up and down. Oh, I felt so free! Then Lil said I must come down immediately. She was very upset and certain it was not right for me to be flying outside the plane like that. I didn't want to come down, but I thought I should do what she wanted. She was so worried. I began to fall and landed in a haystack. I was surprised I wasn't injured at all by the fall. Lil took me to the hospital, but I had no injuries."

Gram's physical condition was deteriorating, but otherwise she remained an alert, spirited lady. Her visitors invariably came away blessed by her insight and faith in the God she had worshiped and loved all her life. Gram was ready to die. She was not frightened. Death seemed practical and welcome. More than that, she believed she would be united with God in a way not possible while in her physical body. At first she felt that she continued to live because there was spiritual work remaining for her to accomplish. This was her understanding of her first dream when she couldn't raise her eyes to see Jesus. Several weeks later, when she had the second dream, this hindrance seemed to be resolved. Now Gram anticipated with exhilaration the freedom of physical death in her metaphor of flying free of the plane. Then, remembering her daughter's love and concern for her welfare, she was brought "down to earth." Gram was saying in her dream that she heard her daughter's earnest desire that she live. The "no injuries" of her dream was perhaps the recognition that despite her yearning to be free, no actual harm would come from staying a while longer within the confines of her body.

Lil talked to Karen and others about the great loss she would feel when her mother died. Slowly she began to accept the inevitable transition it would be for them both. As day followed day, Gram's physical condition continued to decline, while at the same time she planned her own funeral and burial. Gram got in touch with the Saint Francis Center, an organization in Washington D.C., that provides support to people facing personal and practical difficulties associated with illness, death, and dying. She asked friends to make her pine coffin. It was assembled in the home of the Anderson family. Lil came to believe it was right for her mother to die. The coffin was finished, with a small cross carved in the lid of the simple box.

The following day Gram Shriver died.

Dreams can be a seedpod in which the seeds of the past and the plantings of the future are encased. When we crack them open, reseeding of life can begin again. But where, how?

In an era of visual media overload, we do well to also look within for balanced direction. At best, recovery from the pain of life crises is jagged. The gritty demands of ongoing responsibilities need to become coherent with new levels of reality, often dimly perceived, and with sorrow not soothed by pat explanations. A number of national groups extend specialized support to people suffering from death experiences, and I include a partial listing, some with local chapters.

The written word may be experienced not merely as intellectual stimulation, but as a pathway to our inner light. A word, a phrase, a paragraph brought into the silence of our own being may stimulate the self-healing process. It is for this purpose, as you work with your own dreams and reactions to death, that the following bibliography is offered. Some of these books have been a source of guidance and comfort to the dreamers whose dreams you have just read.

Life need not be a slow march toward degeneration and hopelessness. We can look within and without for help. Within, our dreams sharpen the images of our stress until our emotions become defined. Within, our dreams gather together old and new responses to our problems. Some responses, outdated and inhibiting change, need to be discarded; others may, with refinement or repetition, generate change.

We look without to a host of people who have moved through

searing pain, disregarding easy answers, refusing defeat, to emerge with inner strength and compassion. They have helped us appreciate and release our resources as we have shared together in dream workshops and support groups and as friends. And theirs also are the voices of the writers who, reaching deep within themselves, have spread out their discoveries so we might "drink from wells we did not dig."

Our dream theaters are never dark. Against the backdrop of these nightly revelations are the voices of the day, waiting for us to unite with them in courage and hope.

Self-Help Aids, Support Groups, and Organizations Available to People Suffering from a Death Experience

Candlelighters
2025 Eye Street, N.W. Suite 1011
Washington, DC 20006

Candlelighters is part of a worldwide network of parents who have children with cancer, and parents whose children have died.

Compassionate Friends in the United States
P.O. Box 1347
Oak Brook, IL 60521

A nondenominational self-help organization for parents who have experienced the death of a child.

The Grief Education Institute
P.O. Box 623
Englewood, CO 80105

A nonprofit organization whose program includes workshops, seminars, and lectures to help people work effectively with death-related grief.

Shanti Nilaya (Home of Peace)
P.O. Box 2396
Escondido, CA 92023

Founded by Elisabeth Kübler-Ross, its purpose is to see life as a challenge rather than merely a painful ordeal. Workshops are given for bereaved families of children who have died.

Saint Francis Center
1768 Church Street, N.W.
Washington, DC 20036

A nondenominational organization whose purpose is to provide counsel, support, and caring to those facing the personal and practical difficulties associated with grief, loss, impairment, illness, death, and dying. They publish a substantive newsletter, *Centering*.

They Help One Another
Spiritually (THEOS)
Office Building Penn Hills Mall
Suite 306
Pittsburgh, PA 15235

Suicide support groups are a part
of most community mental
health centers. Further information may be obtained from:

Suicide Bereavement
334 Presway Road
Timonium, MD 21093

Suicide Prevention Center, Inc.
184 Salem Avenue
Dayton, OH 45406

References

Grollman, Earl A., ed. *What Helped Me When My Loved One Died.* Boston: Beacon Press, 1981.

Hillman, James. *Suicide and the Soul.* Dallas: Spring Publications, Inc., 1983.

Nouwen, Henri J.M. *A Letter of Consolation.* San Francisco: Harper and Row, 1982.

Shneidman, Edwin. *Voices of Death.* New York: Harper & Row, 1980.

Ullman, Montague, and Zimmerman, Nan. *Working With Dreams.* Los Angeles: Jeremy P. Tarcher, Inc., 1979.

Vail, Elaine. *A Personal Guide to Living With Loss.* New York: John Wiley & Sons, Inc., 1982.

Weaver, Warren. *Scene of Change.* New York: Charles Scribner's Sons, 1970.

Part Two

THE SPREAD
TO OTHER
DISCIPLINES

·4·

Creativity and Dreams
HELENE FAGIN, Ph.D.

It is now over a decade since I introduced experiential dream work as a course in a psychoanalytic training center. Helene Fagin was one of the candidates exposed to this way of learning about dreams. Looking back over the eleven years that have elapsed since then, I think she was the one who was most deeply affected by this approach and the one most responsive to and excited by the aesthetic and metaphorical power of dream imagery. She went on to acquire further training in the process and has conducted her own dream groups. In line with her special interest in creativity she undertook the study reported in this chapter about the dreams of artists and the influence of dream work on their creative work.

Introduction

Since the time Cro-Magnon man first painted the images of bison and unicorns by torchlight deep within the Caves of Lascaux, the artistic vision has distinguished man from his animal forebears. Throughout the centuries, we have admired and stood in awe of the power and magical qualities imbued in these works. Yet, it is only during the last twenty-five years that psychologists have looked at the creative process itself in seeking to understand this human capacity to express feelings, dreams, wishes, and imagination. It is man's unique way of responding to the world around him and of gaining mastery and control over its meaning.

Creativity is a multifaceted phenomenon, a complex group of processes and activities that result in new and innovative ideas and products. The source of this creative endeavor is described by Storr as the split between the inner and outer world that is common to all human beings, and the need to bridge the gap. It is our childhood dissatisfactions that stimulate our rich fantasy life. From this inner world springs the "divine discontent" (Plato) that compels us to seek our symbolic satisfactions in creative achievement. Dreams provide access to this inner world, and when explored and understood, create a connecting bridge.

The Link Between Dreams and Creativity

Creativity has been linked with dreams throughout history long before Freud elaborated on their nature and function. The symbolists—Redon, Ensor, Gauguin—used the imagery of dreams in their work. Goya produced monsters and nightmarish figures from his dreams, whereas van Gogh spun stars and earth in a blue sky. The surrealists, Dali, Ernst, and their followers, took the actual images from their dreams creating bizarre, yet strangely familiar, landscapes. Some artists and writers such as Coleridge and Blake described dreamlike trances that led to their masterpieces.

Dream images were originally thought to be divinely inspired, as were dreams since the time of the Egyptians. The Temple of Konumba in Egypt has a hieroglyphic depicting the gathering of people to share their dreams with the high priest, who represented the crocodile god, Sobek. He could then tell them their ailments and problems and predict their futures.

Many theorists, as well as the artists and writers themselves, emphasize the similarity between dreams and works of art. Rothenberg alludes to some of these elements, as follows:

> the primarily visual nature of dreams and the visual nature of painting, sculpture, etc.; the seeming novelty in the content of dreams and the novelty in art; the particularity and concreteness of dreams and art; the sense of story and sequence in dreams despite shifting time references and the similar sequential sense in art, especially in literature and

music; the sharp contrasts and contradictions depicted in
dreams and art; the extraordinary vividness of dreams and
the vividness embodied in works of art; . . . that dreams like
art have strong emotional connotations. (p. 40)

He describes the creative process as the "mirror image" of the
dream, one that produces order and meaningful images and
metaphors in contrast to the dream thought which produces
confusing chaotic and manifestly illogical images and sequence.
"Unconscious material is shaped and integrated into the resulting creation, and, for the creator, some degree of awareness or
personal insight usually occurs" (Rothenberg, p. 41).

"Incubation," which is mentioned in almost all the descriptions
of creativity, is another important link between the creative process and dreams. This is a stage during which the individual is
not concentrated solely on the work or problem, and before the
new insight emerges. The word "incubate" is derived from a
Latin word meaning "to lie down upon"—thus when we sleep on
a problem, we are, in effect, incubating. In certain ancient Roman rites, incubation referred to lying down on a mat in order to
have dreams in which one communicated with the deities of the
underworld.

The incubation period is part of the dream experience. The
conscious mind is at rest, and long-forgotten memories and experiences emerging in the dream state create new visions and
possibilities.

An Artists' Dream Group

Dreams have always interested me in my work as a psychoanalyst, where patients in speaking about their dreams paint a powerful picture of their inner world. I have been moved by the
beauty and creativity of the metaphorical language of the dream
to express deep feeling. I first became aware of the creative potential of dream work through Dr. Montague Ullman's approach
to working with dreams, an approach that tapped a resource of
human potential so undervalued in our culture. I conducted
workshops on dreams for mental-health professionals throughout the United States and Canada for the American Group Psy-

chotherapy Association. Among my patients were several artists and writers, whose dreams were especially vivid and creative. In the course of therapy, there was a freeing-up of the creative process, which they connected with the dream work.

These two aspects of their lives, dreams and art, seemed strongly entwined. The idea of a dream group limited to painters and sculptors intrigued me. It presented a challenge and coincided with my longtime interest in the creative process itself. It seemed like a natural laboratory to observe directly any connections emerging from dream work that might affect the artist's work.

I decided to offer a dream workshop for artists in Westchester County, where I live and work, and received responses from about fifteen women artists. Twelve of them agreed to work with me for a period of ten months in a dream group to explore dreams and their relationship, if any, to the creative process. I visited each studio in order to answer questions, determine their interest in group participation, and to see their work in process.

During this initial exploration I found that one of the major interests of the artists was to find subject matter for their work through dreams. Each seemed to sense there were rich possibilities that were available but were not being utilized. Some expressed the wish to be freer and less constricted in their work. Others thought the dream might provide access to new sources of imagery for their paintings. For some, who claimed that they never dreamed (six out of the twelve), it was a curiosity about dreams, this unknown aspect of themselves. A few of them felt that "being with other artists might be less lonely," "more stimulating," and even "fun." I accepted them based on their willingness to make a firm commitment and did not evaluate their work.

All were working artists. Their work had been shown at a variety of art galleries in Westchester as well as in two artists' cooperatives in New York City that are specially interested in women artists. Their work represented varied approaches—representational and nonobjective, printmaking, collage, and sculpture. There was also a wide range of ability and experience. Two of them were mature women artists who had gone back to school for degrees in fine arts and art management. Two others would probably define themselves as sculptors rather than painters, though they worked in both media.

There were some variations on the dream-group method described by Dr. Ullman that had special application for the artists. At the beginning of each session, the artist/dreamer shared further insights obtained from working on the dream privately with special emphasis on any stimulus she may have experienced involving her work. Announcements by the artists of their shows or important information relating to the artistic community were discussed.

For the artist her work is often inseparable from her life. For some, art provides an outlet for the release of frustrations experienced in daily living. For others, it is a fulfillment of deepest wishes, needs, and fantasies long buried since childhood. In any case, the dream group helps the artist build that connection, providing access to unknown resources within. By making the unconscious known, we open up the possibility of utilizing a new insight and returning to it at a point when one feels blocked or stuck.

The dream group provides the artist with a chance to experience this. Rather than the "royal road" Freud described, I see it as a river that has been dammed, ready to flow again in the safety of the dream group.

Metaphoric Language in Artists' Dreams

Artists are especially sensitive to visual imagery and seem to respond to the pictorial qualities of the dream in a unique way. They describe vivid, cinematic imagery with attention to light and composition, reminiscent of actual paintings. The dreams presented by this group were unusually imaginative. They had a more aesthetic quality than those of other groups with whom I had worked.

As an illustration, Diane described the setting of her dream as an ocean liner riding high above the water but dramatically listing to one side. The group responded with images of the famous poster of the S.S. *Normandie*, although Diane had told us the ship was the *QE II*. In the dialogue, as the group questioned her more closely, Diane recalled that the *Normandie* had been the setting for a special experience with her father that was significant in understanding the dream. The painting tied past and present experiences, linking the men in her life—her husband with whom she had honeymooned on the *QE II*, and her father, with whom she had visited the *Normandie* as a little girl.

Paintings became the language of the group, and there were a number of references to works of art in the dream imagery. Masochism was represented in a painting of the martyred Saint Jerome. The surrealist qualities of the dream often evoked memories of scenes from the works of Magritte, Dali, or Balthus.

The dreams of the artists seemed to trigger imagery from one to another as each adapted and utilized metaphors in her own way. There were multiple water images starting with the Art Deco poster of the *Normandie* about to capsize in the ocean; walking along the rocks next to the Atlantic in Maine; a pier in Southampton jutting out into the ocean; canals filled with debris; gutters flooded with rain water, dams bursting; stagnant pools, and people swimming in the murky waters of a lake. The artists related many of these images to mother, birth, and the creative process itself. They viewed their creativity as a birth process, a struggle toward delivery similar to childbirth, a natural but often painful experience. Water also represented a harmonious force connected with symbiosis, oneness, and closeness to "mother" nature and the world. The members of the group were curious about the numerous references to childbirth that appeared in so many of their dreams.

Another common metaphor permeating the dreams was "illumination" and the experiencing of color in a distinctive way. In one dream there was a sky exploding with a profusion of color and light over Manhattan. In another there were light beams beneath the water followed by underground swimmers. In still another, night suddenly changed into daylight. Leonora's room in her dream was strangely illuminated without sunlight or artificial light. In Jackie's dream she described the darkness of an archeological dig where the colors were light, sand-color, dirt-beige. In Mary's dream, the sky was a luminous blue-violet color.

I believe that the emphasis on details of color and light has to do with the importance of this aspect of an artist's work. Color and light are essential elements of painting, and the artist cannot help respond sensitively to them in her environment.

Emerging Themes and Issues

One of the major themes in the dreams related to identity conflicts—artist versus woman, wife, and mother. The quest for identity is described by Koestler as one of the motivations underlying creativity. When a person feels divided or split, this interferes with the freedom to express one's talent. This became clear over the course of the meetings of the dream group. The dream is often an attempt to reconcile incompatible aspects of personality. This was illustrated in dreams that focused on the struggle between a woman's identity as homemaker and as artist.

Susan's dream ends with this choice clearly defined—to go toward a crying child or down the steps of the Metropolitan Museum of Art to the world of art. Marilyn's dream involves a mother figure dishing out bowls of spaghetti—more for the husband and less for the wife. Her struggle is between her own needs as an artist, and his for creative expression in his film work. The husband often sees the primary responsibility of his wife as homemaker rather than as artist. The artist/wife struggles with this division within her. Some dreams, such as Diane's, reveal guilt about expressing the artistic side. Only when children have grown and left home can there be a complete acceptance of the self as "artist." Roslyn described a shift in her attitude after working on her dream. "It made me look at things from a different point of view. We are adults now. Our grown children are doing their thing. I feel more aware of their needs as individuals—not as part of me."

The process of "separation-individuation" as part of the development of a sense of identity was another important group theme. Separating from one's grown children seemed to touch on old issues of separation from mother that had not been resolved. Many of the dreams revolved around parental figures, especially mothers. The continued ambivalence toward the maternal figure was a surprise to many. Its emergence in the dreams helped participants become more aware of this and of its relationship to their creative work. The following example deals with the personal and creative aspects of working through a dream and applying it to one's life. It provides an opportunity to see how the process works.

Leonora's Dream

"I am in a sterile, white room. It isn't painted. It is papered white. It is higher than it is wide or long. I feel disoriented; the perspective seems wrong. It is very bright, although there are no windows or lights. It is like a box. I am quite aware that this is a dream. As uncomfortable as I feel, I know that I can awaken if I wish. I think I even say 'This is a dream' in my dream. Suddenly, I see a pile of boulders or stones in the corner. I am surprised because it seems wrong for them to be in that environment. I wonder if I am supposed to do something with them, but I can't imagine what it should be—whether I should try to drag them one by one to another corner. I am really agitated because I don't know what to do with these stones. Now there is a ladder-back chair, white, in the middle of the room. A heavy woman sits in it, her buttocks overflowing the seat of the chair. I only see her from the back, but she seems familiar. I approach, and now I am a child. It is my mother, although there is no expression or welcome. I climb into her lap with difficulty. She seems very large to me and doesn't help at all. Once on her lap, I close my eyes and bury my face in her bosom. Again, I know it is a dream, and I think it is silly that I am expecting protection and nurturing from my mother. I look up at her, but she's changed into my husband. I'm uncomfortable, and I want to wake up. Now I'm seated, and I am the seated figure, and my oldest son is a baby in my lap. He is crying, and I don't know how to soothe him. I'm very upset and wake up."

The dream encompasses some of the issues mentioned—identity in terms of child, mother, and wife and the struggle to express oneself creatively. It sees the maternal figure as unnurturing, and there is an identification with the unresponsive parent. The group focused on the feelings of rejection, impotence, and longing. They picked up on the coldness of the boulder and stonelike woman. The mother was viewed as impersonal, like a Botero painting, the whiteness of unrelenting light, a Mexican setting. There was the identity confusion of mother, husband, and self. The stones were seen by the group as the materials of sculpture, large well-rounded forms, sturdy and massive like Leonora's work. The group's specific responses to the metaphors follow:

> The room has a strange perspective. If I can change my perspective and not be so boxed in, perhaps I would feel better.
>
> The dream feels very clinical, mechanical and sterile, like a hospital. Perhaps it is a womb.
>
> White paper in layers makes me think of papier-mâché.
>
> The forms are so sculptural—the ladder-back chair like in a Balthus painting. The dream is a ladder going back in time.
>
> Lights are the illumination, like going into the center of my own being, descending into a well. The illumination in the other dreams was outside. This is clearly in the center—me, mother. I am the center now.
>
> There are two types of work and two types of problems—one dealing with my art and fitting it into my life—the boulder and the stone. The other is being a mother and wife, dealing with children. There is creation and procreation—my life work .
>
> Where am I in these relationships—with my mother, myself, and my child?
>
> The impulse to create is causing the agitation and is pressing. Perhaps the baby is my new work, what I am giving birth to.
>
> The creative force is my new work—represented by those boulders.
>
> As I approach the rocks in my work, I stay with it. I get some kind of comfort, although they are very difficult to move. When I get into it, it really moves me. It is difficult to approach it, to confront the challenge.
>
> I feel like the child, suppressing my own needs and feelings; there are not sounds. It is so locked up—the sound that wakes me is a silent scream. I feel agitated.
>
> The setting feels like the Mari Galleries; the walls are papered

with paintings. There is the feminine and masculine part of me, the quality of my male and female self. I feel isolated in the center, comforted by the round form of the breasts.

My husband is like my mother, but he takes care of me, and he gave me my son.

I want to be conscious that I am dreaming to bring it to the dream group.

I feel caught with my needs for a nurturing relationship with my son. I am a bad mother, like my own mother and not empathic. My strength is with my work, not my mothering.

Leonora's Response to the Group: "I thought about the dream a lot today. I'm not used to this kind of thing. Originally, I felt it had a lot to do with a need for renewal. After a show, I usually feel let down, but this time I expected to feel differently because of the writing. All my energy has now gone into writing, but I was feeling very sterile. I thought when people were responding that perhaps the white paper was typing paper and I was feeling unable to write.

"The figure in the room was a literal description of what my mother looked like. She was five feet tall and weighed three hundred pounds. The form was beautiful, yet horrible. There was always that combination of beauty and ugliness, almost disgust. I recognized the feeling in the dream. Originally, I thought of the dream literally, that it was silly to expect to get nurturing, but then she turned into my husband. I felt uncomfortable in expecting something from him. An adult shouldn't need nurturing.

"While I was listening, I realized that I was describing the shape of one of my stones, tall and rectangular, and the result is very blank, not any light. I had the feeling that there should be something to release the light in the stone.

"Yes, I have difficulty in dragging the stones. I feel like a pack mule. There is great difficulty and not enough time and energy for both the creative part and the wife-mother part of me. I know that I am an adult and feel I shouldn't need that kind of nurturance, but I want it. The comment about impotence really hit me a great deal; and my relationship with people, something is not clear in that area. Father was more nurturing than mother.

Mother told me that I didn't know how to give love. I am not sure who is right.

"The comment about light being insight, that was something that I hadn't thought of. I'm struggling with that illumination, some realization that is just out of reach. In writing, it is called 'epiphany,' some slight change and realization. I also visualize it as a light going on.

"First, mother is the center, then husband and then child. When is my turn? I want the center, and it is a struggle for me because I feel guilty about it. It frightened me when the words were said about the sculpture being on the side—put aside. I put in a forty- or fifty-hour work week in my work, yet my husband and society do not see it as my 'work.' My main job is wife and family. My husband *is* very supportive and proud of 'his wife's accomplishments.' Also, I am putting aside my writing, which I have always wanted to do and did before my sculpting.

"The baby is the newness of me and still unable to handle it as an adult. Am I abandoning the sculpture for something new? Is that my oldest son in the dream? The new work, the child who is crying, perhaps that is the writing which is crying out.

"I often feel like a little girl, uncomfortable and ashamed. Other times, I am a superwoman and can do anything. I'll take care of the world. I am very uncomfortable about acknowledging my needs—open to everyone but myself about things that happened. I am frightened about acknowledging myself. I guess I don't feel entitled. The feeling of worth is so elusive. I feel I have no reason to expect anything, positive or negative, that feels natural. I did feel anger at that moment in my mother's lap even though I was not expecting anything."

The dialogue stage of the process was very limited because of the completeness with which Leonora connected with her own dream. She did recall the statement her husband had made the night before the dream: "'Did you notice that so and so showed up at our opening?' It went through my head that when he practices law, it is not '*our* case' that is on trial. So I guess I was pretty angry at him when I went to sleep."

The following session Leonora expanded on her response to her dream. It was the first dream she had remembered in ages. She used to have terrible dreams after the death of her mother.

When she awoke, she would go down to the basement and sculpt in clay. The figures were horrifying and not very saleable. The emotion had been unbearable, but there was something positive in working on the sculptures. She thought that perhaps she was containing her horror, not feeling so overwhelmed.

Something important happened to Leonora since working on the dream, and she shared it with the group. It involved her writing.

"One of the associations that hit home for me was the one about the child being my creativity. The oldest son represented my first love—writing. I went home very stimulated and excited by the experience. Tuesday, when I woke up, I sat down and started writing, thinking it might be a short story. I had been suffering from a writing block on Monday, since the teacher had given me the assignment. It just flowed out of me, and I realized that I had the beginning of a novel. I felt as if a stopper had been taken out. It felt so good!"

I should also add an event that followed the dream work, which I only became aware of when I went to interview Leonora after the group work had ended. I saw a sculpture in her studio of a heavy woman on a stool with a naked baby tightly embraced, close to the breast. It was powerful and moving, as I experienced both strength and tenderness in the embrace. I asked Leonora about this new sculpture. She replied: "This is the one I did after the dream that I discussed with the group. It is the opposite of the feeling in the dream, but it *is* the mother and child which was the vision I had—but the other mother was not someone who could hug. My mother was very loving in a Russian sort of way, but she was also very crazy. Well, I was really going to put aside the sculpture for a while and work on my writing and then I said, 'Don't throw something away completely,' and I said, 'I'm going to do something that is not in the round and work on a bas-relief, which does not take as long.' I bought this stone. I guess I was going to do a mother and child. I was working on the drawing, and as I was working, I was laughing and saying 'This is a whole madonna number you are doing.' The more I laughed at myself, the sweeter it became. I kept saying that I was going to work on the stool so I could get the dark in there and the whole thing had nothing to do with stools. This had to be a mother really holding that baby, and the baby had to be naked. It was something I had to do, and in the midst of . . . no, I guess when I got to the polishing, when I no longer could think about what I was doing, I said, 'My God, this is the woman with the big hips sitting on the chair and, instead of saying "no" to the baby, she is really, absolutely hugging the baby.'"

I commented to her that it sounded like an outcome of working on her dream. The dream wish for a loving mother was fulfilled in her sculpture.

Self-Esteem

Another issue for the group of artists was appreciating the importance of their dreams. The dreams were often introduced as "nothing," "unimportant," "weird." As they were explored and understood and seen as one's own creative productions, a gradual sense of acceptance, and even pride, emerged. After the connections were made, there would be an acknowledgment of ownership and recognition of important issues that were confronted honestly. The same reaction was apparent in the denigration by some of the importance of their artistic work. Since this work was often considered secondary to the "real work" of the husband, it also had a diminished value in their eyes.

The growth in self-esteem and confidence within the dream group was one of the most apparent changes that took place. In their self-reports, one after another commented on new-found assertiveness, willingness to risk rejection, and deserving the hard-won prize or acclaim. The issue of confidence and self-assertion was a central one in moving from behind the palette out into the world of art critics and New York galleries.

Even the more successful artists, who had many gallery shows and had earned recognition and awards, had difficulty in this area. This was evidenced through dreams that dealt with childhood experiences, and it revealed the lack of validation from significant authority figures (parents). Each artist had to risk being judged and evaluated and, possibly, found wanting. The healing process of dream work seemed to extend good feelings of value and self-worth to artistic products. Through an improved sense of self, some rather striking things happened.

Jackie sold her first sculpture at a show in New York at the Cork Gallery at Lincoln Center. It was one of her sleeping son called "The Arms of Morpheus," named in response to the dream-group experience. She had enough self-assurance to make several castings of the original and place a good price on her work.

Elaine, shortly after sharing her dream, went off to Florence, Italy. In her dream, she was singing on a stage "There's No Business Like Show Business," and half the audience walked out. The group related to the audience as the critics, and her performance as the struggle with the business of showing one's work, an exposure of an intimate, personal part of the self. She later brought her slides to a gallery, and they agreed to arrange a show of her work. She commented to the group on her new-found ability to sail into an unknown situation and sell herself. Even more significant, after withdrawing from the group for the second half because of other commitments, she had a burst of inspiration and energy and painted a series of works after reading about the Holocaust. These were powerful images of death contrasted with flowers and gardens representing life. She sold more than ten paintings. This was her first success. Her work was described by both the viewers and herself as different from any of her previous efforts.

Susan commented on an increase in self-assertiveness that enabled her to ask for, and be accepted, in a show in a Madison Avenue gallery.

Elyse had her show and received plaudits from critics and teachers. The confidence to try something completely different from anything she had done before was attributed by her to the self-awareness that came through the dream group as well as the support and encouragement of its members.

Diane H. had the confidence to paint her dreams and to try more expressionist work.

The other artists also showed signs of increasing willingness to take risks, each in her own way, and each according to where she was in her artistic and emotional growth and development.

Freedom Versus Responsibility

There is a quality to creativity that taps into the playful part of ourselves, a freedom once experienced as children but often repressed in adult life. Children often express artistic talent without inhibition, use metaphorical imagery, color, and form in ways reminiscent of a Picasso or Klee. When the child part is helped to emerge in the adult, we see the release of imagination and creativity.

The group dealt with this issue in several ways. One was by getting in touch with the inner child through working with dreams. The dream, in its search for resolution of present tensions, returns to the childhood years when these tensions arose. In recalling childhood memories and experiences, we utilize them for our own growth. We can come closer to integrating two aspects of the self—the freedom of childhood and the discipline of maturity.

During the part of the dream group process called "the game," in which the group takes on the presented dream as its own, there is this sense of playfulness and spontaneity. Here we are utilizing what has been described as "right brain function." Intuitive, holistic, empathic responses are being stimulated by interaction with each other. Reason, control, intellectualization, and interpretation are put aside. After ten months of working together, there was a recognizable change—a wider range of associations, greater imagination, and freedom to react spontaneously. Group members were willing to take on the dream as their own and respond to the metaphors with less investment in being right, an important issue for a highly conscientious group. Excitement and mutual interaction developed to an intense level. Part of this is due to the safety of the structure and trust in the leader to control the process and set the boundaries. It bears some resemblance to that first sense of spontaneous play and imagination developed in the safety of the mother's presence. (Winnicott)

Parallels Between Dreams and Creativity

An interesting phenomenon observed in the dream group was the parallel between dreams and creativity. Rugg gives a metaphorical description of the creative process:

> It is as though successive closed doors barred off a passageway of dark antechambers which ranged from the deep unconscious through several sub-, fore-, or pre-conscious

> rooms, into the light of conscious day. We forget our prob-
> lems, sleep on it, let go, relax. In one way or another, we get
> the conscious mind off guard so that contacts on the fringe
> of consciousness can be established. Then, the spark ex-
> plodes the meaning (p. 11).

Several artists had dreams in which they passed through dark
rooms and corridors with passageways leading back into their
childhood and adolescence, arriving finally at a brightly illuminated area representing the future. There seemed to be a parallel search toward growth that would permit fertility and freedom
in the artistic process. The search in life, in work, and in dreams
is to illuminate that process of creativity. The dream group acts
as a stimulus to both dreaming and creativity.

Shirley was the first artist to paint some of the images that appeared in her dreams. In her work, the dream and the creative
process seemed to merge. She did three water colors that were
beautiful, poetic, mythical in quality, in a lower-world setting.
They depicted several small figures in sheer flowing gowns wandering through subterranean caves and archways, ascending toward the illumination above. The group named it "Dream Pas-
sages." Shirley said when interviewed, "The thought of painting
dreams is fascinating. The ideas so many expressed, that they
were wandering through dark rooms and searching for things. I
see it as a metaphor for not knowing what to do in life."

Art depicts the deepest levels of the human psyche. The artist,
like the dreamer, draws on past and present experiences to create something new. There are images that have symbolic significance in a highly personal and idiosyncratic way. Perhaps the
spark that ignites into creativity is the sudden interaction between two electric currents, past and present, as they cross and
make contact.

Some examples of the artists' use of dreams to find creative
sources within themselves follow:

Elyse: "Yes, I may be doing the best work I've ever done. My
paintings used to be saccharine sweet. I never wanted anyone to
know what went on in me. The dreams are allowing me to show
other people what is really going on. The reviews have been phe-

nomenal. One professor commented, 'There seems to be a tremendous amount of growth.' My sculpture teacher thought that
I was using my own struggle to show strong forms. The dream
group opened up feelings, delving into my metaphors, sometimes a little deeper than I wanted. The reception of these pieces
has been interesting. Everyone sees the feelings in them and the
dream images that I worked with. It is the first time that I have
exhibited so many pieces together, actually set up a show with
twenty pieces revealing my personality, exposing my guts."

Elyse's show was a powerful and disturbing one. One sculpture reminded me of a dream she had shared with the group
where she was imprisoned behind a tollgate that separated her
from the world of married couples. When I asked her about this,
she commented:

"Absolutely, I put that dream into a sculpture called 'Agony'
or 'Struggle.' It started as a leaf, and from there it emerged as a
person full of painful feelings—the shell on the outside to deal
with society, and the raw edges representing the inside of every
human being. This was going to be one of the people struggling
from being in the Holocaust—coming out of the mud—not
pretty grass but emerging out of this muddy field. The sculpture
needed some barrier, and the dream of the tollgate stayed in my
mind. The pole with the three spokes evolved from the feeling
of the tollgate. It is not only that we are held in by it but that we
have to pay so much in life for whatever we struggle to get. So it
is emerging not only from the Holocaust but from society's
restrictions."

Jackie: "I went through a couple of dreams, and I thought about
them in connection with my work. Instead of taking the individual metaphors of the dream, I decided to take the feeling from
the whole dream or a particular person in that dream and do a
piece that symbolizes the relationship. I want to pull the
energy and feeling from the dreams and direct them toward a
piece that represents what the relationship means."

Marilyn: "A change developed in my latest work, where one portrait is pasted on top of another and stitched to the paper—a
grandmother and a baby. To me, there were several levels. One

of them was the composition as a whole. Then there was what happens when the first baby is born, when everything changes in the family, and so the addition to the work. The addition was the baby which, of course, is integrated into the whole, which is what happens in the family. That really is a metaphor, so perhaps I am beginning to think in terms of metaphor."

Mary: "There is one painting that has a direct connection to a dream. One of my dreams ended looking out of a doorway, seeing the sky and horizon. It's not that I'm replaying the image, but many of my pieces seem to have an inner rectangle from which the light comes. In some I reverse it and put darkness in the center, looking inward. I have made a direct connection with the dream experience. Also, I guess I was relating it to the insight that I got from the dream, not knowing that I had this power to see something within myself. Sometimes vivid images come into my mind as I'm doing something or happen to see something just as when I was down by the river and the sky was illuminated as it was in Diane's dream of a nuclear explosion. I work more from the inner vision, and I want to explore it further. New stuff comes out because I'm aware of it."

Utilization of Childhood Experiences in Dreams and Art

Childhood experiences and memories are an essential part of dreams. In dreams recalled by members of the group, there were clear references to familiar childhood settings and parental figures. The struggle to grow and change was something that each was dealing with in her daily life as illustrated in the following excerpts from dreams:

Elaine went on stage following a woman named Joy, whom she later identified as her older sister, a famous artist. Joy had her act together and knew exactly what to do. Elaine, on the other hand, had to improvise. The dream pointed up the past rivalry between the two, how it was still holding Elaine back in the present. It encouraged her to face the public and risk rejection. The half-empty house in her dream and the stage setting had to do with where she was, in the middle stage of her life. Although half of it had passed, she could work and focus on the future and her own growth as an artist.

Barbara's dream described a baby crawling on the floor, in danger of pulling the connected cord of an electric iron. In the dream she explored her attempt at differentiation from mother —cutting the cord—while reflecting her as a role model. Her work, a series of books, combines childlike freshness with adult sophistication, both illustratively and in content. They seek to understand the universe adults have created through the simplicity and directness of a child's view. A brilliant young woman, she is searching for meaning in her work, her dreams, and her life.

Nadine had a dream in which the artist, Larry Rivers, substituted for the authority figure of her father. She indicated the dream helped her to clarify unresolved issues with her father relating to a man in her life. The ending of the dream was reminiscent of a Balthus painting, where a young, adolescent girl is at a window, dreaming of the world outside. It is descriptive of Nadine.

Value and Social Applications

Creativity is accorded great value in our culture, whereas dreams are dismissed as unimportant. In the early weeks of the dream group this attitude was observed among the artists. Undeniably, part of the problem is a lack of information and understanding of the importance and value of dreams. The dream becomes an open creative communication, as the group works with the dreamer. Dream groups help to reduce the social polarity between dreams and creativity, bringing them into a harmonious and parallel relationship.

Several of the artists felt that the dream group should and could be used in a larger framework. Mary, who works in a woman's prison, felt that a dream group could help inmates get in touch with their feelings. She saw it as a tool for productive growth and communication. Diane, who teaches art in a grammar school in the Bronx, has begun to use dreams in her classroom. She asks her students to talk about their dreams, then to paint some of the imagery they describe. This provides direct access to metaphor as a source of inspiration and stimulates the imagination.

Artists in the community, including several from the group, have rented space in converted lofts. Although they may work in fairly close proximity, they do not have specific opportunities to share experiences. A creative dream group could add a new dimension to their experience as an enrichment and stimulus to their work. Positive responses indicate the potential value of this type of depth experience to tap creative resources.

The dream group had a powerful effect on its members as you will see in their taped reports.

Marilyn: I found I became more connected with my dreams as I understood more how to approach them—became familiar with the ground rules and became more comfortable with the short-hand. When there were repeated motifs, we picked it up. There were some visual images from our life patterns. I certainly think about them more (dreams).

Mary: I am never going to look at dreams in the same way again. I can see more clearly what the images stand for, though I may wake up and wish ten people were there to help me understand them. Group input is powerful and strong. I think it helped me to know myself better and to recognize the things that bother me . . . to pay attention to what the unconscious is saying. One of the ideas I had in mind in coming to the group was a sort of un-blocking process. I was at a crossroads in my work, and this is providing some specific images.

Roslyn: In the beginning it surprised me that some members of the group shared as much as they did, not having met before. I didn't think that I was going to give much to it or that I was go-ing to get much. I was very skeptical. Now I would like the lux-ury of going into it even deeper. I know I'm very controlled, and that's another thing that works against me as an artist. If only I could get in touch with that old childish freedom! That's hard to get in touch with.

Leonora: I couldn't believe that in this group of ten or twelve artists there was such a feeling of support. I couldn't figure out how that had happened, and I felt that it had to do with the fact that we took each dream on as our own. I kept thinking about that—and that was what made the whole thing nonconfrontational.

Nadine: You realize from the interaction with other people that maybe you wanted to block certain things and not see them.

Elyse: The impact of the dream group for any artist that lives and works alone is overwhelming. When you have a group there is a greater openness and growth and awareness that everybody is going through the same problems.

Susan: All of a sudden, lately, I find these off-the-wall opinions (of mine) are valuable, and I have all these people coming to me for ideas. I had been feeling isolated, and it was important for me to find these other people. I needed the interaction and encouragement of other artists to get myself going.

Barbara: The first dream I shared had such impact for me. It was my introduction to the whole technique, and I was astounded by the amplification of the imagery. I loved the idea that in no other area do all the time spans of one's life come together. In my dream, there was a releasing of a bond (mother-daughter) toward autonomy. It's important for an artist, and it is also a woman's question.

Unanimously, the artists recognized the impact of sharing dreams in a group as a way of knowing oneself and connecting with others on the deepest level. My initial thought that dreams provide access to the rich, fertile soil of creative imagination appears to be supported by their responses and the changes in their work. Their artistic talents seem to have brought a more creative dimension to the metaphorical imagery in their dreams, and the dreams, in turn, illuminated their work. They drew what they needed from the experience and applied it in unique and idiosyncratic ways—on both a conscious and an unconscious level. They became more aware of the creative process, itself, as they focused on their inner world. They understood some of the sources of resistance and enjoyed a concomitant sense of freedom.

Conclusion

Creativity is potentially within many of us, but, along with talent and ability, there must be the courage to reveal ourselves. The dream group supports that kind of risk-taking, sharing feelings and, sometimes, painful memories. The artist's goal is to reveal the truth as he or she sees it, and the dream group enables each one to connect with that inner part of herself and express it in her work.

Kubie describes the creative process as "the capacity to find new and unexpected connections, to voyage freely over the seas, to happen on America as we seek new routes to India, to find new relationships in time and space, and thus new meanings" (p.149). The artist's voyage is both an internal and an external quest that brings order and meaning to his or her personal universe.

Artists have their own metaphorical language that can provide a source of material for painting through both emotional connections and content. Several of them experienced the release of energy after working on a dream or even hearing the dream of another participant. They confirm the impact of the shared experience on the solitary process of painting. The richness of metaphoric imagery stimulated the artists and remained with them when the dream group ended. They felt that these images were stored deep within and could be utilized at some future point as sources of imagery in their work. Susan described it as a "butterfly effect." This refers to the idea that a butterfly flapping its wings in Peking may affect the weather in New York, three weeks later. It is called "sensitive dependence on initial conditions." I have a feeling that a year from now things will happen with the group. One small dream discussed in the group will make a major change.

The full impact is something difficult to predict, but there certainly has been a flapping of wings.

References

Freud, S. *The Interpretation of Dreams*. New York: Basic Books, 1955.

Koestler, A. *The Act of Creation*. New York: Noonday Press, 1958.

Kubie, L. *Neurotic Distortion of the Creative Process*. New York: Noonday Press, 1958.

Rothenberg, A. *The Emerging Goddess*. Chicago, Illinois: University of Chicago Press, 1979.

Rugg, H. *Imagination*. New York: Harper & Row, 1963.

Storr, A. *The Dynamics of Creation*. New York: Atheneum, 1972.

Ullman, M., and Zimmerman, N. *Working With Dreams*. Los Angeles: Jeremy P. Tarcher, Inc., 1979.

Wallas, G. *The Art of Thought*. New York: Harcourt Brace, 1926.

Winnicott, D. *Playing and Reality*. New York: Basic Books, 1971.

·5·

Myths, Dreams,
and Divine Revelation:
From Abram to Abraham

JOHN A. WALSH, D. Min.

John Walsh brings both theological and psychological sophis-
tication to the story of Abraham's covenant with God and its
allegorical reference to the covenant one makes with oneself
through dream work. He likens Abraham's struggle to the uni-
versal issue of individuation and the role that dreams can play
in the struggle toward that goal. He compares the dream to an
inner voice that points the way, a way beset with setbacks and
trials.

Father Walsh's interest in dreams is related to his general
concern with ministry. The title of his doctoral disquisition
was "The Experiential Dream Group as Ministry." In it he
describes his own experiences as a leader of a dream group of
his parishioners.

Introduction

Dreams and visions have always played an important role in
the religious experience of people, for such phenomena put people in touch with a dimension of reality that is other than their
ordinary experience of the physical world. My own dreams have
deeply influenced my development since childhood and con-

tinue to vividly affect my sense of selfhood and union with God in my adult years.

This chapter, then, is devoted to describing the role of dream experience in one's religious development. The contents of the chapter are written within the framework of the Judeo-Christian tradition. The limiting of this survey of the religious role that dreams can and do exercise to the Judeo-Christian tradition stems from two facts. First, I am a devotee of that tradition, and have been formed and schooled essentially within its perspective. Second, the vast amount of material concerning dreams that continues to be contributed from all the great religious movements is too complex a body of literature to be addressed by this present work.

The Book of the Two Covenants, the Old and New Testaments, presents the religious experience of people in terms of conversion. In other words, when a person turns to religion and to one extent or another embraces Judaism or Christianity, he does so because he feels the need to convert, to change his life. The method and motivation that precipitate this turning to religion defy definition, for there are as many reasons, and as many ways in which conversion occurs, as there are people who actually convert. A synonym for the word conversion is our English word, repentance. The word connotes a "doing of acts of penance," a "changing of one's behavior," or, in modern parlance, "cleaning up one's act." This English word, meaning to do acts of penance, is the translation of the Latin verb *poenitemini*, which approximately implies the same meaning. The Latin, however, translates a word used in the Greek scriptures, namely, *metanoia*. The Greek word implies that a person should radically "think around" his life; his heart and mind must do a complete "turn-about." It means that the direction toward which one's life is headed should be changed to the extent that the new direction is diametrically opposite from the former way.

The Greek word, *metanoia*, is the translation of the Aramaic word, *schub*, a word that suggests the sense of "returning." It is frequently used in the Bible, suggesting that a man or woman should turn to God, or return to religious ways. It is also used to indicate that returning to God is actually a returning home, or a returning to a more authentic identity. So Luke in his gospel has Jesus tell the story of the Prodigal Son. The story relates how the wayward son eventually came home to his father and was reconciled. On a deeper level, the story relates how turning to God is actually a returning home. On a personal level, the story depicts a young man finally coming to terms with his own identity; in the strength of that discovery, he is able to return to his physical or geographical center. The word *schub,* in its application to religious conversion, suggests that turning to God, sensing the divine in one's life, and experiencing one's personhood as connected with, or in union with, the divine, is the process of discovering, or rediscovering, the inner core of our personal identity—our true home—our center. At the inner point of this center is the place of union with, and connection with, the Creator-Spirit, referred to as Yahweh in the Old Testament and as Christ in the New Testament.

Religious conversion, then, in the Judeo-Christian system might be interpreted as "finding one's true self," or "getting in touch with one's real identity." This discovery of self is simultaneously a discovery of God and His Kingdom. As the little prayer attributed to Augustine of Hippo states it: "Lord, teach me to know me, that I might know You." The implication here is not that the "finding" or discovery is something that is externally mandated by God, but rather that it arises out of the deepest law embedded in the nature of man and woman. To be truly a man or a woman in the vision of the Bible is to be that person who is in touch with his or her selfhood and with the Creator-God who continues to author that identity. This discovery is not, therefore, a once-and-for-all experience, but rather it can be compared to a journey, a pilgrimage, a lifetime of seeking and searching.

The role of dreams and visions can be essential to this process. The dream experience is uniquely able to enlighten a person on such a journey. Certain dreams or visions surface out of a transconscious source, a source that the religious person identifies as the movement or "workings" of divinity. These occurrences illuminate one's journey of self-discovery; they shed light on the direction of both the exterior and interior paths one should choose; they confirm and confront us in our dealings with God, within ourselves, and with others.

It is, then, with the conviction that dreams and visions can and do possess an essential role in an individual's life that this chapter will present such an experience in the life of the biblical man, Abram.

The origins of the Hebrew people are described in the Book of Genesis in terms of a family tree that is traced back to Adam and Eve. Although the Book of Genesis concentrates on the evolution and development of the Hebrew family, it also constructs a religious view of the creation of the universe and the human family in general. In language that is specifically concerned with the cosmic or physical creation of the universe, the opening pages of this book describe the original act of God as a movement or conversion from darkness into light, from chaos into order, from void into meaning. Thus the dark abyss that exists before creation becomes enlightened by God speaking His creative word, and through that enlightenment the chaos and meaninglessness of the same abyss become transformed into order and purposefulness. The same movement eventually is employed to describe the conversion process, or the "coming to faith" of a person who turns to God. In other words, when a person turns to God, it's a new creation; the "genesis process" occurs in that person's life. He undergoes a transformation in personhood that is a turning from darkness, chaos, and void into light, order, and meaning. This process, then, will be closely analyzed as it touched and affected the life of Abram, a nomadic chieftain who is introduced in Chapter 12 of the Book of Genesis.

Through a series of visions, or experiences of God, something takes hold of Abram's life, something so new that it totally changes him. Through the creative experience of this primitive man a religion was born, and a way of interpreting life was fashioned that became the "tap/root" of the entire Judeo-Christian religious tradition. The process that dramatically changed the life of Abram, converting him in a gradual, but total, manner into a devotee of the one God, serves as a model or paradigm for communities of religious believers and for individuals within those communities. Abram's experience contains a universal for-mat for the genesis of faith, or as the psychologist Jung would say, an archetypal blueprint that serves as the guiding force, enabling a person to discover his God-given identity, and through that discovery, God Himself. Although the Book of Genesis refers to the process as "creation," and the Bible in general calls it "conversion," Carl Jung from a psychological perspective refers to the process as "individuation." Within the context of this chapter the notions of creation, conversion, and individuation will be used in a synonymous manner with appropriate distinctions where they may be necessary.

An essential and highly significant dimension of the account of Abram's conversion is the role that his visions, or auditory experiences of the presence of God, play in the process. Morton Kelsey explains that dreams, visions, and supernatural visitations are "all of one piece" (p. 80), that is, it is difficult to separate and delineate the exact difference. Kelsey also points out that the content or meaning that comes before one's consciousness is more important than the exact state of consciousness in which the experience occurs. Abram's experiences of God will be interpreted along the lines of dream interpretation, although the Bible does not clearly indicate what state of consciousness Abram was in when the visitations from God occurred.

Generally the "round-figure" date of 1850 B.C. is given to the time of Abram. His homeland was Mesopotamia, and his life was that of a nomad, a sheepherder. He resided with his family, his servants, and his flocks in an area then known as Ur of the Chaldees. Abram was a business person of his day. His investments consisted of his family, his servants, and his flocks. These were his security and his power. His experience of himself as a man, his own self-worth and dignity, and the measure by which he gauged these things were dependent on economic success in his own eyes and in the eyes of his clanspeople. All this required continual appeasement of the gods. Abram was a polytheist. He had to worship many gods, and his livelihood rested on their intervention in his life. His gods were those of nature controlling the sun, the wind, the rain, and, in general, those aspects upon which his life as a sheepherder depended. As E. A. Speiser explains in *The Anchor Bible,* "All major decisions in heaven required approval by the corporate body of the gods. And since nothing was valid for all time, the upshot was chronic indecision in heaven and consequent insecurity on earth. Man's best hope to get a favorable nod from the cosmic powers lay, it was felt, in ritualistic appeasement. And as the ritual machinery grew more and more cumbersome, the spiritual content receded ever farther, until it all but disappeared from the official" (p. xlviii).

To challenge the polytheistic religion of the day would demand a tremendous struggle against all the forces of society. To supplant polytheism with a monotheistic belief in one God demanded more than just the logic and vision of reason alone. For Abram to come up with the notion of one God without any known precedent for this unique conviction implied a rejection of everything that was important and dear to him. It meant going against society with all its rules and expectations; it implied standing alone with support only from one's inner convictions.

Most of all, it signaled the removal of the power, security, and success that were woven into his reliance on, and worship of, the gods of nature who afforded Abram economic stability. This is a challenge of almost an insurmountable size for any person. A new vision, a new power, a new security, a new sense of self meant a new birth, a new beginning; in short, a new creation. As recounted in the story of Genesis, the genesis process, conversion, happened in the life history of this man; he was converted. Through an experience, a happening, a process, his old ways took on the semblance of darkness, chaos, and void, and the newness of his vision became light, order, and meaning. The process of creation began to occur in this man's life.

With a concern about the future of himself and his family, Abram's father, Terah, left the city of Ur with his son and family for the land of Canaan. They settled in Hurrian country in a place called Haran. It was at Haran that God spoke to Abram.

> The Lord said to Abram, "Leave your country, your
> relatives, and your father's home, and go to a land
> that I am going to show you. I will give you many
> descendents, and they will become a great nation.
> I will bless you and make your name famous, so that
> you will be a blessing.

I will bless those who bless you,
But I will curse those who curse you.
And through you I will bless all the nations."
(Genesis 12:1–3)

A fundamental question concerning the communication from God to Abram is in what manner it occurred. The scripture gives no clear indication. Was this a dreamlike experience that Abram remembered only as "divine audition," or did it occur while he was fully awake? Was the voice of God heard outside him, or did it erupt as an inner summons? These questions cannot be answered with certainty, but what is certain is that ultimately the "voice" touched Abram in the depths of his personhood. Whether or not he experienced the "voice" as coming from without or within, its resonance was heard from within the depths of his soul.

In the context of Carl Jung's psychology, the voice is at once the voice of Abram's "self-archetype" and the voice of God. Jung describes the central power of the human personality as the "self" or "self-archetype." By this he means it is the representation and central guiding force of the entire personality. It is greater than our conscious ego state, for it not only contains our consciousness and unconsciousness but has its roots in what Jung refers to as a universal or collective unconsciousness. It is within this universal collectivity of unconsciousness that the self is joined or related to God. In other words, the selfhood of a person is that reality within a person that bears the stamp and image of God. From a Jungian psychological perspective, the central source of all consciousness arises out of the collective unconscious and is explained by Jung as the God-image archetype or power. From a religious or theological perspective the mystery of God, which is over and above and beyond any human analogy, reveals itself through this central power of consciousness that is the self-archetype or self-construct in a person. So the "voice" that Abram hears can be understood as both the voice of God and the voice of Abram's greater self. In this sense the summons or demand can be understood as a critical moment, for the voice urgently calls upon Abram to enter upon the greatest journey of his life; namely, self-expansion or, as Jung calls it, individuation. Individuation in this sense can be likened to the profound experience of conversion or re-creation. One implication of this particular understanding of our dream experiences, our imaginings, or even our reflective discourse with ourselves is that such natural phenomena often contain the impetus and direction for the development of our life and our personal growth.

The Bible indicates the contents of the communication; Abram is instructed to "go forth," to take leave of his present situation, to take upon himself a journey. Carl Jung describes individuation as a departure from one's familiar way of judging and resolving problems. It is a separation from the collective mindset of society in service of a greater sense of personal responsibility. Ordinarily the familiar props of our lives afford us fundamental security and consolation. We cling to other people, to our comfortable surroundings, and to the way of understanding life and the world that we have built up over the years. We need to feel part of our society, to be included within its approved attitudes and ways of operating. When confrontation personally enters our life, when a demand for change happens that grasps us in the depths of our being and becomes a conscious conviction, then upheaval and anxiety occur in our inner world. The anxiety focuses itself on both the loss of supporting structures and the unknown aspects of new ways of seeing ourselves. Individuation and/or conversion implies all this and even more. If the journey is responded to in a positive manner, then we are thrown back on our own strengths. Our personal sense of worth and value, our inner strength, comes into play, and we begin the long odyssey of separation, trusting in, and depending on, the self.

The Bible states, "Abram went as Yahweh told him . . . Abram took his wife Sarai, his brother's son Lot, all the possessions that they had acquired, and all the persons they had obtained in Haran. They set out for the land of Canaan and arrived in the land of Canaan " (Gen. 12:4–5).

Abram obeyed the promptings of the inner voice. He responded to the summons and began his journey. In biblical understanding there is no conversion without faith. Faith is a response, a trusting surrender to one's discernment of the voice of God. It implies a redefinition of one's values and securities, and a clarification of "who" or "what" one deems worthy of trust. Abram's discovery of a new trust relationship enables him to start out. The new "godlike" voice becomes a source of energy;

he begins his journey enlivened and quickened by a new-found trust in his own God-image, his self. He is able to expand his trust beyond the experienced realms of his self and fasten it to his sense of God. Faith is born on the experience and promise of a Voice.

Most of us carry "excess baggage" when we go on a trip. Railway stations, bus and air terminals are a daily scene of people dragging their belongings with much effort as they search out their chosen mode of transportation. The scripture indicates that Abram took "all his possessions." Individuation and/or conversion in its earliest stages is often not understood as a radical departure from one's familiar ways. Therefore most of us, like Abram, decide we're going to have the "best of both worlds." This doesn't work, and Abram must learn this lesson. Comfortable habits, attitudes and values, age-old fears and phobias, unreal and illusionary expectations of both God and others must be sacrificed in service of a more genuine expression of one's self. In short, the process demands a new vision, a new way of experiencing oneself and others. Abram begins both his outer and inner journey still holding on to what he feels he needs. His future experiences of this Voice and the events of his outer world will gradually effect a change.

Abram is learning to live on a promise, and the promise is presented in terms of a blessing. The blessing consists of multiple progeny, "I will make of you a great nation" (Gen. 12:2), and the possession of a new land, "Go forth . . . to a land that I will show you" (Gen. 12:1). His trust and faith in this inner voice are strong, if not totally integral at this point. Abram and Sarai are childless; they are beyond the childbearing years. Where will this great nation come from, or how will it originate out of these two people?

Chapter 15 of Genesis begins with another description of Abram's hearing of the voice.

> Sometime afterward, this word of Yahweh came to Abram
> in a vision:
>
> > "Fear not, Abram!
> > I am your shield;
> > Your reward shall be very great."

> But Abram answered, "O Lord Yahweh, to what
> purpose are your gifts, when I continue childless, . . .
> Since you have granted me no offspring, a member
> of my household will become my heir." Then Yahweh's
> word came back to him in reply, . . ."none but your
> own issue shall be your heir." He took him outside
> and said, "Look up at the sky and count the stars
> if you can. Just so," he added, "shall be your offspring."
> He put his trust in Yahweh, who accounted it to his
> merit (Gen. 15:1–6).

This time the scripture refers to the experience as a vision. Kelsey describes the various connotations of Greek words used for vision in the New Testament. He states that the Greek word *horama*, used to translate the Hebrew words for both dream and vision, refers to the state in which one receives a vision, as well as to the dreaming state. Kelsey suggests that the word does not distinguish explicitly between dreams and visions. Whether Abram is sleeping or in an altered state of consciousness is of no great significance; he is experiencing something beyond his normal conscious state. The contents of the message are comforting and of a directional nature. They implicitly deal with an underlying issue of Abram's makeup, namely, his ability to trust. This appears as "unfinished business" in this man's makeup. Dr. Montague Ullman writes of the honesty of dreams,

> While we are asleep and dreaming, our self-healing machinery propels us into a realm where feelings are displayed honestly. They shape images that may frighten or delight us, but that is not their intent. Their intent is simply to tell it like it is. . . . The change from dreaming to waking effects a radical transformation. We move from a realm of honesty to one in which honesty becomes mixed with expediency. While dreaming we have been given a clear lens with which to examine ourself. When awake we often look at the same situation through rose-colored glasses. And to make matters worse we have no way of knowing that our vision is now colored (p.231).

Abram's journey forces him to face himself. Shortly after his initial response to God and his new sense of self, Abram found himself in serious trouble because of his deceitfulness. Forced by famine to temporarily leave the land of Canaan, Abram goes to Egypt. There the Pharoah desires Sarai, and in order to save "his own skin," Abram "pawns" her off as his sister, and gives her to the Pharoah who takes her into his household. The scriptures relate that Yahweh afflicts the household of Pharoah with extraordinary plagues. The Pharoah discovers Abram's deceit and expels him from Egypt.

The vision of Genesis 15 strengthens Abram's original resolve. It addresses his fear. Abram fears the alien powers of his outer world, yet he is also plagued with inner doubts about the process he has begun. Abram still resorts to relying on collective society; he has not yet been able to break from this security. He fears what is innermost to him, the new-found sense of self and God. Jung describes this state of the individuation process as an intermediary stage:

> It would therefore be wrong to regard this intermediary stage as a trap; on the contrary, for a long time to come it will represent the only possible form of existence for the individual, who nowadays seems more than ever threatened by anonymity. Collective organization is still so essential today that many consider it, with some justification, to be the final goal; . . . Nevertheless, it may be that for sufficient reasons a man feels he must set out on his own feet along the road to wider realms. . . . He will go alone and be in his own company (p. 343).

The motivating force of such a journey becomes the individual's secret. Abram is both motivated and frightened by his inner secret. Jung describes such a secret as reinforcing the person in the isolation of individual goals. God has spoken to Abram. Only he knows the experience; only he has felt the urgency and insistency of the promise. As Jung adds, many people cannot bear this isolation. The person who acts on the secret becomes totally engaged by its implication and begins to act as though "driven" by a new and frightening force. Jung says that the person driven by this secret "truly enters the untrodden, untreadable regions" (p. 344) where there are no charted ways and no shelter spreads a protecting roof over his head. In the religious realm, one spiritual writer describes such a journey of faith as "a road without maps."

Abram's vision with its dialogue between God and the soul of Abram brings into relief the conflict between the outer and the inner world. God is demanding fidelity of Abram, and Abram is concerned about the reward or fulfillment of God's promise to him. "Who will be the recipient of all my possessions," asks Abram, or, "when will you fulfill your part of the bargain?" Abram asks of God. The inner process of conversion or individuation so often gets detoured by the religious person as we begin to look for the "rewards" of God in the outer world. This diversionary tactic is doomed to failure, disappointment, and disillusionment in the religious process. Coming to grips with the inner movements of our spiritual development is often understood only through contact with our dream experiences. It is precisely the intention of the dream to correct and adjust one's conscious misapprehensions of personal values and goals. The themes of a person's life such as personal loves, hates, attachments, addictions, and so forth, appear in a stark state of reality within the images and actions of our dream states. Close attention to the feelings and movements of the dream images often reveals the fuller meaning and direction that should be given life's themes. Abram, with his inaugural vision of himself and his God, with his inner secret of possessing a personal promise of fulfillment from God, and with age-old habits of self-deceptive behavior that he has employed for survival purposes in the outer world, finds himself caught. Only a series of dreamlike visions can clearly illuminate his path to freedom.

An additional consideration surfaces in this particular vision. Inner conflict between outer behavior and inner strivings does not necessarily place one at odds with God or oneself. God's reply to Abram in this vision is one of acceptance and understanding. The vision is at once directional and affirming. The concluding scene of the vision attempts to express this man's intimate experience of the divine:

> When the sun had gone down and it was very dark, there appeared a smoking fire pot and a flaming torch. . . . That day Yahweh concluded a covenant with Abram, saying, "To your offspring I give this land. . . ." (Gen. 15:17–18).

The Bible often expresses the experience of God through the symbol of fire. Moses encounters God in the burning bush (cf. Ex. 3:2), and in the New Testament God is referred to as an all-consuming fire (Heb. 12:29). The strength and all-pervasive effect of fire speak of the impact of covenant or union with God. It is, so to speak, the experience of union with God that makes up for what is lacking in a person's ability to live out the commands of God. So, too, the experience of this unconditional acceptance on the part of God, God's desire to covenant with his people, enables them to continue the process of conversion and individuation. The depth of covenant experience is a "knowing" that supersedes all other forms of knowing. It is a communication through which the selfhood of a person is grounded and confirmed by the experience of its divine origin. Such an experience is humanly expressed by confessing that another, or, the Transcendent Other (that is, the mystery of God), has addressed me in my innermost being. This Other as the origin and source of my person and, even more so, as the ultimate dimension of my selfhood, leads me to rejoice in my creatureliness and recognize God as Creator and Father.

One might apply the words of Psalm 2 to this experience, "You are my son, this day I have begotten you" (vs. 7). The verse of the psalm expresses in language this identification of my selfhood with God. I experience within myself the sense of the Other as joined with me, or, part of me, and the communication of the Other to me in the depths of my soul is, "You are my son, you are my daughter—I am continually giving you new birth." The heart of religious mysticism hinges, in a sense, on this realization, namely, that one's life is from another, and that this ultimate otherness is God. Perhaps Jung's theory of the collective unconscious is helpful in this consideration. The transconsciousness, or transpersonalism of one's conscious roots, although present in a person's experience of his selfhood, is ultimately rooted and grounded in God. The revelation or expression of God, then, can be essentially experienced in our own self-experience. God's covenant with Abram simultaneously affords Abram unconditional acceptance on the part of God and profound self-acceptance. Abram's faith or trust in the Voice that continues to speak with him is the medium by which this gracious human experience becomes communicated. The great dreams and visions of our life often act out this inner relationship with oneself and God, and in the religious quest we should look for this profound theme within the contents and plot of a dream.

Jung explains that in such dreams the self, or the central archetype, often appears in images of wholeness or completeness. This is so because the self is the totality of the human personality. Images such as a circle, a square, a quaternity, mandala, or child; any symbol that speaks of wholeness can reflect the wholeness of the self in a dream (p. 398). Jung elaborates on the relationship between the self and the image of God occurring in a dream by stating:

> It is only through the psyche that we can establish that God acts upon us, but we are unable to distinguish whether these actions emanate from God or from the unconscious. We cannot tell whether God and the unconscious are two different entities. Both are borderline concepts for transcendental contents. But empirically it can be established, with a sufficient degree of probability, that there is in the unconscious an archetype of wholeness which manifests itself spontaneously in dreams, etc., and a tendency, independent of the conscious will, to relate other archetypes to this centre. . . . The God-image does not coincide with the unconscious as such, but with a special content of it, namely the archetype of the self. It is this archetype from which we can no longer distinguish the God-image empirically. . . . One can, then, explain the God-image . . . as a reflection of the self, or conversely, explain the self as an *image Dei,* (image of God) in man (p. 395).

Abram's Voice in his vision is both the utterance of God and the articulation of his greater self. The Voice, which speaks of wholeness and greater integration, takes on the same meaning as images of wholeness in a dream. The dream, then, in its religious dimension, potentially leads us far beyond that vision of life limited by human reason, and discloses those "edge situations" where the divine has a tendency to linger and reveal itself.

Karl Menninger, in describing approaches to the interpretation of psychoanalytic resistances, insightfully remarks that people expect the wrong things from the right people and the right things from the wrong people (p. 136). The story of the birth of Ishmael is a concrete example of this fact in the journey of Abram. Abram is psychologically and religiously driven by his desire for offspring. He feels he needs some concrete, permanent sign that the promises of his visions are being fulfilled. This is the classic temptation in the life of faith. As the song from the Broadway hit, *Godspell,* says it, "When Will God Save the People?" Abram in his outer world is an aggressive business person of his own day; he knows how to "take things into his own hands"; he can "get things done." The Bible says he took Sarai's Egyptian maidservant, Hagar, with the supposed approval and urging of Sarai (later Sarai bitterly regrets her benevolent gesture), and has sexual intercourse with her. In this situation, Abram seeks the right thing from the wrong person. Hagar becomes pregnant and bears Abram a son named Ishmael. The Bible describes Ishmael as a "wild colt of a man, his hand against everyone, and everyone's hand against him" (Gen. 16:12). Later on in the New Testament, Paul writes, "man proposes and God disposes." Such is the case with this folly of Abram. Turmoil enters his life in the form of marital disorder and human hurt. Sarai reverses her decision. She scornfully tells Abram, "This outrage against me is your fault! I myself put my maid in your lap. But from the moment she found that she had conceived, she has been looking at me with contempt" (Gen. 16:5). In the life of faith there is a tendency to put aside the inner vision and sense of God and choose, rather, what seems expedient and attainable. This urge reveals itself in motives of ambition, power, status, and achievement. Unconscious issues and urges operate without the control of the inner self's judgment and ultimately lead one to act in haste and without integrity. The result is usually damaging. In the case of Abram, family strife makes his life so miserable that the only solution is to banish Hagar and his son, Ishmael. This Abram does with God's assurance that they will be taken care of under His protection. Abram had to learn that his sought-after fulfillment of the promise would happen in God's time and in God's way. He truly sought "the right thing from the wrong person."

Religious faith rests on relationship, relationship that the Bible calls covenant. Faith is a way of knowing that is characterized by an unusual sense of being-in-God and God-being-in-you. It is a knowledge that the pact or alliance with the divine has no finality to it, but rather continues to unfold its mystery and experience as one enters more deeply into the union. Chapter 17 of Genesis accents a new consciousness for Abram in his covenant relationship with God. In a visionlike dream episode, the Scriptures narrate an intimate moment between Abram and God:

> When Abram was ninety-nine years old, Yahweh appeared to Abram and said to him, "I am El Shaddai. Follow my ways and be blameless. I will grant a covenant between myself and you, and will make you exceedingly numerous. . . . And this is my covenant with you: You are to be the father of a host of nations. Nor shall you be called Abram any longer: your name shall be Abraham, meaning that "I make you the father of a host of nations." . . . And this shall be the covenant between myself and you, and your offspring to follow, which you must keep: every male among you shall be circumcised. You shall circumcise the flesh of your foreskin, and that shall be the mark of the covenant between me and you (Gen. 17:1–11).

There are many interpretations for the name El Shaddai. Traditionally, it has been understood to mean the "Almighty." Another meaning given to the name is "self-sufficient." Our modern interpretation gives the meaning of "mountain" implying the symbol of divinity (Speiser). At any rate, the name implies the greatness and transcendence of the Divine One who manifests Himself to Abram. The change of Abram's name to Abraham surely implies not only a new sense of relationship with God, but also a more expansive sense of selfhood. Symbolically, a name expresses identity. It is the ordinary way that people externally and concretely identify themselves and are identified by others. One's name becomes so intimately wrapped up with one's identity that it becomes almost impossible to separate one from the other. In this vision the man Abram comes to a new realization of himself. Jung states that the selfhood of a person is beyond total comprehension of one's consciousness. "There is little hope of our ever being able to reach even approximate consciousness of the self." says Jung (p. 398). The new name is a hallmark of Abraham's new sense of identity. In his vision or dream he grasps himself in a far wider sense than his ordinary consciousness affords him. He is in a sensitive partnership with God and with himself.

A dream can and does give us energy and power that we never knew we possessed. Some dreams are self-revelatory. They reveal us to ourselves. They picture us in a complementary image that stirs our inner sense of worth and value. Such an image breaks down our more narrow boundaries of self-estimation and challenges us or liberates us to risk experimenting with new modes of growth and development. Just as the change of name in many cultures and religious traditions symbolizes a new beginning, a new way of living, so, too, Abraham, through the medium of a vision, is able to assume a far greater sense of his own identity.

The reference to circumcision as the sign of the covenant relationship speaks of change and integration. The word literally implies "to cut around" or "to cut away from." Within the context of this vision it represents for Abraham a new state of internalizing his sojourn. He must shed his false self and bring forth new light, order, and meaning in his world. The symbol implies the creative process as it personally touches this man. He is called to be the generator, the father of many; he, himself, must first become that creator by cutting around and away from the false world that now appears as darkness, chaos, and void. The vision, in other words, is another image of the genesis process as this process enters into and personally touches this biblical figure. Through his experience Abram becomes Abraham, not through the external change of a name, but by the inner process of personal consolidation and integration which the vision precipitates. The internal coming-together of his selfhood, the experience of having, so to speak, "all the parts fit" for a privileged moment is the fullness of the covenant. Abraham in his selfhood can now be "father" and "generator" to all those who would willingly take upon themselves a similar journey. His outer world of behavior has yet to adapt to the inner experience of consolidation. That is the ongoing process that encompasses a lifetime, and even more, from the viewpoint of religion and faith.

In a delightful narration the Bible next describes a banquet which Abraham and Sarah (her name has also been changed) gave for God and two angels. The story narrates how God and two mysterious figures appeared at the tent of Abraham. Sarah was quickly ordered by Abraham to fix the food, and the visitors ate. During the course of this extraordinary occasion the three visitors informed Abraham that Sarah, who is ninety years of age, was finally going to have a baby. Sarah, the Bible adds, had been listening inside the tent, and when she heard the "men" talking, she laughed at their naïveté. God then confronted Abraham and asked why Sarah laughed. Sarah interrupted and denied laughing—or listening. God retorted to Sarah, "Yes, you did." Frederick Buechner in his book, *Wishful Thinking,* writes of this episode:

> When God told Abraham, who was a hundred at the time, that at the age of ninety his wife Sarah was finally going to have a baby, Abraham came close to knocking himself out —"fell on his face and laughed" as Genesis puts it (17:17). In another version of the story (18:18ff) Sarah is hiding behind the door eavesdropping, and here it's Sarah herself who nearly splits a gut although when God asks her about it afterward, she denies it. "No, but you did laugh," God says, thus having the last word as well as the first. God doesn't seem to hold their outbursts against them, however. On the contrary, he tells them the baby's going to be a boy and that he wants them to name him Isaac. Isaac in Hebrew means laughter (pp. 24–25).

Faith in this instance gives birth to laughter.

What is the meaning of this story? It obviously has many levels. One interpretation would be that even the impossible is possible with God. On a deeper level it implies the readiness and pliability that conversion affects in a person so that God can accomplish His will and plan in his or her life. Jung might interpret it as a scene of wholeness and integrity in the individuation process, a wholeness that is capable of creating new life and new vision in one's world. Individuation as it develops within the life stages of a person enables us to enter lovingly and freely into relationships. Ordinarily our love relationships contain projections that fill us with desires that express themselves in coercion and constraint. The individuation process enables a person to withdraw such projections, and to detach himself from the false expectations that so often distract from relationships and keep us in a state of anxiety and doubt (Jung). Another way of saying it is that individuation allows us to enter into relationships of giving and receiving. So often marriages and friendships are referred to as "a give-and-take proposition." "Taking" is the offspring of unrealistic expectations toward another. Healing unions with others necessarily become the peaceful process of freely giving and freely receiving. This dynamic between persons produces life; it is creative and, indeed, fulfilling. It causes us to lovingly celebrate our own freedom and the freedom and dignity of others. Abraham seems to have reached this stage in his own conversion and individuation; he is ready to give birth, and such a birth produces laughter within him. The promise revealed to him at the beginning of his journey is about to become fulfilled. He knows now that it will come from within the power and energy of his wholeness, his selfhood. His faltering attempts to "force the issue" by impulsively manipulating his world and those around him now seem to be just that—namely, the faltering of a man who did not know himself.

A final insight into the banquet story is Abraham's communion with God. The faith-union with God is frequently described metaphorically as a banquet. The partnership, the covenant, is, in a sense, consummated by eating together. The scene once again heightens the union or oneness that such a faith-relationship creates. Abraham has slowly given room to the development of the God-image within his own personality. In this sense his inner destiny is being fulfilled in him. Contact and understanding and obedience to his visions accomplish communion for him, communion that the Scriptures describe as a banquet. The sense of oneness quickens, energizes, and fertilizes the personhood of Abraham. Similar, then, to the Spirit that fertilized the dark, voidlike waters of the original creation scene bringing forth life, so too, Abraham impregnates the dark, motionless womb of Sarah, and the child of faith is conceived. Isaac, the embodiment in the flesh of God's laughter, is born to two noble people, and the promise of Abraham's dreams and visions is well on its way toward fulfillment.

Separation from others is never an easy task, and yet a major theme of human development is the acceptance of, and even welcome of, the need for relationships to change and possibly end. As John S. Dunne writes:

> It is difficult to grow out of the relationships formed in one period of life and to enter into those appropriate for the next period, to leave behind those of youth for those of manhood, to leave behind those of manhood for those of old age, to leave behind those of old age for those of the dead. It is also difficult to allow someone else to leave a relationship with oneself behind as he grows and moves onward, because a familiar relationship is being abandoned for an unknown one (p.44).

Usually we will resist with the greatest of effort the severance of union with those who have played an intimate role in our life. In the process of psychoanalysis, writes Menninger, one criterion for the success of an analysis is that when the "analyzed person" comes to realize in his relationships with others he "has no need to find satisfactions for childish wishes" (p. 167). He continues: "The 'analyzed person' either comes to realize that he can be gratified without such exertions as he had previously made or that he does not need to be gratified or that he has no further feeling of need for such gratification or that there is no prospect of gratifying them and hence they must be renounced without regrets" (p. 168).

Chapter 22 of Genesis narrates the dramatic extent of Abraham's renunciation and separation from his only son whom he loves. The content of the chapter constitutes a passion and suffering that is only exceeded by the self-emptying and death of Jesus of Nazareth in the New Testament. God asks the impossible of Abraham:

> Take your son, your beloved son, Isaac, whom you hold so dear and go to the land of Moriah, where you shall offer him up as a burnt offering on one of the heights that I will point out to you (Gen. 22:1–2).

The Book of Hebrews states: "It is a terrifying thing to fall into the hands of the living God!" (Heb. 10.31) Abraham is caught, not by some outside force that will violate him and his family, but by an interior knowing that has become all pervasive in his life's judgments. Jung's teaching on the "inner secret" of a person, his self-knowledge, is extremely applicable in understanding Abraham's situation:

> But if a man faced with a conflict of duties undertakes to deal with them absolutely on his own responsibility, and before a judge who sits in judgment on him day and night, he may well find himself in an isolated position. There is now an authentic secret in his life which cannot be discussed—if only because he is involved in an endless inner trial in which he is his own counsel and ruthless examiner, and no secular or spiritual judge can restore his easy sleep. . . . In his case the court is transposed to the inner world where the verdict is pronounced behind closed doors. . . .
>
> Nothing so promotes the growth of consciousness as this inner confrontation of opposites . . . the inner world has gained that much weight by being raised to the rank of a tribunal for ethical decisions. . . . The ego becomes ambivalent and ambiguous and is caught between hammer and anvil. It becomes aware of a polarity superordinate to itself (p. 345).

For Abraham it is no longer a question of manipulating his outer world and ignoring his visions and voices. His journey away from the falsity and illusion of his prior life-style has been too extensive, too conclusive. It is not even a question of whether or not he should obey. He undergoes the anguish of giving up the last vestige of reliance upon the satisfactions of human warmth and human companionship as the ultimate answer to anything in life. The Bible simply says, "He laid him on the altar on top of the wood. He put out his hand and picked up the cleaver to slay his son" (Gen. 22:9–10). Offering the relief of a proverbial "Hollywood ending" to impending doom, the Bible, however, adds, "But an angel of Yahweh called to him from heaven, 'Abraham! Abraham!' 'Here I am,' he answered. And He said, 'Lay not your hand upon the boy, nor do the least thing to him! Now I know how dedicated you are to God, since you did not withhold from me your own beloved son'" (Gen 22:11–12).

A characteristic of childhood, writes Jung, at least in the eyes of adults, is the way that this stage of human development represents paradise; childhood is a time of being carefree, playful, taken care of, provided for, and cherished without anxiety or responsibility (p. 244). This aspect of childhood causes us to expect and unconsciously await some childish dreams of the future. It is the longing to find the "pot of gold" at the end of the rainbow. In an acutely terrifying moment, Abraham tears himself from such fantasies. His son, Isaac, was not to be sacrificed for his personal growth, but rather to show a readiness to relinquish that naive world of paradisiacal solutions to the hard problems of human living. The purity, innocence, and goodness reflected in the child, Isaac, and God's unwillingness to have the child harmed, mirrored for Abraham a more complete picture of himself in his goal of individuation.

Abraham's visions and dreams, thus, carved and shaped him into a whole person, a man of faith, and a father-figure for those willing to inaugurate their own journey.

Conclusion

Faith then is born from heeding dreams, visions, and voices. It begins with a journey, a leave-taking, that actually guides us home to our true self. It is a series of creative moments that gradually change or convert the way we view ourselves, others, and the world. Abraham's sojourn teaches us that such a process opens up an experience of life that is more vast than "counting the stars at night" or "measuring the sands of the seashore." It is learning to live with a promise whose fulfillment seems to be continually changing. Such a promise is continually reinforced, reshaped, and rephrased by the inner movements of our images, voices, and dreams.

The inner power modeled in such a personage as Abraham empowers us to give new life, new birth, to ourselves and to others. It causes us genuinely to erupt with laughter in response to the surprise of discovering new life at the strangest times and in the most uncommon of places. Living life in this sensitive manner allows us to understand the stumbling, faltering, and uncertainties of our travel as necessary to the overall development of adult life. With this sense of inner direction, inner wholeness, and walking with God, we are able to meet, cope with, and, if necessary, surrender and separate from those things that are no longer of service to the inner quest.

"From Abram to Abraham" is the story of a man who found out that the "promised land" of his voices and visions lay in the discovery of his own identity. Through that discovery he came to know and trust in God who weaves His creative word into self-hood. Through that discovery Abram came to realize the short-comings of an abbreviated name. He took personal ownership of the name that fully expressed his identity—Abraham.

References

Buechner, F. *Wishful Thinking.* New York: Harper & Row, Publishers, Inc., 1973.

Dunne, J. S. *The Way of All the Earth.* Harper & Row, Publishers, Inc., 1972.

Jung, C. G. *Memories, Dreams, Reflections.* New York: Random House, 1961, 1962, 1963.

Kelsey, M. T. *God, Dreams and Revelation.* Minneapolis, Minnesota: Augsburg Publishing House, 1974.

Menninger, K. *Theory of Psychoanalytic Technique.* New York: Harper Touchbooks, Harper & Row Publishers, 1958.

Speiser, E. A. *Genesis—The Anchor Bible.* New York: Doubleday & Company, Inc., 1964.

Ullman, M., and Zimmerman, N. *Working With Dreams.* Los Angeles: Jeremy P. Tarcher, Inc., 1979.

·6·

This*Other-Ness and Dreams

JOHN BRIGGS, Ph.D.

John Briggs has talents that flow in many directions. His writings have encompassed poetry, literature, science, and philosophy. I have had occasion to read in manuscript form a penetrating and brilliant study by him of the concept of metaphor. In it he goes into the contradictions involved in the formation of the metaphor and the powerful way a newly crafted metaphor is both expressive of something in the present while, at the same time, it exposes us to a bit more of the mystery of our existence. Deeply immersed in the metaphorical structure of poetry, he turns now to a consideration of the metaphorical structure of the dream.

My self-imposed task in this chapter is to consider whether and in what ways dreams may be like literature. I know something about literature, having taught it for many years during which time I have developed an aesthetic approach that I believe goes some distance toward showing why poems and stories are different from other forms of human communication and why they share with the other arts a mysterious property of being always beyond whatever we say about them.

I know less about dreams. Like almost everyone, I have wondered about my own and other people's dreams and felt the pull of the oneiric mystery. I've written some short stories from dreams and spent several days at different times with Monte in his dream groups. I've also worked with dreams a few times in class.

The analogy of dreams-as-like-literature is an intuitively appealing one to me, and in commencing to think about it I naturally expected to be able either to validate or to falsify it to my own satisfaction. That has not been the case. As a rule, a writer should keep his mouth shut when he has difficulty with his material; however, I have been unable to escape the sensation that my difficulty contains a point. As a result, I have developed not so much a clear line of argument as a record of my reflections on what I see now is a curiously subtle problem.

I began my thinking about dreams-as-like-literature from a point of view I have developed over the years about the second half of my analogy.

Literature

From that perspective, poetry, fiction, and the other arts possess a quality that I have called "this*other-ness." This made-up word is one of several I've attempted over the years in an effort to throw light on the deep structural dynamics of great creative works. (Briggs, 1986)

Let me illustrate what I mean with a short poem by Robert Frost:

A Patch of Old Snow

There's a patch of old snow in a corner,
That I should have guessed
Was a blow-away paper the rain
Had brought to rest.

It is speckled with grime as if
small print overspread it,
The news of a day I've forgotten—
If I ever read it.

Frost's poem turns upon a central metaphor which compares a patch of old snow to a newspaper. It's a poem about a "this" (snow) which is discovered to be in some sense an "other" (a newspaper, the bearer of "news"). The key thing here is not the fact of the comparison; it is the very peculiar dynamic that happens between the terms of the metaphor. To get a sense of this, one can ask, How does the fictional narrator of this poem *feel* about his comparison of snow to a newspaper? Is he expressing regret over not having read the news of that forgotten day or waxing cynical about it?

Consider, for example, the poet's supporting metaphor comparing "grime" to "small print." Is the point that the everyday news we get in newspapers is "grimy"? Is the grime here the variety that's messy and sordid or the kind that's an insignificant nuisance? Was the "news" missed in the patch of old snow a grimy news or has it been made grimy by time?

In trying to interpret, the reader is immediately immersed in an undertow of such questions. Add to this the fact that the grimy, cynical side of the metaphor is offset by other things in the poem which seem to point to quite a different feeling—a feeling that the narrator finds in this patch of snow a sense of poignant loss about the news that's been missed. In other words, the central metaphor seems pervaded by irony. The word "should" is a microcosm of that irony.

"Should" can be read at least three ways: A) The narrator *ought to* have guessed that the patch of snow was a newspaper because making such a guess enables him to enter a metaphoric world where one can realize the kind of news that nature and the passage of time have to offer; B) he ought to have guessed because there is some kind of universal imperative for us to notice the news of things and a guilt associated with our failing to do so, or C) he *might have* guessed the snow was a newspaper (but he didn't) in which case the whole metaphor is much more frivolous, almost a throw-away fancy (Monaco and Briggs).

The point is, literary metaphor and literary irony are fundamentally ambiguous. Possible meanings are not resolved in favor of one of them; rather, they all hang together like the facets of a crystal in dynamic suspension. Another way of putting it is to say that the meanings exist in harmony with each other, harmony in the musical sense, where differences and similarities create a movement and order.

The made-up word, "this∗other-ness," is my attempt to express the dynamics of this harmony. It has seemed to me that the movement of literature is to see the universe in a white whale, a grain of sand, a patch of old snow—in "this" which is an "other" and an "other" which is "this." The back-and-forth simultaneity of meaning between the "this" and the "other" I've represented by the asterisk *. As I see it, the elements in a great literary work are perceived as neither "this" nor something "other" than "this"—they are experienced as (somehow) both. Virginia Woolf in *To the Lighthouse* put the sensation this way. It is, she said, "to be on a level with ordinary experience, to feel simply that that's a chair, that's a table, and yet at the same time, it's a miracle, it's an ecstasy." This*other-ness in the dining room and kitchen—the kind of effect that abounds in Woolf's novels.

In the case of the Frost poem, I could describe the movement of this*other-ness as follows: The central metaphor tells us explicitly that the patch of snow is something other. First, the other is a newspaper, then it's a more mysterious "news." At that point the snow becomes so much an other that it might seem almost an abstraction, an image of the fleetingness of time and the slipperiness of memory. Just there, however, we encounter the irony. The snowpatch is a "this," covered with grime like an old newspaper. It's not a vast abstraction; it's one of the perfectly ordinary objects of life. And yet this ordinary object can bring us news of a forgotten day. And so on. The snowpatch is a this*other-ness without resolution.

In other words, a great work of literature always expresses a kind of ambivalence toward its subject. In ambivalence of a psychological kind, if we feel two ways about something or someone (love-hate, secure-insecure), we want to resolve the contradiction because it creates conflict or leaves us with a sense that we're powerless. We usually resolve an ambivalence by giving precedence to one side and suppressing the other (insisting we feel secure and denying our insecurity, for example), or by finding a new way of thinking about the ambivalence that joins the thesis and antithesis of the conflict into a synthesis of resolution. Literary ambivalence is of a different sort.

It is not a conflict of meanings or an immobility of meanings which have been jammed into each other. Neither is it a synthesis of previous contradictions. It has no resolution. Rather, it is a richness of meanings, none subordinated to the other, all standing together. It is something like taking the wild inhabitants of a zoo and bringing them all close enough so they can be in the same picture. Literary ambivalence is a sense of meaning beyond meanings. It might better be called "*omni*valence." Omnivalence is an order which arises subtly out of the piece like a fragrance. This∗other-ness is the dynamic from which a sense of omnivalence emerges.

I have found that this∗other-ness and omnivalence are related to another important aspect of literature which I've already alluded to in the discussion of "should" in the Frost poem. The elements of a piece of literature are isomorphic, that is, they reflect one another. "Should" is a microcosm of the overall ironies of the poem; grime like small print also contains these ironies, but from another direction; the word "news" contains them. Thus each element is a microcosm of other elements and of the poem as a whole.

Now we come to the crux. For me to accept as valid an analogy between literature and dreams I'd need to see that isomorphism, omnivalence, and this∗other-ness actually exist in the dream. Of course, I'm not saying one could not make this analogy based on some other criteria, but for me these are the most fundamental, the most important, aspects of literary order. I see them as so crucial because I see them as intimately connected with my experience in literature of universality and truth.

Dreams

A poem or a novel is an artifact. Embedded in the structure of that artifact, I believe, is an isomorphism, this∗other-ness, and omnivalence which evokes a reciprocal sense of this∗other-ness, omnivalence, and order in the reader. Upon the dreamer's awakening and remembering it, the dream is an artifact, too. So, the most obvious question is, can these two types of artifacts be compared?

Knowing of my interest in dreams, a neighbor of mine, Joanne Fuller, brought me a long, panoramic dream that seemed perfect for the comparison. In one passage of the dream, the dreamer visits the apartment of a friend, Bob, who is living with a girl the dreamer thinks might be mentally retarded. This girl "stayed in the background, very humbly, not looking into our eyes. He (Bob) ignored her, I think." A little later in the dream:

> The mentally retarded girl was very quietly and shyly moving around like a servant who is not supposed to be talked to. We started talking. She was very nice and quiet, intelligent. She told me she was a queen. We went to her planet and she turned very beautiful and peaceful. It occurred to me that this was Mars and the queen probably had a mask on so as not to frighten me. She took it off. The body was the same but the face was like a "comedy and tragedy" drama mask. The eyes had no eyes, just holes. The mouth did not have a smile but a sad, blank look. I turned to the queen and said, "I'm not afraid."

The passage is striking and seems as close to being a literary artifact as one could hope for. It is evidently a wonderful nocturnal parable on the theme of disguise, reality, and illusion. There is metaphor in the retarded servant who is also a queen. There is irony in the fact that beneath the mask of the queen is a sad, blank look (like the look of a retarded girl?). There is irony in the dreamer's statement, "I'm not afraid," which raises the question of whether she is really not afraid or is trying to convince herself she's not, in which case she *is*. All this reeks of omnivalence and this*other-ness—for example, is the retarded girl a queen or a retarded girl? a "this" or an "other?" In the Frost poem we were introduced, among other things, to the mysterious transience of news in the world. Here we confront, among other things, the elusiveness of identity.

There is isomorphism in the dream as well. In the segment I'm considering, for example, the "comedy and tragedy" drama mask is a microcosm of the comedy and tragedy tone of the whole passage. If the girl is really retarded, it's a tragedy; if she's really a queen, it's a comedy in the Shakespearian sense of that word. In fact, it seems both and neither. The isomorphism also extends to the other parts of the dream, which I have not presented. In the opening section, the dreamer is walking down a street with a friend and sees homosexuals, one of them wearing "long insulated underwear." *Under*wear is a mirror of masking, as is homosexuality, where a person of one sex might be seen as in effect masking himself as another.

This*other-ness, isomorphism, omnivalence. So far it looks as if a dream is very much like a piece of literature. However, at this point I find myself perversely growing a bit nervous. I am beginning to feel that I'm reading in.

I ask myself, as lyrical as this passage is, what if I didn't know the images were from a dream, what if I thought they were from, say, a sketch by a writer, would I find them so intriguing? The answer is clearly no. There's no plot, no character development, no dramatic context for this scene. Taking into account the whole of Joanne's dream, I realize, would only make this problem worse. There, in a manner typical of dreams, scenes and characters change without any accessible internal logic. In great poems and poetic literature—no matter how experimental—there is always an internal logic that can be apprehended in some fashion by the reader and which requires little or no input of information from outside the work itself (presuming one understands the language in which it is written). In other words, each great work creates or evokes its own context. In the Frost poem the context economically evoked is the familiar three-dimensional world where patches of old snow can easily be taken as looking like blow-away newspapers. In Kafka's *The Trial*, a dream*like* context is created. But *The Trial* is not a dream. Joseph K is seen in various situations which, though extremely bizarre, are all connected in some way to his trial. The trial is the context which supports the contextual development and revelation of Joseph K's character. Context creates a this-ness from which the existential other-ness that is the whole elusive meaning of the trial emanates, and the this-ness and the other-ness are always in harmony.

Every writer and every piece uses different means for establishing a context and making it relatively self-consistent and self-contained. Not so with the dream. I mentioned that in the section of Joanne's dream just preceding the mask passage, she is in Bob's apartment. Bob does not appear again in the dream, and his contextual significance evidently lies outside the dream-as-artifact.

The dreamer's life experience is, of course, the actual context of the dream. Many of the images, words, personalities, objects, have a private significance for the dreamer which the artifact of the dream itself does not provide. Poets and fiction writers use a very public language, with shared connotations; or they find ways to make their private language accessible. Dreams are filled with images that have idiosyncratic connotations. I can try to gather enough detail about those connotations to supply a context, but then I feel myself stumbling toward a different dilemma. If I knew who Bob was then I would be on my way to having a specific meaning for Bob in the dream; I would be on my way to seeing the dream as a kind of code, an information game in which the dream's apparent other-ness can be reduced to an apprehensible and relatively unambiguous this-ness.

In fact, decoding is the common way the dream artifact has been handled by the waking mind. The image of a snake in a dream was decoded by the Greeks as a sign of disease; the Egyptians saw it as a sign that a dispute had been settled; Freud saw it as a symbol of the penis and sexual drives. The Iroquois engaged in "dream guessing," which assumed that the dream expresses some unfulfilled wish that needs to be placated. All these approaches assume the dream has a hidden valence, not omnivalence. Even the Jungian approach sees the dream as a code. The idea, for example, of a feminine aspect and a masculine aspect to a dream is not omnivalent unless one were to see that the masculine *is* the feminine and that the dream is expressing something beyond *both* aspects and including them. Joanne's dream would yield easily and splendidly to a number of decoding systems.

Could all these decoding approaches be wrong? I cannot be so bold as to draw that conclusion. In fact there seem good reasons to suppose that a dream does contain information and that it can be decoded. Certainly when a dreamer begins to make his dreams public, some kind of encoding seems to occur. There seems to be truth to the old joke about the patient in Freudian analysis who begins to dream in Freudian symbols. So the dilemma is this.

In so far as a dream is a code, it threatens my analogy because a poem is not a code. Of course, not everyone agrees with that assertion. Certainly many critics think of works of literature as codes. But writers traditionally dispute this position, and I strongly take their side. When someone asked Robert Frost what one of his poems meant, he replied sharply with something like, "What do you want me to do, say it again in worse English?" In effect Frost was saying the intended meaning of his poem is immediately apprehensible and irreducible. It is not some valence but an omnivalence, a simultaneous sense of order and ambiguity which should strike the reader's mind with the vividness of the warmth on a spring day or the abruptness of an auto accident.

So what worries me about my analogy is that although poets usually bridle at attempts to approach their work as a code, dreamers on awakening generally have the opposite reaction. They welcome any help in making sense of the dream. Unlike a poem, the order of its ambiguity is not immediately apparent. It seems that when a dream is brought out of the night into the day as a crystallized artifact, it either begins to fade away into pure other-ness ("Wow, it was too weird") or its other-ness is transformed by some process, theory, or sign system into a this-ness and information.

Does that mean my analogy has failed, that the dream as an artifact can't be apprehended the way a poem is? No. I can't go that far. Indeed, I've worked with dreams as poems and, I think, had some modest success. The process I've used involves developing contextual connotations from the dreamer's life (who Bob is, for example), spinning out all kinds of interpretations about the images and their connections, seeing how these interpretations are mutually exclusive or contradictory, and then letting the sheer immensity and elusiveness of meaning emerge. In that way all specific meanings are dropped and what is left is a this*other-ness in which omnivalence pervades. Obviously the last step is the most important one. The process is a lot of work and tends to make the dream a poignant but somewhat impersonal and public thing, like a poem. Unlike traditional dream work where the point is to connect the images of the dream to the dreamer's personal life dilemmas, here the point is to experience the dream as a window into the this*other-ness of existence in general. For that purpose it seems better to have an older dream rather than a fresh one so that the dreamer, like an author, can have some "distance" on its material. By employing some such process, we make the artifact of the dream, as dream researcher Ellen Fore-man puts it, a "first draft" that has to be worked on in order for its poetry to emerge.

The analogy of dreams-as-like-literature can be rescued by this approach, but frankly for me the rescue is not entirely satis-factory. This is because I think of a piece of literature as some-thing that has an immediate effect. The this*other-ness is simply *there* as the reader perceives the work. If this immediacy is not in the dream as an artifact, I wonder, is it somewhere in the dreaming process itself? What about the experience of the dreamer in the throes of the dream? Do omnivalence and this*other-ness reside there?

When Joanne told me her dream she reported feeling a shift-ing anxiety and uncertainty as the events of her dream unfolded. This typical kind of dream *angst* is closer to ambivalence than omnivalence. Nightmares are an even starker example that the dreamer inside the dream is generally in no poetic position. It might be possible to view a nightmare poetically in the light of day, but in the dream it is a literal, not a metaphoric, event. It's a "this," not an "other." It may be a very strange "this," but the dreamer is in no shape to see if it is "other"-wise ironic. Of course the same could be said for Joseph K, who fails to see the metaphoric other-ness of his life and for whom the bizarre events of his trial are so literal that he is left full of paralysis and conflict. That is an interesting similarity between a dream and a work of literature. The characters *in* the work are like dreamers in a dream, caught up in their reality. The writer and the reader, however, are in a different position. They have distance. They can experience the this*other-ness and omnivalence.

For some reason, this line of thinking suggests to me a rather extraordinary possibility. Perhaps that immediacy of this*other-ness and omnivalence, that isomorphic perception which poets and artists of all kinds participate in and evoke in their works isn't in the dreamer in the dream; it isn't in the dreamer awake who is trying to decipher the dream—it is in the act of dreaming itself. That would mean that the dreamer in the dream is not aware of the omnivalence because he is immersed in the omni-valence, like a character in a story. Perhaps the act of dreaming, making a dream, is our immediate perception that the world as a whole is a this∗other-ness, a grand ironic epic in which we ourselves take a part. Living our basically categorical, nonironic, valent lives, we only become aware of the irony through the act of dreaming or art. In dreaming, however, we awaken to forget, and the artifact of the dream that we remember is merely a residue of an insight which no longer illuminates us, like a conch shell left after the conch inside has vanished. It is beautiful but in some sense lifeless (omnivalent-less), though we could put life back into it if we worked on it as if it were the draft of a work of art.

Alas, I find all this appealing but I am stubbornly suspicious of it. The evidence seems strong that both dreaming and the dream are a coding process which gives information about the particular situation of the person who has the dream. Then again, one might propose that the act of dreaming is both encoding and omnivalent. However, I find this proposal peculiar. Why? Because it seems merely contradictory to me to say we can have determinate information and yet at the same time undercut that information by recognizing it is ironic. How can something be both a determinable this-ness and an indeterminable this∗other-ness? It would be like saying a literary work could be both an allegory and an ironic metaphor. The one cancels out the other. But I wonder.

In any case, my analogy seems neither proved nor disproved by my reflections. I suppose at this point I would be inclined to argue with anyone who denied that dreams are like literature as much as I would be inclined to argue with anyone who thought that they were. So far, no one knows for certain why we dream and perhaps we will never know, though there are many theories. Some even say it's simply a random discharge from the brain.

Rereading a draft of what I've written, I am startled by my opening statement that literature has the quality that it is always beyond what you can say about it. I perceive a certain irony to my sudden thought that I might have proven my dreams-as-like-literature analogy after all.

References

Briggs, J. "Reflectaphors: The Universe as a Work of Art," in B. Hiley and D. Peat (Eds) *David Bohm: Physics and Beyond*. London: Routledge and Keegan Paul (in press).

Monaco, R., and Briggs, J. *The Logic of Poetry*. New York: McGraw-Hill, 1974.

·7·

Dream Work and Field Work: Linking Cultural Anthropology and the Current Dream Work Movement

DEBORAH JAY HILLMAN, M.A.

Deborah Hillman is a young anthropologist, a prolific dreamer, and a talented dream worker. She has been close to the dream scene as it has emerged in the United States in recent years, a fact that shaped her doctoral studies and her plans for the future. With fresh vision she assesses current developments in dream work and reassesses the role anthropologists might play as they take cognizance of a new sociocultural happening, namely, the increasing interest and activity around dreams in the community at large. Paradoxically, it is an easier task for the cultural anthropologist to become immersed in dreams of vastly different cultures than it is to study dreams in the context of her or his own social milieu. A start has to be made, and here we have just such an effort.

Anthropological Fieldwork

Anthropologists* are concerned with the cultural context that shapes and defines our human experiences. They seek to un-

---

*This chapter refers to cultural anthropology and cultural anthropologists. Anthropology, as a whole, embraces four separate but closely related subfields: archeology, linguistics, physical (biological) anthropology, and cultural anthropology.

derstand the cultural frame of reference that gives meaning to particular beliefs, customs, attitudes, and ways of life. Anthropological fieldwork, whether it is carried out in a small, nontechnological culture, an agricultural community, or a complex urban environment, is a research method in which the anthropologist plays a direct, personal role. Through the technique known as participant observation, she or he studies the activities, principles, and values of a group of people by taking part in their world and attempting to see it from their point of view.

Ethnography describes a cultural setting in terms of the concepts and values of its members, and in terms of the perspective derived from the anthropologist's own cultural background and training (Evans-Pritchard, p. 148; cited in Wagner, p. 189). In ethnography, analytical insights are combined with narrative description, and the overall viewpoint is a holistic one. It takes into account the interaction of the various cognitive, emotional, and social patterns found to exist in the setting, and it recognizes the varied perspectives of people who occupy different roles. In all cultural domains there are ambiguities, inconsistencies, and situations that are considered anomalous or exceptional, and ethnography helps to illuminate these complex and subtle aspects of social reality.

Anthropologists have traditionally traveled by some combination of boat, plane, jeep, donkey, foot, to arrive in an alien culture, their fieldwork destination. They have, in the vernacular, "gone to the field." Once there, the boundaries between personal and professional life are lost. The ethnographer is immersed in the culture, and in an effort to grasp what is "going on" there, every experience is revealing. It is increasingly common, however, for American anthropology to be concerned with cultural and social issues at home in its own civilization. The traditional model in which the ethnographer plays the dual role of participant observer in a small, preliterate foraging or horticultural society is adapted to various kinds of social, cultural, and geographic settings in the United States. Melinda Bollar Wagner, for example, has studied the Spiritual Frontiers Fellowship, a "nonmainstream" religious movement currently active in this country. In her ethnography, *Metaphysics in Midwestern America*, she writes, "One purpose of anthropology is to make the concepts that make up one culture understandable to readers in another. As anthropology 'moves into' the American scene, perhaps this function can be extended to promoting understanding among the various factions of our diverse culture (p. ix)."

My exploration of the dream work movement in the United States was in keeping with the trend to apply traditional fieldwork methods to aspects of American culture. At the same time, it brought anthropological dream research into a new and unorthodox setting. It also stimulated my thinking about what it means to do fieldwork as an "insider." In this case, I was an "insider" not only because I belonged to the same culture as my informants, but also because we shared an experience-centered knowledge of dreams. These issues, and their relationship to the future anthropological study of dreams, are discussed in the following sections of this article.

Dreams and Anthropology: An Overview

Since anthropologists must "attend to those things which have meaning for the people [they study]," and since "many of the peoples encountered by anthropologists have attributed significance to their dreams" (O'Nell, p. 38), it is not surprising that dreams have always found a place in anthropology. Yet, despite evidence of an interest in dreams throughout anthropological history (see Kennedy and Langness for a review of the literature), "dreams remain relatively neglected in the ethnographic descriptions of non-Western peoples" (Gregor, p. 353). Furthermore, the subject of dreams in Western culture, including American society, has been virtually ignored (Collins). Several modern anthropological approaches to the study of dreams are represented in the Winter 1981 (vol. 9, no. 4) issue of the journal *Ethos*, published by the Society for Psychological Anthropology. This collection of papers extends our cross-cultural knowledge of dreams and affords a comparative look at the kinds of dream research methods (including ethnography, psychoanalysis, and content analysis) currently employed by anthropologists. At the same time, although it shows a commitment to dream research on the part of at least a handful of contemporary anthropologists, it stays within the confines of the traditional focus on dreams in non-Western cultures.

The limited scope of both past and present anthropological research on dreams reflects the cultural assumptions that influence the way in which anthropologists, and others in our society, view dreams. Except in those cultures where dreams play a prominent social role and are seen as having particular "native significance" (see, for example, Lincoln's classic study), informants are seldom asked questions about their dream lives. So, whereas the outwardly visible realms of cultural life such as kinship patterns, modes of subsistence, and religious rituals are routinely examined in the ethnographic literature, dreams and dream beliefs are not. As a result of their own cultural conditioning, most anthropologists think of dreaming, in general, as a subject better dealt with by psychologists.

Dorothy Eggan's (1949; 1952) mid-century challenge to social science, and to anthropology in particular, i.e., to study the manifest content of dreams as reflections of the interaction between personality and culture, had little impact on the discipline. I think that Eggan was not correct in imagining that the difficulties of psychoanalytic theory, as a framework for cross-cultural investigation, stood most firmly in the way of anthropological research on dreams. Rather, I think the problem was (and is) the fact that "[a]ll anthropologists wear the blinders of their own civilization in approaching other cultures; our eyes are as conditioned as those of the people we study" (Reiter, p. 13). Among the many factors that shape anthropological fieldwork are the methods and theories chosen as the means of gathering and analyzing data. Yet these choices, along with the very selection of a research topic (and decisions regarding what to look for in the field), are affected by a host of unarticulated and assumed ideas about what is relevant, interesting, and valid. Only when these attitudes and assumptions are examined can fresh perspectives be admitted.

The dream work movement sets the stage for a new view of dreams within anthropology, and for the development of a multifaceted "anthropology of dreams." Just as the feminist movement inspired the growth of an anthropology of women, examining blind spots and distortions in the discipline's view of women's lives, so can the dream work movement provide the necessary stimulus for anthropologists to take a look at their biases regarding dreams. In turn, anthropologists, by applying their methods and concepts to the study of dreams in both Western and non-Western cultures, can contribute more fully to our understanding of the nature and importance of dreaming.

A Note on My Fieldwork

Initially, I intended to limit my attention to the experiential dream group and to study the way in which gender issues— cultural concepts of femaleness and maleness—are reflected in both dream content and the interactions of dream group members. Then, as I began to explore the recent popular dream literature (including the [no longer published] *Sundance Community Dream Journal*, edited by Henry Reed), I discovered that my dream group was part of a developing social trend: an emphasis on the value of dream sharing and on the creative and practical uses of dreams. I decided to make this "movement" my focus since it seemed like a good foundation for future anthropological research on the role of dreams in American culture.

Most of my participant observation in dream groups and workshops occurred in or near New York City. It was supplemented by several open-ended interviews, primarily with people who did not belong to dream groups, about the significance of dreams in their personal lives. In addition, I talked and corresponded with people who are professionally involved in dream work, and I spoke with many others about their personal experiences with dreams. The material that I gathered during this early period in the dream work movement's history (1979–1982), combined with my own experiences as a dream worker (both during and since that time), have formed the basis of my thinking about the relationship between anthropology and dreams.

Fieldwork is by nature an activity that is both interpersonal and introspective. It brings to light many of the anthropologist's own beliefs and assumptions about the world. For me, this process of self-examination was intensified by the level of personal revelation inherent in doing dream work. It has been suggested that paying attention to dreams in the field setting, both one's own dreams and those of one's informants, can illuminate subtle and hidden aspects of the research relationship that influence the process of fieldwork (LeVine). Since I was involved with my own and others' dreams not as an adjunct to fieldwork, but rather as one of its main facets, I experienced a "built-in" sense of these deeper psychological issues. On several occasions, informants reported that they had dreamed about me, and I often dreamed not only of my informants, but also of the topics we discussed during our meetings. It was through the merging of my roles as anthropologist and dream worker that the process of fieldwork unfolded.

The Dream Work Movement

Background: The Cultural Bias Surrounding Dreams. One of the reasons I chose to study anthropology was to learn how cultural influences help to shape and define our *inner worlds*. In the spring of 1978, as a result of a talk given by Montague Ullman at the New School for Social Research in New York City, I began to consider the impact of Western culture's attitude toward dreams. In his lecture, Ullman spoke of the way in which our society both mystifies and devalues dreams, honoring their role in psychoanalysis, where they are considered the province of "experts," and denying them a place of importance outside this specialized arena. Since anthropologists (like others) are conditioned to think in light of the biases of their own culture, it struck me that these insights into the nature of Western dream ideology were describing the very situation that had influenced anthropology's approach to dreams. That evening, Ullman also discussed the group process he had developed to help people become more familiar with the metaphorical language of dreams. This experiential approach to dream appreciation, in a nonclinical setting, sounded like an excellent way to start altering the personal and social effects of the biases surrounding dreams in our culture.

A member of the dream group observed, during my fieldwork, that "nobody *talks* about dreams, really." Although the dream work movement has begun to change this situation (at least in some circles), it is generally not expected that during the course of our everyday lives we will remember our dreams and share them with others. In my own day-to-day life, telling people about my fieldwork often meant that I functioned as a "catalyst," turning conversations to the subject of dreaming. This usually evoked curiosity and lively discussion (and became the occasion for some spontaneous fieldwork). I found that my willingness to talk about my own dream life helped to gain the trust of informants. Conversations about dreams often led to other topics like out-of-the-body experiences (see, for example, Gabbard and Twemlow) and waking déjà vu. The fear that these kinds of experiences might be seen as "weird," or thought of as signs of an emotional disturbance, increases the sense of vulnerability many people feel about exposing the contents of their private worlds. "One of the things that frustrates me about the culture," said one of my informants (a member of the dream group), "is that I can't talk about the things that interest me in social situations without being thought of as eccentric." She added that the dream group gave her "energy to go into those other situations."

Despite a social climate inhospitable to the sharing of dreams and related states of consciousness, many people have privately nurtured an interest in these realms. One informant, a thirty-year-old man who grew up in a rural New England town, felt that paying attention to dreams was a "natural outgrowth" of the artistic encouragement he received from his parents. "I often tell people my dreams because they *excite* me," he said, "but I also hesitate because, while they have power for *me*, they often don't for others." He explained that when his dreams are "particularly intense," it is as though "everything's pregnant with possibilities . . . there's life . . . you feel in rapport with things . . . it's what you call being 'high.'" Another informant, a thirty-eight-year-old woman who came to the United States from Latvia at the age of three, had begun several years earlier to keep a journal that included dreams. For her, dreams are "like going to a movie at night. You just never know what's going to happen." She finds that they "set a tone for the day" and "often work like a catalyst," leading to "new thoughts" of the people about whom she has dreamed. Neither of these informants felt inclined to join a dream group, yet both expressed a keen appreciation of the ways in which dreams influence and enrich their waking lives.

In a self-help resource guide on dreams, published in 1976, Dick McLeester reported that "scattered individuals" were "starting to listen to their dreams to see what they might offer" (p. 7). He regarded this trend as an early sign of a changing cultural attitude toward dreams. He wrote:

> People are looking to other times and cultures to see what different attitudes they had towards their dreams and what value [they] got from them. Dreams are being used as inspiration for art, theater and poetry. People are gathering in groups with the specific intention of sharing and working on their dreams, and exploring ways of integrating them into all areas of their lives (p. 7).

These were the first visible stirrings of the current dream work movement.

History and Description of the Movement. Since the early 1970s, a growing number of people in the United States have become involved with dreams, and a popular dream literature, guiding and encouraging this activity, has been steadily proliferating (see, for example, Delaney; Faraday 1972, 1974; Garfield 1974, 1979, 1984; McLeester, Taylor; and Ullman and Zimmerman; Taylor includes an extensive annotated bibliography). In January 1982, Bill Stimson, of New York City, published the first issue of a grassroots newsletter known as the *Dream Network Bulletin*. Its purpose was to provide information and ideas about dream work, to make practical suggestions for starting dream groups, and to enable dream workers with similar interests to "find" one another. At the same time, the Dream Community of New York was formed to give people in the New York City area who were interested in dreams an opportunity to meet and learn from one another. This loosely structured organization initially sponsored free dream workshops on one or two evenings each month. The New York City area, along with other parts of the country, was beginning to draw attention to the idea of dream work through a variety of dream-oriented events offered locally.

For two years, publications affiliated with the parent newsletter in New York City were issued from other parts of the country. *Lucidity and Beyond* began in New Jersey and later moved to California; *Fusion* came out of Washington State; and *Dream Craft* originated in Virginia. During this period, the network of subscribers, in both the United States and other countries, grew to six hundred (Bill Stimson, personal communication), and the *Dream Network Bulletin* became a prominent and lively forum for the developing grassroots dream movement.

In 1984, Chris Hudson assumed the editorship of the *Bulletin*. He unified the publication and started producing it on a bimonthly basis from his home in Brooklyn, New York. By June of 1985, about seven hundred people were regularly receiving the newsletter (Chris Hudson, personal communication). The May/June 1985 issue marked another editorial transition, and the *Bulletin* is currently in the hands of two well-known dream workers in Virginia, Robert Van de Castle (who acts as senior editor) and Henry Reed (manager and associate editor). It continues to provide a heterogeneous dream work community with a vehicle for sharing diverse perspectives on dreams.

There have been many paths of entry into the dream work movement. One of the earliest routes was involvement in the human potential movement that was active during the 1960s (see Domhoff, pp. 3 & 4). Some of its members, advocating the concept of "personal growth," recognized dream work as a valuable source of insight into themselves and our human condition. Other people have likewise encountered dream work in the context of a metaphysical or spiritual organization, such as the Association for Research and Enlightenment (dedicated to furthering the work of the American psychic, Edgar Cayce) or the Spiritual Frontiers Fellowship. Still others have been inspired to pursue dreams further as a result of their experiences in therapy. For many women, the feminist movement has become an avenue to dream work, prompting them to explore dreams and fantasies for a deeper understanding of their identities as women. Now, with the expansion of the dream work movement itself, more people are "discovering" dreams as a result of direct exposure to it, through publications, workshops, classes, lectures, dream groups, and simple word of mouth.

So far, there has not been a sociocultural analysis of the dream work movement, showing how factors such as sex, age, ethnic background, and social class influence one's relationship to dreams. It is clear, for example, that although the ratio of women to men in dream work is shifting toward somewhat greater balance, the majority of dream workers are, and have been, women. In the early 1980s, they outnumbered men seven to one in Montague Ullman's experiential dream groups (personal communication). This is not surprising, since the gender role traditionally assigned to women in our society calls for sensitivity to emotional issues and a concern for the quality of personal relationships, themes that play an important role in dream work. On the other hand, more men are beginning to cultivate these traits, and for some of them dream work is seen as an opportunity to explore the "feminine" side of their personalities. People of many different ages engage in dream work, and there has been some attention to the benefits of doing dream work with children (see, for example, Garfield, 1984; Ullman and Zimmerman, Ch. 9). The potential value of dreams in the lives of the elderly is a topic that still needs to be pursued (see Van de Castle for a review of research concerning dreams and aging).

While participants in the dream work movement come from predominantly white, middle-class backgrounds, the appeal of the movement has not been limited to this segment of the population. We can expect individuals' responses to the dream work movement to vary according to their past experiences with dreams, and according to the particular feelings and ideas they have about them. These are of course influenced by one's ethnic and cultural background and the role that it assigns to dreams. One of my informants, an Afro-American woman in her late twenties, said it was taken for granted in her family that dreams lend insight to ordinary conversation. She had the impression that in her culture dreams are "talked about and accepted" more readily than they are among most white Americans. We need to examine such variations in the ways dreams are handled by different cultural groups in our own society.

The term "dream work movement" became popular during the years 1982 and 1983 to designate the growing number of people who were becoming aware of their dreams and who were beginning to advocate this new awareness to others. At the heart of this social movement is a belief in the intrinsic value of the dream as a source of knowledge about ourselves and the world we inhabit. Though a basic sense of the communicative power of dreams underlies all the diverse approaches to dream work, the specific goals of this activity are expressed in a variety of ways. In the group I belonged to, Montague Ullman spoke of the emotional repair and healing brought about by dream work. Another dream work leader, whose interests were more narrowly focused, stated that dream work was the "safest, quickest way to develop the psychic faculty." A third teacher of dream work techniques preferred to view dreams as a "direct line to the soul," enabling us to contact a deep source of inner wisdom. The principle uniting most nonclinical approaches to dream work declares that dreams can be understood and appreciated by the lay person, without recourse to the professional dream analyst. Montague Ullman has referred to this principle as "deprofessionalizing the dream" (Ullman).

Within the dream work movement, the stress is on experiential methods rather than didactic and intellectual approaches. In the broadest sense, experiential dream work encompasses all the activities involved in developing an active relationship with dreams. These include learning to recall dreams, keeping a dream journal, and sharing dreams with others. At the same time, special emphasis is placed on techniques that encourage the dreamer to reenter the dream and to experience it again from a waking perspective. This "felt sense" of the dream, combined with an exploration of its symbolic content to discover which of the possible meanings "ring true," is the experience that is thought most conducive to genuine insight. Montague Ullman, in particular, stresses that dream appreciation "requires work and takes energy" (personal communication). His approach to experiential dream work is unique in its step-by-step structuring of the group process in order to create a "safe" emotional environment for accomplishing the necessary work.

Collectively, the various styles of nonclinical dream work share a greater affinity with Jung's view of the dream than with Freud's. They assume, like Jung, that dreams are constructed to reveal, rather than hide, their messages, and they concur with his emphasis on the positive, healthy dimensions of the self embodied in dreams (see Ullman and Zimmerman, Ch. 3). The Jungian technique of "amplification," which one workshop leader described as a "process of enrichment of the [dream] symbol" (by means of exploring its various facets), is among the popular dream work methods borrowed from particular schools of therapy.

Many dream workers are also attracted to Jung's theory of archetypes. It refers to a universal and inherent tendency to produce powerful, unconscious images in response to facing such significant psychological issues as birth, death, struggling with an enemy, or searching for wisdom. Some feminist dream workers have begun to rethink the notion of archetypes and to revise it in order to avoid the gender stereotypes found in Jung's formulation (see Lauter and Rupprecht). They believe that at a time when women's personal identities and social roles are changing, it is especially helpful for them to be aware of their unconscious attitudes and feelings. They view the formation of specific archetypal images as a process influenced by particular social and historical circumstances. Modern women are encouraged to participate in the creation of new archetypal images capable of speaking to their current situations as women.

The Gestalt techniques of Fritz Perls have also captured the attention of dream workers. Based on the theory that all dream elements represent parts of the self, these methods invite dreamers to identify with, and to act out, the various characters and objects that appear in their dreams. One exercise derived from the Gestalt approach involves "dialoguing" with a dream character in order to experience what it is like to "be" that character.

In addition to creating new contexts for sharing dreams outside the realm of therapy and teaching new ways of becoming attuned to the language of dreams, the dream work movement encourages investigation of the full range of consciousness that can occur during sleep. The orthodox view holds not only that dreams are unintelligible to the lay person, and that their importance lies solely in the diagnostic insights they bring to therapy, but also that they constitute a "unitary phenomenon" (Tart, 1969, p. 171) in which qualitatively distinct states are not possible. Recent experimental research (LaBerge) shows, for example, that it is possible to experience a waking-like consciousness while dreaming, as people throughout history have reported, and as I, and many of my informants, were accustomed to experiencing on occasion. Since the academic world both reflects and validates conceptual biases prevalent in the culture, its initial skepticism about the possibility of "lucid dreaming," generally defined as the state of knowing, while one dreams, that one is dreaming, pointed to a more pervasive social view of the nature of consciousness (and dreams).

Within the dream work movement, there is a strong current of interest in lucid dreaming and its relationship to several other "altered states." Jayne Gackenbach, of the University of Northern Iowa, edits a publication known as *Lucidity Letter*, which focuses exclusively on lucid dreaming and related topics. *Lucidity and Beyond* (edited by Sally Shute) was one of the original quarterly newsletters of the *Dream Network Bulletin*, and it also concentrated on the phenomenon of lucid dreaming. This particular branch of the dream work movement, perhaps more than any other, has been calling attention to the philosophical and spiritual aspects of our dream lives. It has also begun to investigate the phenomenological links among lucidity, out-of-the-body consciousness, and near-death experience (on the phenomenon of near-death experience see, for example, Ring).

Experiential dream work can increase not only one's emotional openness and sensitivity to dreams, but also one's level of "sophistication" in terms of actual dream experience. The anthropologist Roy D'Andrade observed that "[c]ultural beliefs and theories about dreams . . . appear to affect [both] the content of dreams and emotional reactions to [them]" (pp. 314–315). We can witness this malleability of dream content within our own society in the well-known tendency for a client in therapy to produce dream imagery that fits easily into the theoretical framework of the therapist. Likewise, it appears that the quality of consciousness experienced during dreaming is amenable to the particular expectations we hold. Several of my informants reported an increased amount of lucid dreaming simply as a result of their desire for the experience and their belief that it was possible (coupled, no doubt, with the added power of suggestion stemming from regularly reading and talking about lucidity). By learning to value our dreams, and by exploring realms of consciousness previously unknown to us, we challenge the cultural demand to limit our attention to the ordinary waking state.

The Social Dimension of Dream Work. Many dream workers feel that they are involved in a process with far-reaching implications for social change. In his handbook on dream work, Dick McLeester devotes two sections to the subject of consciousness-raising and social change (pp. 21–24; pp. 53–64), reminding us that "[o]ur dreams reflect the world around us as well as within us" (p. 21). Attending to the cultural as well as the personal messages in dreams helps to shed light on the intimate connections between social reality and personal experience. Furthermore, as Montague Ullman and Nan Zimmerman point out, the "rigorously honest reflections of personal and social truths that appear in our dreams present us with the opportunity to reexamine both personal and social myths and to begin the process of dismantling them and moving forward" (p. 22). Despite a wealth of cultural information inherent in the dream, this dimension is rarely explored in dream work settings.

Jeremy Taylor devotes a chapter of his book on dream work to the question of "dream work and social responsibility," and it highlights some of the concrete ways in which this theme can be put into practice. In summary, he states that dream work can help to effect social change by "breaking down our prematurely closed prejudices, opinions, ideologies, and world views. Group dream work can also create a community of support and understanding which can sustain us in the efforts to remake global society in a wiser, more humane and just form, as well as [offer] specific creative insights and ideas to accomplish this vitally important task" (p. 19).

The Academic Realm. The dream work movement, like the feminist movement, has both academic and grassroots segments, and these two aspects represent complementary approaches to the same broad goal (Hillman 1984a). Both are concerned with making dreams more important, culturally: the academic through the development of new avenues of research and practical application, and the creation of a multidisciplinary perspective; the grassroots through the encouragement of dream sharing, group dream work, and networking among people who are involved with dreams. As the movement grows, an increasing number of people find themselves in both dimensions.

The Association for the Study of Dreams (ASD) was founded in 1983 by a small group of dream workers who sought a means of fostering and supporting professional interest in dreams. Its first annual conference was held in San Francisco during the summer of 1984. Charlottesville, Virginia, was the host site of the second annual conference, which took place the following summer. As I write this chapter, plans are well under way for the 1986 conference in Ottawa, Canada. The creation of this organization elicited concern among some grassroots dream workers that the egalitarian spirit of dream work might be undermined by a focus on professionalism. In this regard, it is noteworthy that Robert Van de Castle, who succeeds Gayle Delaney as president of the ASD, is also the senior editor of the *Dream Network Bulletin*. That one individual publicly represents both aspects of the dream work movement may be symbolic of a trend toward integrating them more fully.*

Creating an Anthropology of Dreams

Consciousness-raising. Underlying all the potentials brought about by the dream work movement for nurturing the relationship between anthropology and dreams, there is the important factor of "consciousness-raising." The presence of the dream work movement and the existence of new techniques for incorporating dreams into our daily lives have allowed dreams to become more accessible. The increasing social awareness of dreams is significant for anthropology because it means that, as members of a society whose attitude toward dreams is changing, anthropologists as a group can be expected to become more interested in, and sensitive to, dreams. The personal awareness of dreams that results from exposure to the various concepts and ideas expressed by the movement is deepened and enhanced by another

---

*The ASD publishes its own newsletter under the editorship of Jayne Gackenbach.

form of consciousness-raising, the kind that is derived from experience.

The Importance of Experiential Dream Work. I believe that a subjective knowledge of the dream world is as important as fieldwork skills for anthropologists who question others about the nature of their dream lives. Anthropologists must ultimately rely on their own perceptions in sorting out the events and information they encounter in the field. These will be more finely "tuned" to the subject of dreaming if they are rooted in personal experience.

The dream work movement offers anthropologists a practical training ground in experiential dream work. Bringing into the field firsthand knowledge of many of the things my informants told me about the nature of their own dream lives made it easier for me to ask questions and to interpret responses. The vocabulary used to talk about dreams is subject to wide variation in meaning. Expressions like "good dream," "bad dream," "strange dream" mean different things to different people. Furthermore, categories of dream experience, like "flying dream" and "lucid dream," do not have single, standard definitions shared by everyone (Tart, 1984, discusses this problem in regard to lucidity). It is important that both the anthropologist and the informant clarify their use of terms.

Another benefit of having an experiential background is that it enhances rapport with informants. Dream sharing is a very personal form of communication, and empathy on the part of the listener is necessary in order to establish trust. Being an "experienced dreamer" and a skilled dream worker, in the context of one's own culture, is useful for dream research in any cultural setting. The anthropologist who has explored her or his own dream landscape is more likely to respond with intuitive, "felt" understanding to other people's dream beliefs and experiences.

Cognicentrism and Ethnocentrism. The union of experiential and academic perspectives helps to minimize the problem of cognicentrism: ignorance and prejudice stemming from the "narrowness of someone's *conscious* [inner world] experience" (Harner, p. xiv). Cognicentrism is closely related to ethnocentrism: bias resulting from the limitations of one's *cultural* experience. We must guard against imposing our cultural beliefs on societies other than our own, and we must be careful not to assume that our personal notions of reality apply to the experiences of everyone else in our own culture. In an ethnically diverse society such as ours, our inner worlds reflect the variations in our outward customs and habits. This was illustrated in my relationship with a Puerto Rican informant who had the gift of mediumship. For her, dreams were a means of receiving guidance from the spirit world, and as I considered her advice about how to contact my own spirit guides, I learned to appreciate the similarities and differences between our separate views of the dream world.

As researchers, it is important for us to ask not only whether people's experiences fit our categories and definitions, but also whether our categories and definitions adequately contain the experiences people describe (Hillman 1984b, p. 2). For this reason, it is appropriate to question whether concepts such as "lucid dream" are valid phenomenological categories for cross-cultural research. We may discover that members of another culture do experience what we call "lucid dreams," for example, but we may fail to learn what, if anything, those experiences mean to *them.* One of the most valuable contributions that anthropologists can make to the study of dreams in general (and to the study of lucid dreaming, in particular) is to provide ethnographic descriptions of dream experiences as they are understood in their own cultural contexts. In this way, dream-oriented anthropologists can bring back to the dream work movement some of the fruits of their growing interest in dreams. The result will be a greater appreciation, within the dream work movement, of the cultural context of dreaming.

Ethnography of Dreaming in America. An interesting exception to anthropology's emphasis on dreams in non-Western cultures is an article by Larry Peters entitled "The Role of Dreams in the Life of a Mentally Retarded Individual," based on ethnographic research in a California workshop for the mentally retarded. This fascinating account of the significance of dreams in a young man's religious life exemplifies an approach that can be widely used by anthropologists in studying the role of dreams in our society. Many people give dreams a special psychological and social function in their lives, though these personal meanings may not be articulated. Some of my informants, for example, said that they had deliberately done in their waking lives things corresponding to the content of particular dreams. They telephoned people they had dreamed of calling, and in one case an informant traveled to a town in another state where she had dreamed of taking a vacation. Several people said that their dreams provide insight and guidance in matters concerning close personal relationships. For one informant, dreams often serve as an entrée into topics that she finds difficult to broach more directly.

Calling for anthropological studies of dreaming in "contemporary middle class America," Kathleen Collins points out that, " as is true cross-culturally, dream telling in America has a variety of purposes and patterns" (p. 3). Anthropologists can analyze the varieties of dream narration, both within and outside the dream work movement, and among different segments of the population, as forms of oral communication. Like collecting life histories from informants, gathering dream stories during a one-to-one interview can have a strong emotional impact on the person being interviewed. Anthropologists in this kind of dream-sharing situation have a special responsibility to their informants. Avoiding the role of the therapist, they must nevertheless provide a supportive context for dream sharing to unfold and, if necessary, for it to do its own healing work. One of my informants looked forward to a second interview so that he could continue "going through a lot of hard stuff" in the process of recounting some of his dreams.

There are many other aspects of the sociocultural role of dreaming in America that anthropologists can help to illuminate. They include such questions as: What is the relationship between dream work and other daily activities like going to work, spending time with friends, exercising, doing housework and errands? What role do dreams play in shaping an individual's personal philosophy and world view? What purposes are served by keeping a dream journal? In addition, the significance of the dream work movement as a social phenomenon merits ethnographic study.

For anthropologists with a parapsychological or transpersonal orientation, the changing attitude toward dreams is particularly exciting. It has brought about a greater recognition of the psychic and spiritual dimensions of dreams, and of dream work's potential to help guide the quest for knowledge in these realms. Thus the dream work movement presents anthropology with both a stimulus and a field for exploring the connections between dreaming and other forms of experience that point to a level of awareness beyond the confines of ordinary consciousness.

Dream Work and "Practicing Anthropology." The employment of anthropologists in settings outside academia, in both the public and private sectors, has become increasingly common. There are several opportunities to practice anthropology within the context of the dream work movement. The need to devote more attention to the cultural dimension of dreams has already been mentioned. Anthropologists can help to guide the process of group dream sharing toward more explicit examinations of the dream's cultural meanings. Those anthropologists who are trained in experiential dream work techniques can teach them to other anthropologists. It has been observed that "[i]f dreams are in part social and not merely individual psychological products . . . then both the issues and the resolutions presented by dreams must be culturally contextualized" and that this will be "central to the development of an anthropology of dreams" (Kuper, p. 650). The dream group setting provides an excellent laboratory for exploring the social and cultural context of dreams.

Furthermore, since the dream work movement is interested in the dream-related rituals of other societies (for example, those of traditional North American Indian cultures), anthropologists can help to clarify the meaning of these practices in the contexts in which they originated. In this way, dream groups and workshops can become the occasion for examining the concept of *culture* and for considering the change in meaning that results when a technique is "borrowed." In addition, as dream work enters such social institutions as schools, hospitals, prisons, and senior citizens' centers, anthropologists who are involved with dreams can play an important advocacy role. They can act as consultants regarding the introduction of dream work programs into existing cultural settings and assist in the development of educational programs on dream work for health care, teaching, and human services professionals. In my present job as a health care counselor/educator in a public high school setting, and in my work as a hospice volunteer, helping to care for the terminally ill, I find many opportunities to talk about dreams and dream work with a variety of people. This kind of spontaneous and informal "fieldwork" helps pave the way for more formal introductions to the idea of dream work. By openly discussing their interest in dreams in the particular settings in which they find themselves, anthropologists (and other dream workers) can begin to get a sense of the specific role dreams might play in those settings.

Anthropological Imagery in Dreams and Dream Work

The interpersonal ties, challenges, and unexpected events that occur in the field setting make the process of fieldwork a rich source of dream material. Any of the emotional responses elicited by the circumstances encountered during the course of fieldwork can find expression in dreams. Furthermore, dreams can serve to highlight and clarify some of the conflicts and questions raised by the fieldwork situation itself.

Dreaming regularly about my contacts with informants helped to reinforce my emotional commitment to the process of fieldwork. At the same time, as a beginning field-worker engaged in a nontraditional type of study, I sometimes questioned whether my work was really "anthropology." In response to this concern, I dreamed that my "true" ethnographic purpose was to travel to the country to carry out research on the nature of farm life. Besides highlighting my doubts about my role as an anthropologist, this dream offered a humorous and insightful comment on my initiation into the practice of fieldwork. The idea of doing anthropological fieldwork on a farm immediately suggests a pun: "fieldwork" is something that farmers do, too! In a metaphorical sense, I was a farmer cultivating the field that would make me "grow" into an anthropologist.

As I continued to explore the dream work movement, I found myself dreaming not only about fieldwork but also about the nature of anthropology and the significance of working with dreams. In a dream that occurred while I was working on a rough draft of this article, I used a sculptural metaphor to describe the difference between experiential dream work and traditional modes of dream interpretation. In the dream, I was attending a conference where an exhibit had been set up to represent these two modes of dream work. It consisted of two square boxes in which identical dream scenes had been fashioned. One of the sculptures—the one representing experiential dream work—was mechanical. When a button was pressed, the box lit up, and the various parts began to move. The other sculpture—the one representing orthodox dream interpretation methods—had no such moving parts. It stood completely motionless while I delighted in watching its companion come alive.

The message of this dream is summarized in a passage that I came across several months later: "*Working with* dreams is a dynamic and constructive response to the whole potential of the dream, whereas *interpreting* dreams may become a static or passive response to a limited portion of that with which the dream deals" (Puryear, p. 137). Anthropologists do not always "know" how much they intuitively sense about the world they attend to in the field. My dream, set as it was in a public place, revealed not only my personal feelings about experiential dream work, but also how I perceive its "meaning" for others involved in the dream work movement.

Paying attention to one's dreams while conducting and analyzing fieldwork can be a source of ethnographic insights and hunches. Furthermore, the subjectively experienced links between dreams and anthropology are not confined to the dream's ability to illuminate ethnographic concerns, or to monitor and reflect the complex feelings that accompany fieldwork. Just as *dreams* can contribute to the anthropologist's self-understanding, and to her or his grasp of events that occur in the field, so can *anthropology* lend itself to metaphors capable of enriching our understanding of dreams. In one of my dreams I suggest that an analogous relationship exists between the experiences of doing dream work and fieldwork. The dream included a conversation about dreams which is described in the following excerpt from my dream journal:

> I explain . . . that meaning is inherent in the *making* of a
> dream, and that, although the images and symbols may lend
> themselves to metaphorical description of a particular cir-
> cumstance in the dreamer's life, that does not necessarily
> mean that the dreaming mind *intended* such a connection. To
> get at the dream's own meaning, the dreamer has to suspend
> waking judgment and learn to "think" with the "dream
> mind."
>   What I am saying (my journal entry continues) is that the
> dream world constitutes its own reality, and one has to be an
> "ethnographer" of that realm in order to understand it.

For me, one of the most interesting aspects of doing regular
dream work with a "dream partner" or "partners" has been the
mutual exploration of two distinctly different dream worlds. Just
as a single dream expresses the uniqueness of one's inner being,
so does the dream world—defined by a body of dreams that occur over time—bear the stamp of one's individuality. Along with
an ability to appreciate the meaning and creativity of a single
dream, dream work can foster a sensitivity to the qualities con-
stituting the dream world as a whole. In experiential dream
groups, the more familiar the dreamer's inner landscape is to the
rest of the group (as a result of frequent dream sharing), the
more often will the projected meanings supplied by the group
flow from their sense of familiarity with the dreamer's "style."
The kind of awareness involved in this process resembles "ethnographic" understanding—the ability to imagine thinking and
seeing with the mind and eyes of an "insider." Even in my private work with dreams I find an anthropological metaphor: my
dream journal is like a set of field notes describing the world I inhabit every night in my dreams.

Conclusion

Anthropologists can make an important contribution to the field
of dream research and to the grassroots effort to change our
Western cultural attitude toward dreams. Besides expanding the
scope of cross-cultural research on dreams and helping to clarify
our understanding of the cultural context of dreaming, anthropologists can provide practical support for the changes that are

occurring in the settings and methods of dream sharing. To accomplish these goals, anthropologists need to start lifting the blinders that have conditioned their perspective on dreams in the past. They need to strengthen their curiosity about the role of dreams in human experience, in both Western and non-Western cultures. The dream work movement establishes a social context for bringing about this kind of anthropological consciousness-raising, and it sets the stage for creating a full-fledged anthropology of dreams.

An experiential knowledge of dreams is a vital adjunct to fieldwork skills for anthropologists who do dream research. To be familiar with the language of dreams, and with the multidimensionality of the dream world, enables one to develop greater sensitivity to the emotional and cognitive subtleties of dream sharing. This, in turn, enhances rapport with informants and increases the ability to both elicit and clarify information about dreams.

Dream work offers the field-worker an added perspective on the fieldwork situation, in both its ethnographic and personal dimensions, and fieldwork offers the dream worker some metaphorical images to use in exploring the dream world. The combined roles of dream worker and field-worker demand that the anthropologist, an observer who must constantly shuttle between "objective" and "subjective" realities, become more fully attuned to the ethnographic paradox. Inherent in looking at the world "out there" is our own unavoidable subjectivity. Our dreams can help us to understand the nature of the personal and social lenses through which we are accustomed to see.

References

Collins, K. "Anthropology of Dreaming in America." *ASD Newsletter,* 1984, *1*(4), 1 & 3.

D'Andrade, R.G. "Anthropological Studies of Dreams." In Francis L. K. Hsu, ed. *Psychological Anthropology.* Homewood, Ill.: Dorsey Press, 1961.

Delaney, G. *Living Your Dreams.* San Francisco: Harper & Row, Publishers, 1979.

Domhoff, G. W. *The Mystique of Dreams.* Berkeley: University of California Press, 1985.

Eggan, D. "The Significance of Dreams for Anthropological Research." *American Anthropologist,* 1949, *51*, 177–198.

Eggan, D. "The Manifest Content of Dreams: A Challenge to Social Science." *American Anthropologist*, 1952, *54*, 469–485.

Evans-Pritchard, E. E. *Social Anthropology and Other Essays*. New York: Free Press, 1962.

Faraday, A. *Dream Power*. New York: Berkley Publishing Corporation, 1972.

Faraday, A. *The Dream Game*. New York: Harper and Row, Publishers, 1974.

Gabbard, G. O., and Twemlow, S. W. *With the Eyes of the Mind*. New York: Praeger Publishers, 1984.

Garfield, P. *Creative Dreaming*. New York: Ballantine Books, 1974.

Garfield, P. *Pathway to Ecstasy: The Way of the Dream Mandala*. New York: Holt, Rinehart and Winston, 1979.

Garfield, P. *Your Child's Dreams*. New York: Ballantine Books, 1984.

Gregor, T. "A Content Analysis of Mehinaku Dreams." *Ethos*, 1981, *9*, 353–390.

Harner, M. *The Way of the Shaman*. New York: Harper & Row, Publishers, 1980.

Hillman, D. J. "Making Room. A Perspective on the Existence of a Professional Dream Association." *Dream Network Bulletin*, 1984a, *3*(4), 10–13.

Hillman, D. J. "Lucid Dream Consciousness: A Subjective Account." *Dream Network Bulletin*, 1984b, *3*(5), 1–5.

Kennedy, J. G., and Langness, L. L. Introduction. *Ethos*, 1981, *9*, 249–257.

Kuper, A. "A Structural Approach to Dreams." *Man*, 1979, *14*, 645–662.

LaBerge, S. *Lucid Dreaming*. Los Angeles: Jeremy P. Tarcher, Inc., 1985.

Lauter, E., and Rupprecht, C. S., eds. *Feminist Archetypal Theory*. Knoxville, Tenn.: University of Tennessee Press, 1985.

LeVine, S. "Dreams of the Informant About the Researcher: Some Difficulties Inherent in the Research Relationships." *Ethos*, 1981, *9*, 276–293.

Lincoln, J. S. *The Dream in Primitive Cultures*. New York: Johnson Reprint Corporation, 1970 [orig. pub. 1935].

McLeester, D. *Welcome to the Magic Theater*. Amherst, Mass.: Food for Thought Publications [self-published], 1976.

O'Nell, C. W. *Dreams, Culture, and the Individual*. San Francisco: Chandler and Sharp Publishers, 1976.

Peters, L. G. "The Role of Dreams in the Life of a Mentally Retarded Individual." *Ethos*, *11*, 49–65.

Puryear, H. B. *The Edgar Cayce Primer*. New York: Bantam Books, 1982.

Reiter, R. R. Introduction. In R. R. Reiter, ed. *Toward an Anthropology of Women*. New York: Monthly Review Press, 1975, pp. 11–19.

Ring, K. *Life at Death: A Scientific Investigation of the Near-Death Experience*. New York: Coward, McCann, and Geohegan, 1980.

Tart, C. T. "The 'High' Dream: a New State of Consciousness." In C. T. Tart, ed. *Altered States of Consciousness*. New York: Anchor Books, 1969, pp. 171–179.

Tart, C. T. "Terminology in Lucid Dream Research." *Lucidity Letter*, 1984 vol 3, No. 1, pp. 4–6.

Taylor, J. *Dream Work*. Ramsey, N.J.: Paulist Press, 1983.

Ullman, M. "On Relearning the Forgotten Language: Deprofessionalizing the Dream." *Contemporary Psychoanalysis,* 1982, *18*(1), 153–159.

Ullman, M., and Zimmerman, N. *Working With Dreams.* Los Angeles: Jeremy P. Tarcher, Inc., 1979.

Van de Castle, B. "Dreams and the Aging Process." *Dream Network Bulletin,* 1985, *4*(4), 1, 3, 4.

Wagner, M. B. *Metaphysics in Midwestern America.* Columbus, Ohio: Ohio State University Press, 1983.

·8·

Dream Reflection and Creative Writing

RICHARD M. JONES, Ph. D.

Several decades ago Richard Jones chose as the setting for his interest in dreams a small experimental college on the west coast, the Evergreen State College in Olympia, Washington. At that time he had already published his first book on dreams, Ego Synthesis in Dreams. *Two more books were to follow. In* The New Psychology of Dreaming *Jones developed his own theoretical ideas against the background of the new experimental work on sleep and dreams.* The Dream Poet, *a most original contribution, was based on a college course Jones developed that combined what he referred to as dream reflection and literature. His goal, a successful one, was to help students tap into the creativity that goes into the fashioning of meaningful dream images, to use dream work both as a way of deepening their appreciation of literature and to strengthen writings of their own creation.*

Jones's studies have led him into a deeper pursuit of the connection between the metaphorical potential of dream imagery and the origin of language. In a book now in preparation he has further developed his ideas on the relationship of literature, dreams, and the nature of metaphor.

The program he initiated at Evergreen, introducing dream reflection into a literature course, is unique and one that could profitably be emulated at all institutions of higher learning.

Creative writing requires transcendence, or at least subordination of self. This truism is the foundation of creative writing.

Dreams, we are told by Freudian psychologists, seek to hide us from ourselves; and, we are told by some post-Freudian psychologists, dreams seek to reveal us to ourselves. Neither view can illuminate the relation of dreams to creativity, because both raise the self to the focus of their attention. This was inevitable in view of the fact that dreams were rediscovered in modern times by the first psychoanalyst, and the study of dreams has since continued almost exclusively in psychotherapeutic settings. People go to psychotherapists for help in getting more satisfyingly *into* themselves—not for help in getting more creatively out of themselves—although this sometimes does also occur as a result of successful psychotherapy.

What if dreams had been discovered for our time not by a psychiatrist but by, say, an epistemologist? An epistemologist would not feel obliged to pursue his interest in dreams by reference to ego defense or ego synthesis or *ego* anything else. He need not even feel obliged to begin his study of dreams by asking what they might *mean,* or be made to mean, to their hosts. He could simply start by recognizing dreams for what they are. I believe such a basic epistemological view is that a dream is an effortlessly and unself-consciously produced series of potential metaphors connected by a story line.

In dreams we kiss ourselves good-by. *Of* us dreams are; *for* us they are not. They are neither more honest than we are (Fromm) nor more dishonest than we are (Freud). Dreams can be made to respond to our selfish wakeful interests in the insightful ways with which psychotherapists and their patients are familiar, because dreams are *not responsible.* They are not irresponsible either; dreams are simply and sublimely indifferent to the only locus of responsibility that makes any sense in the modern world: ourselves. Dreams are metaphorical visions of being alive cleared of the shades of being alive inside a self.

This might now be obvious had dreams not been rediscovered for our time as a part of the invention of psychoanalysis. For example, Erich Fromm: "In dreams we need not look at the outside world; we look at our inner world, are concerned exclusively with ourselves. . . . In sleep the realm of necessity has given way to the realm of freedom in which 'I am' is the only system to which thoughts and feelings refer" (p. 27). Freedom?! If freedom to think and feel nothing but my "I am" system was truly what my dreams did for me I should here and now resolve to perform the very easy task of forgetting them forevermore.

To have to think and feel the unending noontime of self is the necessity placed on my wakeful life by the society into which I was born that I most regret. I don't go sulking round about this ever-pressing injunction to hold the treasures of being alive fast on the spindle of my little view of life, but I do mean to avoid the necessity whenever possible. My dreams, I find, provide ingenious guidance in pursuit of this avoidance. Whenever I find myself having traversed the morning distance from the bed to the bathroom with nought but thoughts of relieving my bladder and shaving my whiskers; whenever I notice my lady and I to have repeated the same sequence of love moves; whenever a whole day passes in which I have not recalled a line from Shakespeare; whenever my reading of the daily newspaper begins to seem an activity of some durable significance; whenever, that is, the burdens of being nothing but myself become noticeable—I try to remember a dream. Wherein I may discover something akin to the illuminating confusions of Bottom, whom Shakespeare* had say: "I have had a most rare vision. I have had a dream past the wit of man to say what dream it was. Man is but an ass if he go about to expound this dream. Methought I was —there is no man can tell what. Methought I was—and methought I had—but man is but a patched fool if he will offer to say what methought I had. The eye of man hath not heard, the ear of man hath not seen, man's hand is not able to taste, his tongue to conceive, nor his heart to report, what my dream was."

It is not our "I am" systems to which our dreams refer; it is our "I am *not*" systems to which our dreams refer. Fromm is exquisitely wrong in this matter of what it is that dreams free us from. Dreams take us not into ourselves but *out* of ourselves. Therein lies their potential value in preparing us for creative thought.

A Midsummer Night's Dream.

I share this perspective with Montague Ullman, who has expressed it as follows:

> While awake, our view of ourselves is one in which we see and stress our autonomy, our individuality, our discreteness. . . . (Our dreams are) organized by a different principle. Our dreams are more concerned with the nature of our connections with *all* others. . . . The history of the human race, while awake, is a history of fragmentation, of separating people and communities of people . . . nationally, religiously, politically. Our dreams are connected with the basic truth that we are all members of a single species.

> While awake we move through our lives in a sequential, linear moment-by-moment fashion with a point representing birth and another point the present moment. But when we go to sleep and begin to dream we create pictures of what's going on in our psyche from points in space and time which are outside of our waking organizations (p.1).

There's the truth: In dreams our sentence to the individual view of life is suspended, as our perceptions of living are reconnected with those of our species, by way of a transcendent mental function which has united the human race over all human space and over all human time. No wonder that even some "bad" dreams leave us feeling more whole, more human.

I may now refine my thesis: In dreams, where ego was shall species-feeling be. Our dreams are authored from within our individual lives merely to the extent that our self-interests provide their materials, their stuff, exactly the extent to which Shakespeare's plays were authored by the stuff of old histories and legends. Indeed, it was Shakespeare from whom I learned what I am trying to say here: "We *are* such stuff as dreams are made on. And our little lives *are* rounded with a sleep."* ("Rounded," in Elizabethan time, meant rounded *out*, not rounded *in*.)

It is also true, though, as Fromm and others are right to emphasize, that in this modern time of psychological, I-am systemmed man, we can use the selfless creations of our dreams to amplify the intricacies of pressingly self-centered problems. For

---

*The Tempest.

example, I recently went to sleep after a vexing (over how long television could be watched) evening with my two sons, resolving, as I dozed off, that I really did love them anyway, and would always love them, come what may. In an ensuing dream there was a newspaper article which said that the United States Congress has passed a law declaring a turkey farmer's turkeys worthless, and also requiring that he continue to feed his turkeys for the rest of his life. A few minutes of reflection on the dream enabled me to sharpen the implications of my mixed feelings toward my sons: Yes, I love them, and I shall always love them; but I need not, therefore, overlook that they are, at times, a couple of turkeys. And so, at times with them, am *I* a turkey. As a consequence of that brief dream reflection I shall now enjoy a more honest relationship with myself. And with my sons. But I will not so demean the poetic license of my dreams as to assign the intention of bringing that element of honesty into my life to the dream. That intention was mine, first in remembering the dream and then in projecting my personal life into it. The dream could not care less.

Do I split a superfluous hair, here, in dwelling on this distinction between dreaming and reflecting on dreams? It is admittedly a sad thing that our society belittles dreams; and, if we can counter that bias by perceiving dreams as intending us more honest lives, what can be the harm? The harm could be, as Hamlet foresaw, that in taking up arms against one ill we might invite another ill that we know not sufficiently of. What then could be the harm in assuming that, because we can extract more honest living from our dreams, our dreams must mean for us to do so? It is the harm in continuing to deny Herman Melville's Dionysian insight that we are, as a species, alone in this vastly uninterested universe. Because we are the species that experiences life in words, that is, which connects its experiences by way of disconnecting and reassembling than—through the making of metaphor.

This tendency not to distinguish the purposelessness of dreaming from the purpose of reflecting on dreams parallels one to which Morse Peckham brings our attention in the fields of art and aesthetics. The popular assumption of aestheticians has for centuries been that art reveals the essential quest for order of the unconscious human mind. Peckham refutes the assumption as follows:

> That order is a defining character of art is so utterly untrue that it is downright absurd. . . . Not art but perception is ordered. . . . Since we value—and often madly overvalue—whatever is ordered, we tend to impute order to whatever we value. . . . Man desires above all a predictable and ordered world. . . . But because man desires such a world so passionately, he is very much inclined to ignore anything that intimates that he does not have it. . . . It is clear that art is useless, that perceiver and artist are arrogant and indifferent. . . . Art tells us nothing about the world that we cannot find elsewhere and more reliably. Art does not make us better citizens, or more moral, or more honest. . . . Clearly the perception of art and the affective response to its signs and its discontinuities prepare us for no mode of behavior, no role, no pattern, no style. But it is preparation. . . . We rehearse for various roles all our lives. We rehearse our national, our local and our personal styles. These things we rehearse so that we may participate in a predictable world of social and environmental interaction. But we also must rehearse the power to perceive the failure, the necessary failure, of all those patterns of behavior. . . . Art is the reinforcement of the capacity to endure disorientation which makes innovation possible (pp. 313–314).

The same may be said of dreams—almost verbatim: Remembering and reflecting on dreams reinforces our capacity to endure selflessness, which makes creative processes possible. Or *can*, of which more below.

Another example of our tendency to attribute to nature what we choose to find in nature is at the heart of no less than the scientific method, the Null hypothesis, which arbitrarily defines knowledge as that which cannot happen by chance. Enter Jacques Monod, the Nobel-Prize-winning biologist, who has shown that the Null hypothesis will lead us to knowledge of organic life only if we restrict our interests in organic life to those of its forms that are presently, as the biologists say, "selected in"—a kind of Baba Ram Dass, be-here-now biology. It is true that the processes that govern the developments, the behaviors, and the per-petuations of these established life forms, while exceedingly complex, are unambiguously lawful and not influenced by chance. However, as scientific knowledge moves into questions of how *new* forms of organic life are introduced onto the planet—occurrences more frequent in evolution than are the occurrences which perpetuate the established forms—the Null hypothesis must lead us astray of knowledge. Because the intro-duction of new forms of organic life onto the planet is entirely and exclusively governed by chance. The complete view of or-ganic life consists, then, of the macromolecular realm of estab-lished life forms *feeding into which for at least the last four billion years* have been vastly more frequent micromolecular changes occurring by chance alone.

> We call these events accidental; we say that they are ran-dom occurrences. And since they constitute the *only* possible source of modifications in the genetic text, itself the *sole* re-pository of the organism's hereditary structure, it necessarily follows that chance *alone* is at the source of every innovation, of all creation in the biosphere. Pure chance, absolutely free but blind, at the very root of the stupendous edifice of evolu-tion (Monod, p.112).

"Absolutely free but blind." The same is true of dreams. And correspondingly, dreams may be at the root of the stupendous edifice of human language—of which more below.

In summary: we can and do so perceive art that life feels more unified, but it does not follow from that that art intends to unify life. Similarly, we can and do order our relations with nature by applying the scientific method to our observations of nature, but it does not follow from that that all of nature is ordered. Like-wise, returning to our subject, reflection on dreams can help us to live more honest personal lives, but it does not follow from that that dreams intend for us to live more honest personal lives.

"In dreams we kiss ourselves good-by" wants a systematic statement in psychological language. Jean Piaget's will serve. Ac-cording to Piaget, dreams are composed almost exclusively of "ludic (Greek for playful) imagery." Other mental functions, such as those that support artistic perception and the play of children, are composed *predominantly* of ludic imagery; dreams are composed almost *exclusively* of ludic imagery. What is ludic imagery? It is, writes Piaget, "that form of symbolization which originates in conditions of suppression of consciousness of the ego by absorption in, and identification with the external world" (p. 209). *Suppression of consciousness of the ego by absorption in, and identification with the external world.* I interpret that to mean that dreams show us our *external* worlds *un*self-consciously imbued with the desires, the beliefs, the interests, and the values of the self. Thus, dreams are *of* the self, but they cannot be either by or for the self because they originate in conditions in which there is a complete lack of differentiation between the self and the external world, and consequently, a state of nonconsciousness of the self as differentiated from the external world in waking life. The comparison between the turkey farmer's strange relationship with his turkeys and my familiar relationship with my sons could be as refreshing to my waking life as it was, *because* the imagery of the turkey farmer's predicament was imagined in a mental state in which such a comparison is not possible. The infinite freedom of imagination characteristic of dreams is thus a consequence of their blindness to the self-interests of their makers. It is in the course of *reflecting* on dreams that we may accommodate their strangely interesting views to the familiar self-interests of our "real" lives.

Reflecting on dreams cannot, in our time, be unself-conscious, as may once have been so in Homer's time. (Read *The Odyssey* as a series of dreams and see what you think.) Our post-Cartesian culture has made the importance of self-centeredness much too compelling for that to be possible. *But* reflecting on dreams can be *only* self-conscious, and almost always is so, for the reason that reflecting on dreams, as a culturally sanctioned activity, has been largely limited in modern time to psychotherapeutic settings. Thus, the literature on how dream reflection may set its sights *beyond* the pursuit of self-knowledge is just beginning.

I daresay the little knowledge I can share on the subject is primarily due to my having chosen to follow my professional interests in dreams within educational as well as within clinical settings. College students, I discovered, welcome discussions of their dreams in class, and they prize the liberating personal insights that grow from these discussions; but, over time, they come to suspect the motives of a professor who expects no more of them than this.

Bootlegged psychotherapy is not what they signed on for when they enrolled in my course, and the ambiguity surrounding our commitments as students and teacher would in time make "interpreting the resistance" inane. Consequently, I orient dream reflection seminars as much to a piece of good literature as to the dream. I also require that the seminar participants augment their sometimes startling insights into their own developing lives with a piece of interesting writing out in the world. The element of paradox introduced into the dream reflection process by these expectations is what most clearly distinguishes my approach to dream reflection from "sensitivity training," "encounter groups," "self-consciousness raising" and other forms of abetting our society's addiction to "I am" systems; they invite the seminar to begin with a private production completely lacking in self-consciousness and to end with public productions that extend self-consciousness beyond the self.

It seems to me only right that as dreams are given to us from outside ourselves we should express our gratitude to them outside ourselves. Writing to and from reflections on dreams can remind us of the power we have over our language, and of the responsibility that goes with that power. Responsibility for what? Responsibility for using language as an organ of perception as well as a tool of communication. Language enables us to see as well as to say; and, if we do not use language for both purposes, language suffers.

I need not explain what is meant by using language as a tool of communication. We have heard of nothing else from English teachers our whole lives. Thus the current "literacy crisis" in America, as generations of school children are given nothing but utilitarian reasons for wanting to cultivate literacy. How can language also serve as an organ of perception? By lending itself to the making of metaphors, that is, to the employment of the words for a familiar experience to express the perception of a novel experience. The life of every word in every language began as someone's metaphor. Every word, before it became useful

for the communication of a common experience, was first someone's way of expressing the perception of a novel experience.

Do you catch my drift? I say, do you catch my drift? Probably,
but wait a minute. Have you ever seen a "drift" "caught"? Has
anyone ever seen anyone "catch" a "drift"? No, because it is not
physically possible to catch a drift. But you know, when I use
those words, that I mean: "Do you anticipate the direction in
which my thoughts are moving?" And I knew that you would
know that, and so I could use the phrase as a tool of communication—and save six words in the bargain. But first, someone had
to perceive that image, which only words could be used to perceive it with, by way of making a metaphor. Someone, that is,
had first to use language as an organ of perception so that I
could later improve my use of language as a tool of communication. And this prior function of language must be exercised frequently. And we should all feel obliged to see that it is exercised
frequently. Else our language will get tired. Species-feeling.
Species-feeling. Where ego was shall species-feeling be.

My drift is that reflecting on dreams must instruct us in the
use of language as an organ of perception. Because dreams
make nothing but the stuff of metaphors. And they make them
for nothing; and, according to recent scientific reports, they
make them in extravagant supply. I have speculated from these
scientific reports that dreaming may have played a generative
part in the evolution of languages for probably millions of years
(Jones 1980). If so, then the future that lies in our power, which
Auden's exiles long for, might be the future of our language. I
like to urge, therefore, that whenever we feel a debt of gratitude
to a dream for helping us to live more honest personal lives, that
we seek to pay that debt *in writing*.

For example, the following dream provided the metaphors for
a dream reflection seminar:

"I am driving a big old rounded car. I am also taking care of a
friend's child. Suddenly the child is naked and multiplies into
two babies. One of the babies crawls up my chest and puts its
arms around my neck, desperate like.

"The babies disappear, and I am still in the car. A child's voice
from the back seat says, 'I want money.' I park the car, get out

and open the back door. The two babies have turned into white paper penguins, about the size of writing tablets, one of them wearing a top hat. I reply, 'You always want something.' It feels like I'm talking to my schoolwork."

For the next hour each seminar member tried to articulate the focal conflict in their own lives which the dream could have symbolized, and how it did so—as the author of the dream kept her silence. One man, the father of two adolescent boys, saw in the dream a metaphorical expression of his painful awareness that he enjoys a close relationship with one son and a distant relationship with the other; and that both sons, as they have grown older, have come to love him increasingly as a source of money. The dream reminded one of the women of a pregnancy scare she had recently lived through, and the acute conflict that this experience had brought into focus over whether she will ever want to have children. Other such projections into the dream centered on the making of irreversible decisions, the consequences that inevitably follow, and the equally inevitable doubts which must then respond to the question of "what if?" What if I had not registered for the draft? What if I had not had the abortion? What if my wife *had* had the abortion? And so on.

We then turned to the dreamer to hear of the focal conflict for which the dream had in fact been a metaphor. She had dreamed the dream on the anniversary (sure enough) of her abortion. She thought she had resolved her mixed feelings, but the dream showed differently. With long pauses for tears and calmings of voice, she admitted to herself for the first time the love she had felt for the not-to-be-born child and the guilt she later felt for having "killed" it. She knew the decision had been right, and she would make it again in the same situation. After all, having the abortion enabled her to stay in school, which explained why she felt in the dream as if she were talking to her schoolwork. "But there was that baby crawling up my chest and wrapping its arms around my neck as though holding onto *me* for its *life*." As always happens, the dreamer received much empathy, support, and acceptance from her friends around the table. And, as also always happens, her understanding of the dream was deeply amplified by her friends' projections of their lives into it.

It had been a very therapeutic two hours for us all, and we could have counted the time very well spent had we left it at that. However, anticipating that we would need a piece of good literature through which to pay our debt to the dream, we had previously read and discussed Mark Twain's essay "Taming the Bicycle." So, after lunch, we each went off for two hours to compose something in writing that sought, as artfully as possible, to relate the morning's dream to Twain's essay. And then we came back and read to one another what we had written.

Here are a few lines from the essay, to give you its flavor:

> The bicycle had what is called the "wobbles," and had them very badly. In order to keep my position, a good many things were required of me, and in every instance the thing required was against nature. . . . There are those who imagine that the unlucky accidents of life—life's experiences—are in some way useful to us. I wish I could find out how. I never knew one of them to happen twice. They always change off and swap around and catch you on your inexperienced side.

And here is how one student sought to give something back to our language in return for the gifts of self-knowledge we had taken from the dream:

> I agree with Mark Twain's nihilistic assertion that the useful portions of life's experiences, or "accidents," are not readily available to the layman. My past has consistently done a very patchy job of preparing me for current events. For example, how do I stop my kid from abusing me? I could wear a sign: Please be gentle, you're dealing with an inexperienced good example. But he can't read yet, so the effect could be limited.

> It doesn't seem fair when most insignificant domestic considerations force me to become—Parentman. I really don't enjoy hurried changes in the cramped quarters of my patriarchal phone booth. Child rearing could be revolutionized by simply reversing the speed of life. We could start slow and finish fast.

> Slowly merging with life's energy at birth would have the immediate advantage of eliminating the bright roaring clash of post natal shock. You could enter the world like a slug with

a hangover; irritated by the obstreperous jolt of transition, but not moving fast enough to be affected. Physical activity would very gradually increase with age, while the rate of intellectual growth could maintain its present rate.

The advantage of a late blooming metabolism could recivilize civilization. The emotional intensity of childhood would seem like a day at the zoo. There could be some problems with late-middle aged street gangs; or an occasional geriatric rock concert may take a rowdy turn—but a slower more deliberate youth would have to pick up and absorb a little more of life along the way. The despondence and infirmity of old age would vanish, as we would, with our bodies speeding toward a flaming and glorious demise, like meteors with a mission—Kamakazi comets.

Don Mills

The writing will not stand comparison with Twain's essay as a work of literature, but that is beside the point. The author merely sought, in two hours, to extend the occasion of understanding a dream beyond his understanding of the dream—and to do so in writing. Along the way he had of necessity to use language to see as well as to say ("like a slug with a hangover"; "like a day at the zoo"; "like meteors with a mission—Kamakazi comets").

I have sought to combine dream reflection with the teaching of creative writing for the past ten years. This is the sequence of activities as it has evolved to date:

1. We read a work of great literature and discuss it in a seminar, from the points of view of the possible meanings intended by the author, the meanings suggested by the text, and our personal responses to the work.

2. On a subsequent morning, someone brings a dream to the seminar—typed and dittoed, so that everyone has a copy.

3. The dreamer reads the dream aloud.

4. As we close our eyes and try to visualize our own versions of the dream's imagery, the dreamer reads the dream again. This

has the effect of calming inevitable personal jitters and getting us into a studious frame of mind.

5. As the dreamer listens, volunteers (including the teacher) state the feelings the dream aroused in them and how the dream's various images might have functioned as metaphors for personal conflicts in their lives if the dream had been their own.

6. The dreamer then identifies the day residue and shares his or her understanding of the dream as this has been amplified by the various projections into it.

7. We then discuss the dream from two points of view: What it may be saying to us and what we may be prompted to say back to it. Thus, our objectives are to understand the dream and to enjoy it. In this latter venture we learn to respond to the dream's play on words and images; its sound symbolisms and flourishes of synesthesia; its visually alliterative sequences; its deployments of the figurative and literal; its double entendres, stagings, artifices, puns, and jokes.

The discussion is guided by the rule that we are free to advance any hunch, speculation, or intuition; ask any question; or offer any interpretation or outright guess that may help us to achieve the two objectives: understanding and enjoyment. This freedom is limited only by the common acknowledgment that the dreamer will be the ultimate judge of the correctness of the understanding and of the tastefulness of the enjoyment.

8. Then we go off individually and write for two hours—a poem, an essay, a letter, a story, some dialogue—that links our reflections on the dream to our understanding of the week's common reading assignment. This is the most challenging step in the sequence, and when successful, the most rewarding.

9. Then we reconvene as a seminar, and read to one another what we wrote. The writings tend to be of such startlingly liberated quality as to generate a mood of uncommon mutual respect —sometimes falling not far short of shock.

Here is an extended example of the complete sequence: We read and held a seminar on two of E. B. White's essays: "The

Ring of Time" and "A Report in January." Next, we reflected on the following dream:

"I'm at a football stadium sitting in the grandstands with some of the players and the coach. We are the only ones there, but people will soon be coming and a game will be played. They explain to me that they like to come early to get the feel of the place, especially when not playing a home game. One of the players goes down on the field, and suddenly he is in a game from the past that we are watching. He is in an amazing play, and runs a long way down the field, where he is finally tackled and sustains a shoulder injury. He is then back in the grandstand, and I ask the players if they ever get cold while playing. They say that they are always trying to prevent frostbite, and sometimes when the coach puts his hand inside their jerseys to see if they are OK, he gets so hot that he begins to hyperventilate. I see him pale from this. Now people are arriving, and I go down to get some food. I walk by where one buys tickets and see a press agent buying one. I ask him why he's doing so, because I thought that the press gets in free. He says normally this is so, but here everyone knows each other, and they check. He puts a card into a machine (like he's done this before) and receives a ticket. I figure that I better buy a ticket or I might get caught, so I go to a window. The cashier is Walter Matthau. He asks me where I'm sitting, and when I point to the area, he tells me it costs four dollars. I look into my wallet and there is only a five-dollar bill, which I give to him. After fumbling, he gives me back sixteen dollars. I realize his mistake and start to walk away, and then upon seeing the five-dollar bill, he also realizes his error, and calls out my name, which I pretend not to hear, and keep walking. After a minute, I think better of what I've done and walk back to return the money. As I'm going in the door of the ticket office, he is walking out, apparently going out to find me. I tell him I've returned with the money, and he gives me a cynical look, but says nothing. I walk inside with him, and ask him how he would have found me. He looks at me with an air of confidence and replies, 'I would have found you; I know people.' He asks me if I want something to drink and I tell him soda water. He then puts dry ice in a large glass and fills it with water so that the mixture bubbles, and then transfers it to a smaller glass with regular ice. Before I drink it, I wake up."

As the dreamer listened, a sample of the feelings aroused in the group by the dream were as follows:
"I get a strong feeling of guilt."
"Secretiveness."
"A feeling of superiority, of being able to put things over on people."
"Trickiness; treachery."
"I get a feeling of trying to be very macho, with just a hint of fear."
"Curiosity, mistrust, mystery."
"Vindictiveness and guilt."
As the dreamer continued to listen, here is a sample of the personal conflicts projected into some of the dream's metaphors by other members of the class:
"The part about coming to the stadium before the game is to be played and then seeing a game from the past would be a metaphor for my trying to decide whether to take the GRE this year or next, whether I'm ready, whether I'll ever be ready, whether I even want to go to graduate school. Taking stock of myself, sizing myself up, so as to make the best plans."
"The players always trying to prevent frostbite, and the coach getting hot to the point of hyperventilation when he puts his hand into their jerseys is a perfect metaphor for my relationship with my boyfriend. Our passion times are out of this world. For both of us. Neither of us has ever experienced anything like it with anyone else—exhilarating, fulfilling, and confident. But much of the rest of the time we bore each other. We don't have much in common except the way we enjoy each other physically. The dry ice could tie into that metaphor, too. It looks like ice and feels like ice, but it really burns you."
"I sense some homosexual overtones in the image of the coach getting hot putting his hand inside the players' jerseys. A male friend of mine recently told me that he is gay. I would never have guessed, because he is such a fraternity jock. He said I was the only person he has ever told. Just wanted to share it with a woman he trusts. It put me on the spot, because I can't help

him. He didn't ask for help, but even if he had, I wouldn't have known how. And now I've got this unwanted secret to keep. Which makes the press agent who has to buy a ticket the key metaphor for me, if it was my dream. Most things that friends tell you, you feel free to do something with. This one made me feel stuck, trapped, wary. No free pass. Now that I'm talking about it I'm getting angry. I'm angry because I feel guilty, and I didn't do anything to feel guilty for. I just listened. Jesus!"

"The press agent who has to buy a ticket because everyone knows each other, and they check, is a nice metaphor for a life-long situation of mine that may be coming to a head soon. All my life I've had a free pass. My family is wealthy and I can have anything I want. I have friends like that who feel guilty about it, but I never have. For example, I know I got into Cornell because of my family, not because of my grades. But that's OK with me. I like it here and I'm getting a good education. Sometimes I've thought they might be buying me into their way of life, but, like in the dream, it usually turns out they know me very well. Like what they want for me I usually end up wanting for myself. (Hah!) They 'check.' The dream, if it were mine, gets pretty cute there. My father sure does 'check' me, i.e., write me checks!

"What may be coming to a head (Hey, I really like this, because I've been avoiding thinking about it) is this: My father and I have always just assumed that when I graduate I'll start working in his brokerage firm. I probably will, too. I've never questioned it— even looked forward to it. Why not? The money is good and the life is easy. My father's had a good life. But I have this friend who grew up in China who is going to get a Ph.D. in the School of Agriculture—water conservation. His heart and soul is in it. I'll have a good life on Wall Street. No, I'll make a good *living* on Wall Street, and have a good life doing something else. Like my father. But will my heart and soul be in anything? Like my friend? I don't know. I have another year of college. What if something really grabs me, like teaching or social work? How will my father react? I don't think he'll stop 'checking' me, but I do know I wouldn't feel so entitled to the free passes I've always taken for granted. . . . Transferring the soda water from the large glass with dry ice to the smaller glass with regular ice also fits in."

"If this was my dream it would relate to my deciding to drink soda water instead of soda pop. It's cheaper and healthier. I also found five dollars on the road last week. But the whole dream would symbolize for me my efforts to regard my life as a game. It helps me to resolve a lot of conflicts when I succeed, but it isn't easy. Because the *game* of life is confusing. You can't be absolutely sure what skills you need, what the rules are, or what winning or losing means. I've been watching people lately to see who is doing well and why. Does doing well mean getting ahead? What does getting ahead mean? By whose standards—theirs or society's? I'm getting ahead in my own game, dance, but I'm doing it dishonestly. My parents were skeptical, but I convinced them I would someday dance professionally. I love dance and I'm getting very good, but I know I don't have the talent to dance professionally. What I really expect to do is *teach* dance. I'll be good at it, and I'll be happy doing it, but, as often as not, I allow myself to feel less than good because I'm following my private plan—not the public one. I should realize that that kind of dissembling is an important skill in playing the game of life, and give myself credit for it. I would prefer to judge myself from the inside only. In my best moments I do. But, if this were my dream, it would represent those times when the outside is doing the judging—getting a cynical look after returning the money, being checked up on, found out, known."

The above does not exhaust the various simulations of the dream, but it will suffice.

We took a short break and then turned to the dreamer to hear what he had made of the dream and of our various translations of it:

"I was only able to make a few connections after I wrote the dream down:

The day before I quit my job in the lab. This, I'm sure was the dream's day residue.

Sometimes, when no one is around in the lab, I sneak a piece of dry ice into a glass. I like to see the vapors rise up.

My dad and I used to go to the N.Y. Jets football games a lot. Sometimes it was bitter, painful cold.

The part about giving the money back reminds me of a time in Israel when my girlfriend paid an undercharged bill at the right amount. It pissed me off.

"That's all I had when I came to class. Now the whole dream is much more coherent. First, last year, while working in the lab, I cut my finger very badly when I broke a glass. A nerve was severed. Just by luck one of the top neurosurgeons in the country happened to be in the lab at the time. He had me rushed to the hospital and reconnected the nerve. If he hadn't been there on the spot I'd have had a permanently damaged finger, which would have ruled out a lot of possible medical specialties. Then my dad called a lawyer friend of his who got me sixteen hundred dollars in compensation. Hell, sixteen hundred dollars was more than I made at the lab in a whole school year! That memory of being lucky, mixed with guilt, put the whole dream in perspective. The dream is all about guilt. My dad had given me permission to quit the lab job, and that made me feel guilty. He's paying for everything here and I feel I should be contributing something. I also felt guilty about quitting because my boss had gone out on a limb to give me the job.

"But what Chris said about possibly not joining his father on Wall Street, and Kim's seeing the game as the game of life, really hit me where I live. The dream is a guilt dream, all right, but what it's really doing, metaphorically, is raising the question of whether I'll do what I *should* do with my life or what I *want* to do with it. That's a question I haven't even let myself ask, consciously. As far back as I can remember I've wanted to become a doctor. My dad is a doctor. I'm his only son. I've always been in love with the idea of being a doctor, too. I never thought of any other possibility. I'm taking the Med School exam next semester, and I know I'll score in one of the top percentiles. What my family expects me to do and what I *want* to do have always been mirror images of each other. What your projections into the dream have forced me to verbalize is that I quit the lab job so I'll have more time to read philosophy and to write. Those are two things I've discovered at Cornell that I do just because I *want to do them*. I'm good at them and I enjoy them. I don't seriously think I'd decide to become a philosopher or a writer instead of a doctor, but I shouldn't be following those interests on the sly. Hell, I can follow my philosophical and literary interests *avocationally when* I'm a doctor. But I'm less likely to actually do that if I start letting myself feel guilty about them before I even graduate from college. You're right, Kim, life *is* a game (or should be), so we ought to leave as much room for play in it as we can.

"Thank you all, very much."

Then followed about ten minutes of dialogue between the dreamer and the rest of us on some of the dream's niceties (for example, "hyperventilation being as appropriate a term for what occurred in the dream reflection seminar as for what occurred in the dream; 16 + 5 equaling the dreamer's age; dry ice possibly playing on the sound of dry eyes, and so on).

Another round of thank you's between the dreamer and his classmates followed as they left class.

Here are two representative pieces of writing connecting the dream reflection seminar and the E. B. White essays, in the form of letters to the dreamer:

Dear Barry,

In trying to understand your dream as well as E.B. White's *The Ring of Time*, I think it necessary to do what you were attempting in class—to peel back the layers to get to the core underneath.

White describes the circus as the world in microcosm, but he could also be describing the football game of your dream. "Its magic is universal and complex, out of its wild disorder comes order; from its rank smell arises the good aroma of courage and daring; out of its preliminary shabbiness comes the final splendor. . . . It is at its best at certain moments when it comes to a point, as through a burning glass, in the activity and destiny of a single performer out of so many." White watches the rehearsal and becomes painfully aware of the element of time; which itself began running in circles. You watch a pregame warmup but are suddenly seeing a game from the past. Perhaps you are the single performer who makes an amazing play, whose destiny is being observed in both the past and the future.

But the complexities of living in the world intrude on that destiny, on the sense of timelessness. White describes the apparent idyllic South as contrasting sharply with the softness of its music; as also being cruel, hard and prickly. The football players guard against frostbite but their skin is hot to touch. Dry ice looks hot but is cold and gaseous. Things are not what they seem—the familiar is unfamiliar. The Florida days are models of beauty, wonder and comfort but the treatment of many of its citizens is appalling. White perhaps feels the guilt that you do from taking too much change as he lives in the midst of a great social crisis and sees hardly a sign of it. He tries to discharge his duty to society by observing, commenting on and recording it. You try to pursue your personal goals, to find your place in the world, to play in your own game but feel pulled by expectations of others. And all the while the world and time are spinning. Or are they moving in a straight line down the playing field?

Dear Barry,

If I were an automobile, my motor oil would consist of guilt. I could operate adequately when it is low, but sooner or later, I'll need a whopping dose of it to continue. Guilt is a funny emotion. It's right there like my shadow, following me, leading me, depending on the time of day.

Some people were born with original sin. I was born with guilt. It comes with the territory. From day one I was eating bagels and lox with a side order of guilt. Grandma prepares a wonderful dish of guilt. A culinary masterpiece. She serves it at almost every meal, and if you don't eat it, she wails, "What's the matter, don't you like my cooking?"

The anxiety you felt about quitting your job and your subsequent dream tell me that you must have eaten guilt soufflé in the near past. Parents make delicious guilt soufflé, carefully nurturing their creation, giving it the best in life, teaching it to be independent. Finally, father places the soufflé in the oven, and it begins to grow. It develops into a mature dish—self-supporting, high, beautiful. Then, it wants to make a decision for itself, and father slams the oven door. Good-bye soufflé.

I believe E.B. White's venison was seasoned with a bit of guilt. He is determined to remain a naturalist of sorts, "yet slips into the role of a murderer" and uses steer to feed a woodpecker (not to mention himself). He must feel that twinge of guilt. In his struggle to remain simple and unaf-

fected, he also makes a large amount of money. Maybe this is why the wealthy woodcutter is in his essay; an easy way to absolve himself of his guilt by showing another victim of affluence as untouched.

So Barry, don't fret. Guilt will forever find its way into your kitchen and will ruthlessly contaminate your food. "OK," you think, "I won't eat." But what about those starving people in India, just dying for your food. Won't you feel guilty?

There is not space here to systematically compare the post-dream reflection writings of these students with their other school writings. My impressions are that the two examples are representative of the differences: They are not technically "better" pieces of writing; but they are less hurried, they have more voice, they are more personally particular without being egotistical. They seem to have been written with more pleasure than obligation. They take more risks. They amplify rather than merely reflect the views of E. B. White. Best of all, they are much, much more metaphorical. They use language to *see* and not just to say. So what, for now, that the metaphors threaten to become mixed and are in less than exquisite control? Students must first try to use metaphor before they can learn to use it well.

The tone of the seminar sequence tends to be one of scholarly good humor. Therapeutic gains in self-knowledge are expected and accepted, but the prevailing expectation is that personal insights will be extended to grace some aspect of our academic commitments with creative meaning. Here is the way one student, Lloyd Houston, described the experience:

We come in alone and we go out alone, but in between we have each other; the tight throats, the full and empty days, the tears, the unions of minds and hearts, the laughter, the limbo of chaos—the magic. Feeling the moment as it breaks on the nerve of the heart, turns time timeless, as here and now cease to matter and we grope for the mysteries—the magic. Of sharing and knowing, and sharing the knowing and knowing the sharing.

Hear a quiet woman talk of her life and feel the thread that binds her to me, as though we'd loved. Hear a tender man who turns his dreams—and mine—into wriggling, flashing poetry. To find a watch pocket we thought the world had taken from us, or a blue tin cup we thought our childhood had lost, or a new blue streetcar named desire, or a hidden hinge hitched to integrity, or the real thing in a coke bottle . . .

The uncertainty is still there within each of us, every Friday. But rather than holding us back, spontaneity stifled, we become instead almost child-like in freedom and vitality of mind. And then the afternoon writing shows that we are anything but children. The quality of uncertainty characteristic of the dream reflection seminar seems to act as a catalyst freeing our thoughts from their usual musty pathways. The integrity and quality of "the play" becomes the prevailing concern. Everyone becomes more sensitive to everyone, more civil, more thoughtful, more human. And as is true of a good play, the sign of a good dream reflection seminar sequence is lots of hearty laughter.

Here are some excerpts from written statements by students who were asked to describe the effects of the dream reflection seminar sequence on their writing:

"What I like most is the intellectual fencing with the dream poet. I enjoy the free form parrying between seminar members. Colliding associations forming a fascinating kind of fusion."

"I love the mood—relaxing and exciting. After the dream seminar I feel creative."

"I enjoy the surprise connections that occur. When seemingly obscure images come to form a logical and relevant relationship."

"It's a good exercise for getting the brain loosened up."

"I had to let go of a lot of rigid ideas of what writing was, due to seeing the credibility of confused and scrambled but creative dreams."

"I've always written a lot, but dream reflection has given my writing a richer backbone—made it more concrete, less flowery. Dreams are oblique to normal associations, as art tries to be—a good balancing."

"I attribute my success in writing this year to the dream poet. I was so amused by the metaphors utilized in the dreams that I was inspired to let go and give him a little competition."

"I can place the responsibility for what I write on the content of the dream. It provides proof that the subject is of interest (at least to the dreamer) and worth thinking and writing about."

"I guess one of the main causes for everybody's amazing creative output is tied in with the tremendous energy flow and excitement of the seminars. Bantering with key words from the dream; playing with phrases and images; reversing clichés."

"Dreams are very creative pieces of work that come from you. Never thought you could dream up something this original, did you? But you did! So you write."

"Having to force a connection between a dream and an essay seems so impossible, but it turns out to be so excitingly easy."

"Dreams are so intrinsically interesting. They make anything seem possible when you start writing."

"Connecting a product of the unconscious with a product of the conscious does what comparing two pieces of literature can never do."

"Language is usually used to describe concrete images in unconcrete ways. Writing after the dream seminar prevents that."

"It helps me write from the heart. Not just the mind."

"More personal, more reachable, less hurried, less tense."

"One feels free to push aside all of that English class stiffness."

"My writing becomes more colorful, more intense, and more salient to my life."

"It allows me to use metaphors in my own way—not in the way the author makes me feel I *should* use them."

"Getting inside the dream makes metaphorical thinking less foreboding."

"After toying with the metaphors of the dream, forgotten as well as new experience is generated."

"It gives me more confidence. There is no mock or menace in writing after overcoming the fear of the dream. After that, the fear of self-exposure in writing seems less."

"For once, if only for the moment, I can give patience to my words."

"I don't know if the dream reflection seminar is an operator or a catalyst in my writing. Some of both, I think."

"I feel more open to communicate in this class. I really know the audience. . . . Also the realization that I *could* have dreamed the dream and could *not* have experienced the essay."

"I had to write more honestly, because I felt so honored, so dignified, by the responses to my dream."

How, theoretically, may this approach to writing produce these effects? I think an adequate answer will not be forthcoming until a satisfying epistemology of dreams has been formulated. My presently incomplete answer is that the approach to writing by way of reflecting on dreams requires the employment of language as an organ of perception as well as a tool for communication. In this I have been instructed by Julian Jaynes, who has amplified this observation as follows:

> The most fascinating property of language is its capacity to make metaphors. But what an understatement! For metaphor is not a mere extra trick of language, as it is so often slighted in the old schoolbooks on composition; it is the very constitutive ground of language. I am using metaphor here in its most general sense: the use of a term for one thing to describe another because of some kind of similarity between them or between their relations to other things. There are thus always two terms in a metaphor, the thing to be described, which I shall call the *metaphrand,* and the thing or relation used to elucidate it, which I shall call the *metaphier.* A metaphor is always a known metaphier operating on a less known metaphrand. I have coined these hybrid terms simply to echo multiplication where a multiplier operates on a multiplicand.
>
> It is by metaphor that language grows. The common reply to the question "what is it?" is, when the reply is difficult or the experience unique, "well, it is like—." In laboratory studies, both children and adults describing nonsense objects (or metaphrands) to others who cannot see them use extended metaphiers that with repetition become contracted into labels. This is the major way in which the vocabulary of language is formed. The grand and vigorous function of meta-

phor is the generation of new language as it is needed, as human culture becomes more and more complex.

A random glance at the etymologies of common words in a dictionary will demonstrate this assertion. Or take the naming of various fauna and flora in their Latin indicants, or even in their wonderful common English names, such as stag beetle, lady's slipper, darning needle, Queen Anne's lace, or buttercup. The human body is a particularly generative metaphier, creating preciously unspeakable distinctions in a throng of areas. The *head* of an army, table, page, bed, ship, household, or nail, or of steam or water; the *face* of a clock, cliff, card, or crystal; the *eyes* of needles, winds, storms, targets, flowers, or potatoes; the *brow* of a hill; the *cheeks* of a vice; the *teeth* of cogs or combs; the *lips* of pitchers, craters, augers; the *tongues* of shoes, boardjoints, or railway switches; the *arm* of a chair and so on and on. Or the *foot* of this page. Or the *leaf* you will soon turn. All of these concrete metaphors increase enormously our powers of perception of the world about us and our understanding of it, and literally create new objects. *Indeed language is an organ of perception, not simply a means of communication.* (Italics mine—R.M.J.)

. . . . In early times, language and its referents climbed up from the concrete to the abstract on the steps of metaphors, even, we may say, created the abstract on the bases of metaphors.

It is not always obvious that metaphor has played this all important function. But this is because the concrete metaphiers become hidden in phonemic change, leaving the words to exist on their own. Even such an unmetaphorical sounding word as the verb "to be" was generated from a metaphor. It comes from the Sanskrit *bhu* "to grow, or make grow," while the English forms "am" and "is" have evolved from the same root as the Sanskrit *asmi*, "to breathe." It is something of a lovely surprise that the irregular conjugation of our most nondescript verb is thus a record of a time when man had no independent word for "existence" and could only say that something "grows" or that it "breathes." Of course we are not conscious that the concept of being is thus generated from a metaphor about growing and breathing. Abstract words are ancient coins whose concrete images in the busy give-and-take of talk have worn away with use.

Because in our brief lives we catch so little of the vastnesses of history, we tend too much to think of language as being solid as a dictionary, with a granite-like permanence, rather than as the rampant restless sea of metaphor which it is. Indeed, if we consider the changes in vocabulary that have occurred over the last few millennia, and project them several millennia hence, an interesting paradox arises. For if we ever achieve a language that has the power of expressing everything, then metaphor will no longer be possible. I would not say, in that case, my love is like a red, red rose, for love would have exploded into terms for its thousands of nuances, and applying the correct term would leave the rose metaphorically dead.

The lexicon of language, then, is a finite set of terms that by metaphor is able to stretch out over an infinite set of circumstances, even to creating new circumstances thereby (pp. 48–52).

What was the *biologically* evolved process that abetted this function of the use of words as an organ of perception? I have speculated elsewhere that it was rapid eye movement sleep, which served the development of certain singularly mammalian neurophysiological functions, which, in turn, and in time, became the psychophysiological foundations for the evolution of human dreaming (Jones 1970).

The possible merit of this speculation is unimportant for the purpose of understanding the influence that dream reflection has on writing. The important fact is the obvious one: Human dreaming produces the stuff of metaphors infinitely. A dream, I repeat, is nothing but an effortlessly and unself-consciously produced collection of metaphorical images connected by a story line. To pay attention to a dream (any dream), to reflect on and discuss it, to simulate it as your own, to try to understand and enjoy it and then to write to and from it is to be steeped in the use of language as an organ of perception—while incidentally also using language as a means of communication.

Indeed, the very act of remembering, much less recording, a dream requires the use of language as an organ of perception. Words do occasionally figure in the composition of a dream in sleep, but only infrequently. The fundamental aliment of dreams is that of emotion-charged images, largely, although not exclusively, visual images. The only way a dream can be remembered is to translate its images into words, that is, to employ language in its perceptual function. Whatever else is then done with the remembered dream in a social setting must seek to coordinate the use of language as an organ of perception *with* the use of language as a means of communication. Bear in mind, moreover, that this coordinating sequence of events must proceed along a gradient, and must resolve problems of communication, which are next to impossible to experience in modern civilized waking life. Thus, this approach to dream reflection puts a premium on the inherent selflessness of dreams by requiring that, having used them to project further into ourselves, we then also use them to get further out of ourselves.

There is one more observation to make, which I think may be the most important to understanding why the approach to writing described above works as excitingly as it does. Reflecting on dreams in a social setting requires not only that we engage metaphors in intimate proximity to the unconscious level of their production, but, by virtue of doing so, *we must cope with a metaphorical strategy that is the reverse of conscious metaphor production.* In conscious symbolization a metaphor is, as Jaynes says, "always a known metaphier operating on a less known metaphrand" (p. 48). The symbolization which produces dreams employs the reverse of this strategy. The metaphors that constitute dreams consist of *less*-known metaphiers operating on *more* known metaphrands. In the vocabulary of dream psychology the dream's metaphrands are its "day residues," those incomplete, or unresolved or problematic or new experiences from the preceding day which precipitated the dream and with which the dream is playing. (This is why the dreamer *must* be regarded as the ultimate authority in a dream reflection seminar. No one on God's earth can possibly know what a dream's day residues are, except the author of the dream, who almost always does. The dreamer is, therefore, the only person who has access to the information necessary to confirm or disconfirm the relevance and interest-values of the various projections, simulations, and hypotheses to which the others may subject the dream.)

For example, what was the day residue, that is, the metaphrand of the dream of the two babies who turned into white paper penguins the size of writing tablets? It was the fleeting recollection of the day before that it was the anniversary of the dreamer's abortion. Nothing unknown or mysterious about this—as far as it went, but it obviously needed to be *more* known. So, now we have a metaphrand that is more, not less, known than the metaphiers that made up the manifest dream. It is these metaphiers that were mysterious, at least at first. In the process of reflecting on the dream, and with the help of her friends' projections, the dreamer came to see how these metaphiers amplified the metaphrand, making it even *more* known, more vivid, more conscious as she came to appreciate the relevance of the dream's visual metaphors to the choice she had had to make between her maternal desires and her responsibilities to her schoolwork.

This reverse strategy in the use of metaphor may be unique to the symbolization process characteristic of dreaming. And it is the invitation of the dream reflection seminar not only to embrace the metaphorical process but to embrace it, as it were, *from the inside out,* which, I believe, accounts for the excitement and enthusiasm with which the students turn to their writing assignments *after*ward. Thus: "Getting inside the dream makes metaphorical thinking less foreboding." "I enjoy the surprise connections that occur. When seemingly obscure images come to form a logical and relevant relationship." "I had to let go of a lot of rigid ideas of what writing was, due to seeing the credibility of confused and scrambled but creative dreams."

References

Auden, W. H. *Collected Shorter Poems,* Faber and Faber Limited, 1966.

Fromm, E. *The Forgotten Language.* New York: Rinehart and Co., 1951.

Jaynes, J. *The Origin of Consciousness in the Breakdown of the Bicameral Mind.* Boston: Houghton Mifflin, 1976.

Jones, R. M. *The Dream Poet.* Cambridge, Mass: Schenkman, 1980.

Jones, R. M. *The New Psychology of Dreaming.* New York: Grune and Stratton, 1970.

Monod, J. *Chance and Necessity.* New York: Knopf, 1971.

Peckham, M. *Man's Rage for Chaos.* New York: Schocken Books, 1967.

Piaget, J. *Play, Dreams and Imitation in Childhood.* New York: Norton, 1951.

Ullman, M. "Psi Communication Through Dream Sharing." *Parapsychology Review, 12,* no. 2, 1981.

·9·

Dreaming and Learning:
The Dream in a College Classroom

EDWARD F. STORM, Ph.D.

Edward Storm is a computer scientist who has taken to dream work. His special concern is the language of the dream and what this can tell us about the way the brain works.

This chapter, along with the chapter by Richard Jones, represents an effort to link dreams to creativity and learning, two issues central to the student experience. Both authors present cogent arguments for introducing the study of the dream into a college curriculum and for shifting dreams away from the trivial position they generally occupy in the mind of the student to the significance they can acquire once they are taken seriously. In Storm's case, what at first seems a most unlikely linkage, namely, the connection of dreams to computer science, turns out in his hands to offer rich returns to both disciplines. An analogy is drawn between the content that has to be mastered in computer work and in dream work and the appropriate way of talking about that content, namely, its grammar. In seeking the grammar that shapes the manifest content of the dream Professor Storm is taking a step toward identifying the language base of the dream.

Professor Storm's concerns extend beyond the dream's relation to computer science to a broader consideration of the significance of dream work to learning in general. Let us hope that he is correct in seeing this linkage of dreaming and learning as a "newly forming tradition" that can bring "insight, encouragement, and perspective for the learning student."

For the last three years I have taught an elective course in the School of Computer and Information Science at Syracuse University. This course might be called "The computer in the mind." As part of it the students read about and discuss the phenomenon of dreaming. In this chapter I will describe the course, indicate why dreaming constitutes a natural topic in a course about the mind's computer, and summarize some student responses. I will close with some proposals for a course built around the implementation of interactive computer systems that may help the dreamer in his efforts to understand his dreams.

The subject matter for this course and the student responses to it form the body of this chapter. But just as interesting, and perhaps just as important, are my reasons for continuing to offer such a course in a high-technology curriculum. As a result of giving these courses, I have concluded that dreaming and learning (as the latter occurs in many college classrooms) have much in common. This chapter may be understood then as standing in a newly forming tradition in which dreaming is an important source of insight, encouragement, and perspective for the learning student.

I first came to appreciate the significance of dream work in 1979. Since then I have been involved with experiential dream group work both as a group member and as a leader. I have guided a number of small student groups and two adult groups and have participated in three leadership workshops. In addition, I regularly discuss dreams with individuals, in person, by mail and through interactive computer networks.

The most powerful motive for studying dreaming, of course, is that doing so may enhance our understanding of human nature and the human condition. Among other things, dreams sometimes point to sources of conflict and tension and do so in a way that underscores the significance of those sources for the dreamer. The dream helps us to approach the underpinnings of our suffering. In its role as a source of insight the dream is a powerful instrument for healing.

From a more specifically scientific perspective dreaming is of great importance for our efforts to understand the nature of the mind and its relation to brain and matter. The surprising originality that invests the dream reminds us again and again that spontaneous creativity is a central and universal capacity in the human mind. We are forced to recognize this creative capacity no matter what may be our beliefs about the biological or psychological function of dreaming.

My efforts to identify a relationship between dreaming and the computer science curriculum in a high-technology setting were stimulated by Richard Jones's beautiful study on the use of dreams in a creative writing program. Although the opportunity for experiential dream work is limited in a computer science curriculum, the dream capacity can be observed and described by means similar to those used for language, music, reasoning, and other functions of the mind. If the grammar of one's native language is in important ways described as a computational mechanism, then perhaps so may be described the instrument that assembles dream sequences. And they are both managed by the mind. This then is the scientific topic that brings the dream into the course I will describe.

Dreaming and Learning

The course offerings and the student responses have led to one observation that I find of considerable interest: Dreaming and learning are similar in a number of important ways. Before turning to a discussion of the course itself I will summarize these common points.

When I speak of learning, I am thinking of the situation where a student is confronted with a mass of symbolic, abstract, conceptual material. For example, the science student is expected to master his material in such a way that mathematical principles can, in new and novel situations, be correctly applied to obtain useful solutions to real problems. Or he may be required to understand the mathematics as a source of new combinatorial puzzles. A history student faces a similar task. He must deal with a mass of material that must be approached without prejudice—indeed, with little interpretation of any sort. And he must organize and summarize it so that something new can be obtained. The student in literary criticism confronts a mass of strange and unfamiliar symbols (metaphors). He must understand their references, and how those references fit together into a piece of creative writing. In short, my notion of learning is the one appropriate for a college student in a "conventional" classroom situation.

In the first place, the individual occupies a place of primacy in both the dreaming experience and the learning experience. The dream may inform us about our relationships with others, but the dream (under ordinary circumstances) is addressed to exactly one individual, and it speaks to the dreamer in his own unique language. And as every thoughtful student knows, no one participates in the learning experience except the student. We have classrooms, blackboards, libraries, computers, professors, laboratories, and whatever. But the learning experience itself takes place in the privacy of one mind.

Indeed, the privacy of the experience is a second point of similarity. Even if we allow for the occurrence of dream telepathy, no one shares in the dream experience itself. Like the unrecognized beliefs, fears, and desires that subtly influence our actions and our conscious thoughts, the dream maker presents the scenario to the dreamer alone.

Perhaps we will one day have a device, a learning observer, that we will fasten to the student's head. It will indicate to us, through various quantitative readings, that the student has now grasped how to solve this or that kind of differential equation. Or that he now understands why light bends in its path near the sun. I suspect that if we ever get this device, we will be able to tinker with it enough to use it as a dream observer. Fastened to the dreamer's skull, it will indicate (as usual through quantitative measures) that the dreamer is now dreaming of a seedy and tacky deserted lunchroom that serves to remind the dreamer of the seedy and tacky aspects of his current and past life situations. We may have these devices someday, but we do not have them now. And it is not technological inadequacy that is keeping them from us. The significant part of the experience of dreaming, like the significant part of the experience of learning, is not only private, but there are no known means to observe it instrumentally.

In the third place, both experiences involve comprehending a complex system of unfamiliar ideas. When we come finally to understand exactly what we have dreamed about, it is often a surprise. Dreams do not speak to us in the languages of science or of mathematics, and what they say is rarely simple. Calling, as they do, on subtly intrusive elements from immediate experience, on habits of long standing, on forgotten experiences in the distant past, the dream can assemble a complex of factors into a meaningful whole. I think we don't need to review the complexity of what confronts the college student in many of his classes.

A fourth similarity is found in the fact that in both cases the important material is concealed in a highly structured and systematic code, where the code is unknown to the individual who is experiencing it. For the physicist the code is the language of mathematics, a language in which functions are applied to arguments, in which functions are added together to get other functions, in which functions are assumed to be well behaved and orderly in ways that are commonly taken for granted. For the dreamer, the code is just as obscure, just as complex, and just as hidden as is the code of mathematics from the physics student. It does not make the dreamer's job any easier to tell him that he is dealing with elaborate and hidden metaphors. Most of us have only a superficial grasp of metaphor, just as most students have only a casual grasp of what it means to apply a function to its arguments.

Another similarity is found in the spark of recognition that accompanies the breakthrough in learning. Too many times to mention we have the experience of dealing intensively with a body of material, but without any genuine "insight." Fortunately, there is often a critical moment when separate factors come together and the whole begins to make sense. Just so with the dream. We may examine this or that detail, turn over one or another aspect of the dream, until finally just one incisive piece of insight seems to decipher a large part of the puzzle.

In my own experience, both of learning and of dreaming, this spark of recognition is accompanied by an unanticipated affect. In the case of grasping a dream this affect is more or less strong depending on the issue that the dream has addressed. It sometimes expresses a great sadness, that so much of the past brought so much unhappiness. Sometimes it expresses a great sense of relief—a hidden source of anxiety is brought to light. Sometimes this affect provokes laughter. In the Sunday newspaper there is a little game in which the letters in English words are scrambled. The goal is to identify the unscrambled word. This experience is in many respects like trying to understand a dream, or fathom a set of mathematical theorems, or recognize the metaphors in a poem, or recognize the phrase structure in a Beethoven piano sonata. The letter string "LEMPOC," for example, resisted a number of attacks throughout one whole afternoon. I wanted to shout for joy when the "proper" arrangement sprang out! The affect that accompanies the jolt of recognition is more intense, the longer we have had to wait for it.

Dream work, like learning, also benefits from a small group setting. Such an environment is itself supportive, at least for a dream group, and it certainly ought to be in a college classroom. Moreover, if the context is not too saturated with competition, students benefit from the direct intellectual experiences of other students. It is a commonplace that one student often helps another much more effectively than does the professor.

Finally, both dream work and college classroom work are bound up very much with relationships with others, with judgmental issues, and with questions of self-worth. I have even known people who felt inadequate because they could not recall their dreams, and people whose dreams were "not as rich or exciting as everybody else's." Indeed, if we consider the subject matter of dreams, we find that issues of judging and being judged, of self-worth, and of the pain or pleasure associated with the dreamer's relations with others are almost universal categories for dreams. In a similar way, the classroom is often (improperly, I think) concerned with competition, with scoring points, with coming out on top, with demonstrating self-worth in terms of performance at a technological skill.

The Learning Experience

Now that we have considered how closely related are dreaming and learning, we ask if the study of dreams can shed any light on the learning experience. One of the most serious defects of the educational system is that despite earnest pronouncements to the contrary, very little respect is shown for the individual apart from his possible roles in social structures. One way to appreciate this defect is to contrast the perspective of the individual who learns with the perspectives of the institutions with which the individual is or may become involved. These include the family, the school, its faculty, staff, and administrators, possible employers, the communities of classmates, friends, companions, dormitory mates, and a variety of other social structures. In the primary grades, the focus is necessarily on the individual. The child is conditioned to cultivate reading and writing skills, the principles of simple quantification, "correct" reasoning, and even social and personal skills in hygiene and the management of the individual's affairs. As the student advances through the primary grades into secondary school and then into college, the focus shifts to the needs and values of the institutions that surround him. Almost nowhere in the formal learning experience, after the primary grades, is there a substantial commitment to the individual, unqualified by institutionally administered social and political influences.

For many, the entire college experience is expressed as a set of "requirements." There must be so many credit hours, so much of this, and so much of that. This course must be taken ahead of that course, and such and such must be done sometime in the sophomore year. And there are those grade point average requirements! What is much worse, the content of these requirements is often determined by the condition that the graduate must be equipped to take his proper place in some institutional structure. "The employers expect them to know how to do that." It sometimes seems that the school is embarrassed by the possibility that the individual may have any independent value.

Now there is a lot of value for the individual in acquiring a new skill or a new body of knowledge. Each time one learns a new thing the opportunity is presented to refine and sharpen personal skills in attention, in analysis, in the inspection and appreciation of detail, in expressing what has been learned, and even in explaining it to someone else. Unhappily, the learning experience as I have known it ignores these issues and indeed pretends they have little or no validity. The predominant measure of value is in terms of "career preparation," a euphemism for the idea that we go to college in order to learn how to behave as we are instructed by society's institutions. Not until the student reaches graduate or professional school does his individual integrity play any important part, and even then only to the extent that his analytical and creative skills can be exploited to institutional advantage.

It may be important for the educational enterprise to develop practices to enhance the status of the individual, even if some restraint has to be exercised in teaching employable skills. When closely considered, the individual student is often experienced as a vague and confused personality, unmotivated, inarticulate, insecure, and unaware. The vagueness and inarticulateness manifest themselves in low test scores, reflecting an inability to use verbal and quantitative tools beyond a minimal level. Lack of motivation shows up in an attitude expressed in one prevalent inquiry: "Why do we have to know that? Will we need that to get a job?"

If academic institutions were to ignore the muscle structures of their athletes as diligently as they ignore the "mental muscles" of their students, athletic performance would be as appalling as is performance in the simple skills of reading, writing, and arithmetic. In general, of course, these and similar deficiencies are part of what it means to be a finite and fragile human being, acting out an undefined part in a sometimes ludicrous bit of theater. But in an institutional setting where the individual has no value except as a player in that physical drama, these characteristics lead to frustration, anxiety, and hostility. Learning can hardly be expected to flourish in such a setting.

Acknowledging a problem does not solve it. But learning deficits cannot be managed unless the learner is himself aware of the nature of the deficiencies and how they are manifested in performance. Careful and close self-inspection is an essential first step toward the development of insight, surely a critical ingredient of successful learning. Indeed this kind of insight is essential for quality experience and quality action in all aspects of human affairs. Now the study of one's dreams is a paradigm for self-inspection. I have already described the marked similarities between the experience of dreaming and the experience of learning. In addition, like dream work, learning requires patience and diligence, and profits from skillful guidance. Each is an experience of discovery, and like all discoveries, the attainment of success is accompanied by a spark of recognition. In short, the strong and significant connection between dream work and learning may and ought to help us understand better how to introduce fundamental and badly needed improvement into the educational system.

The Computer in the Mind: Course Outline

The course itself begins with a discussion of the nature of computing. We are not here concerned with any particular technological artifact, however commercially attractive (or unattractive) it might be. We look rather to understand the very nature of computing, much as a physicist looks to understand the nature of motion, or a literary critic the nature of metaphor. So we begin with a presentation of the simplest adequate computing machine we know about. This is a little device designed by Alan M. Turing and described to the world in 1936. His machine does all its "figuring" on a strip of tape marked off into squares, each square capable of holding either a Zero or a One. The individual acts that this little machine can commit include: inspect a square to determine whether it holds a Zero or a One, mark a square with a Zero, or with a One, shift its attention from the square it currently inspects to the square adjacent on the left or on the right. Finite sequences of these acts are then organized into "programs." Alternative paths through the program are chosen by distinguishing what occurs in the currently inspected square. A computation takes place when one "activates" such a set of instructions on a machine that is looking at a suitably prepared tape. We note that there is no arithmetic involved in this machine's activities, and that there are no alphabetic characters available to it. The behavior of this machine and of all machines like it, for all possible programs, is simply described: to rearrange, copy, and erase sequences of Zeros and Ones solely by marking individual squares, by inspecting squares, and by shifting attention from one square to another. In the half century since Turing offered this machine as a paradigm of a digital computer no evidence has appeared to suggest that his model is not adequate. That is, all known computations can in principle be carried out by a suitably prepared (and sufficiently fast!) Turing machine. One may build a computer that can in fact "do" arithmetic. But Turing's description tells us that arithmetic is not a part of the essence of computing. It is merely a cultural fascination that we find it convenient to build in.

One reasonably asks how it is, that if we do not have arithmetic built into the machine we can still use the machine to "do" arithmetic, since numerical processing is surely something we want the computer to do. Just so. And in answering this question we explain how *anything* that is done on a computer is actually done. We adopt a *convention* whereby certain arrangements of Zeros and Ones are to be *interpreted* as numbers. These arrangements "represent" numbers. Suppose, for example, that we want to provide a facility for adding two numbers together. Keeping the convention in mind, we assemble a sequence of instructions which will manipulate and rearrange the Zeros and Ones that represent the two numbers in such a way that at the end of the program the sum of two numbers is what is represented by the resulting sequence of Zeros and Ones. Now it is a fact that all the arithmetic we will ever want to do can be encoded in this way on a Turing machine. Alphabetic characters are similarly "represented." In one current standard, for example, the capital letter "E" is represented by the sequence "1000110." Complex operations that search for things in alphabetical order, for example, need only know about the conventions for representation. The programs may be complex and tedious to write, but that, as they say, is the way things are.

In general, then, in order to compute something we first decide how to represent the relevant things as sequences of Zeros and Ones. Then we write the programs to manipulate these sequences, remembering all the time what these sequences are supposed to represent. When we are all finished, if we have done everything correctly, the representation of the correct result will be represented in a specified sequence of Zeros and Ones on the machine's tape. We can now see what is meant by the statement that a computation is the manipulation of an uninterpreted symbolic structure. Whatever meaning there is in a computation, that meaning resides in the minds of those who choose representations and what to do with them. It is worth noting that we cannot envision a computing system in which the representation convention is somehow incorporated into the program. For then the representation would vanish into the resulting enlarged meaningless manipulation of even more complex symbolic structures.

I have summarized the concept of representation here in somewhat loose and condensed form. In the course itself, a more complete treatment of this material is presented to the students, together with illustrative examples. Considerable emphasis is also placed on the central observation in the theory of computing. This is the observation, or definition, that in order to compute something we first decide how to represent it and then write programs to manipulate the representations. (The reader will find a rigorous treatment of the topic in Davis.)

The second technical result presented explains the relationship between formal deductive logic and computing. This relation is so intimate, in fact, that we see that deducing (or inferring) and computing are but two sides of one and the same coin. This is a mathematical and theoretical result also expressed in Turing's original paper. If you can deduce something, that deduction can be constructed by a computer, and if you can compute something with a set of programs, that same thing can be deduced from a suitable set of hypotheses. It is easy to see that this is the case. A formal logical inference generates a new expression from ones that occur earlier in a proof. For example, consider the familiar inference that "Socrates is mortal" follows from the pair "All humans are mortal" and "Socrates is human." We put these expressions into a precise syntactic form and say that "Mortal (Socrates)" follows from "(For all x) (If Human(x) then Mortal(x))" and "Human (Socrates)." It is clear that if we adhere rigorously to syntactic rules of this kind the individual steps in any logical inference can be carried out by a suitably programmed computer. It is a bit more tedious to see that every computation can be described as a deduction, where the role of inference rules is taken over by the built-in basic operations that turn one state of a computation into its successor state. But the principle is the same for both deductions and computations. This formal identity of logic and computing is exploited later in the course in specific applications.

Following these very rigorous and technical topics, the focus shifts to selected readings. In the fall semester of 1983, four books were read in a specified order. First, the students read Erich Harth's treatment of the central nervous system from the point of view of the mind-brain problem. This book surveys the state of the art in neurophysiology, discusses what is known about sensory processes, and explores the relations between traditional views about the mind-brain puzzle and the current state of neurophysiology. Next, the students studied Chomsky on the relation between mind and language, and the assumption that there is a species specific and species universal element in the human mind that can acquire a generative (computational) grammatical capacity. The reading is successful if the student appreciates the importance of the questions of fact that Chomsky raises: What is the structure of the sound-meaning correspondence? How is it physically realized? What is common to all human languages—species specific but universal? How does a normal child acquire his native language? The third book concerned the experience of music (Sessions), and constituted a shift from the physical to the mental, but without surrendering an interest in precisely specified structures. The last book was the treatment of dream work by Ullman and Zimmerman. There is a natural progression in the reading selected—from the concrete to the abstract, from the experientially unfamiliar to the personally intimate. The chain begins with anatomy and physiology, moves to grammar, then to the structure of music, and finally to dreams.

For each topic the students were asked to consider what they read from the point of view that there is some kind of computing agent at work in the human mind. From the physiological perspective one asks how the computing agent is to be identified in the central nervous system. From the Chomskyan perspective one asks what it means to identify a generative (computational) organ in the mind. The treatment of music is challenging. There is well-defined structure in music, but we have to look very carefully to identify it. One way to appreciate this structure is to compare a piece of music with a piece of prose with attention to the structural details. Apart from context, a sentence has a meaning that is determined by the meanings of the words that occur in it (in a definite order). It is undisputed that subsequences of words form units—phrases—that have meaning germane to that of the sentence as a whole. But the individual letters that make up these words contribute next to nothing to meaning. Similarly, the individual notes in a musical score contribute almost nothing to the significance of the music. It is the orderly grouping of notes into musical phrases, and these into more complex units, serially and in parallel, that provide the meaningful elements in a piece of music. In the Western musical tradition there are "grammar rules" as well. The principle of voice leading (briefly—a requirement that one changes as little as possible to achieve as much effect as possible) is like a universal grammar rule governing not only chord progressions but contrapuntal elaboration as well. Certain chord sequences (for example, cadences) occur in preferred positions. And the unfolding of rhythmic patterns is far from arbitrary, not only in traditional music but in more contemporary musical forms as well. (For an interesting discussion of the foundation of musical forms, see Pierce.) To the extent that these structures can be logically described, they can also be incorporated into computations, for we already know of the intimate connection between logic and computing.

When dreams are discussed in the course, I try to cover at least the following: The principal value of the dream is that it gives you insight into your self, and a prominent characteristic of the dream is that it is essentially a private experience. The dream state may have physiological accompaniments that can be observed, such as rapid eye movement, changes in pulse, oxygen consumption, and so on. The substance of a dream—the staging, the cast of characters, the plot, and the peculiar style in which the characters and the props express the plot—is directly perceived only by the dreamer. A dream, with its complex elaborated story line, intense affect, and sometimes richly decorated and significant texture, is a model of private experience.

These are encouraging times for the dreamer and for the study of dreams. Essential realities about the unconscious are once again allowed to affect the attitudes and life-styles of intelligent and compassionate men and women (Ferguson). The flourishing of underground movements in healing, meditation practice, dream sharing, and spiritual development in general all signal an awakening of interest in the not so material aspects of human affairs. At the same time, we are more fully aware that there is at present no general theory of dream structure that provides an adequate account for the biological function of dreaming. Nor do we have any real understanding of the precise means by which a dream is delivered to the sleeper's awareness. The physiological accompaniments of dreams have been investigated in some depth. The psychiatric aspect of dreaming has been appreciated at least since the discoveries of Sigmund Freud. If the psychological dimension of dreaming is not so well understood, it is only because the psychology of human nature itself remains imprecisely characterized. Mystical and religious aspects of dreaming are receiving increasing attention, and the paranormal dream has been studied in the controlled setting of the experimental laboratory. (For a current summary of what we know about dreams see Wolman.)

It is important to appreciate that dreams do not instruct us with respect to what is right or wrong. The dream draws attention to conflicts, to sources of fear, anxiety, and tension. Or it may draw attention to a source of great joy, or to an available means of self-expression or personal development. In general, the dream points to significant and often intense issues in the dreamer's current life situation. In this respect, the dream is a means of clarifying our appreciation of ourselves. The dream shows us what the realities are and leaves aside any judgment of what is good or bad, and any direct suggestion of treatment or therapy. The dream is a powerful instrument for the experience of personal insight.

A dream also has a form, I think, that is distinct from its substance. Its substance is found in feelings and in emotions, in the linkages between the bits and pieces of experience that show up in the dream and issues in the waking life of the dreamer. The substance is what is supplied by a cogent and compelling interpretation. If the dream is a sometimes elaborate complex of symbols, then an interpretation specifies what these symbols stand for. The form of a dream is that part that is subject to interpretation. It is the part that is constant as interpretations vary. If the same object or situation can mean different things to different dreamers at different times, then the form of a dream is that part that is the "same." We might look for this form in the verbal report of the dream, but the verbal report is not the dream itself. It seems more natural to take the "cognitive content" of the dream as an approximation to its form. We particularly mean, however, to exclude all subjective and affective aspects of the dream experience. The form is what may be organized by an emotionally neutral capacity in the mind, such as grammatical structure is organized by a syntactic mental capacity.

If we postulate a mental capacity for organizing this cognitive structure of dreams, and if we can describe the forms generated by this capacity, we will have gained new insight into the formal structural capacities of the mind. And we may further enlighten our understanding of the process of dreaming and of the way in which dream forms arise in sleeping. But we note that this understanding in no way accounts for the metaphorical aspect of dreams. The proper analogy is informative. A computation is itself a meaningless manipulation of symbolic structures, one that takes meaning only when some external agency assigns a coherent interpretation to these structures and to the computing processes that act upon them. Similarly, the scenario for a dream may be expressed as the script for a theatrical performance. This script might be acted out by a collection of actors and "special effects" men. When shown to an audience of people unacquainted with the dreamer, the event could be regarded simply as a piece of entertainment, or it might be interpreted by the people in the audience each according to his or her own disposition at the time. The important associations and the metaphorically expressed connections felt by the dreamer are in general not derivable from a doctrinal framework. It is this script, apart from the individual's interpretation, that makes up the formal structure of the dream. In short, this formal structure is what could be controlled and generated by a computing machine.

We separated out the form of a dream from its substance with reference to the notion of sameness—the idea that two different dreamers would interpret the "same" dream fragment in different ways. It is natural, then, to try to determine when two dream forms are alike or different. When are two dreams (or dream fragments) the same?

Although it is true that no two dreams are ever exactly alike, it is also true that many dreams have similarities to other dreams. Indeed, at the most comprehensive level all dreams are alike simply because they are dreams—they all belong to the category whose name is "dream." But some dreams are alike in a more interesting way. Corresponding relatives or similar house pets appear in the cast. A forest is a forest in anybody's dream. Common familiar settings turn up in dreams—my seventh-grade classroom, the avenue in my hometown, the rented room, the snake, the faceless man. And of course, there are the common dreams—to dream that one's teeth are falling out, to dream of running breathlessly without going anywhere, to dream of weightlessness, to dream of public nakedness.

In view of these facts about dreams, it seems reasonable to ask if we can specify in a precise way when two dreams are alike in a given respect. The idea that two dreams are alike in any sense at all is made difficult by the metaphorical connections that the dreamer establishes between his dream and his waking experience, and even more by the feelings and emotions that the dreamer experiences with the dream. The simplest step is to exclude these aspects of the dream from the idea of similarity. This step is hardly unreasonable. There is no common inherent affect associated with teeth, rooms, streets, weightlessness, nakedness, or indeed with any object. If we set all emotions and feelings aside, then a cigar *is* just a cigar, a key is only a key, and a bridge is nothing more than a piece of the infrastructure. At some level of description there is a script for the manifest content of the dream, a precise and objective specification of what would be perceived if someone could see someone else's dream. It is just this kind of structure that can be specified in an elaborate computational form. In fact, these forms are similar to the "frames," "scripts," or "scenarios" that are common in the efforts to make computers understand natural language. It is tedious but straightforward to represent such scripts as otherwise uninterpreted patterns of occurrences of signs. (The reader can explore these structures starting with Barr and Feigenbaum.) It is reasonable to conclude that a dream has a well-defined form that is independent of its substantial significance to the dreamer, and is not entirely contained in a verbal report of the dream.

Student Responses

Student participation is not easily arranged with such a body of material. Formally, the students are asked to write two or three papers throughout the course, and at the end a single paper that integrates the topics covered in the reading with the technical ideas presented at the start. In other years, some students elected to make class presentations on related topics, and a few asked to be permitted to carry out some kind of computer implementation, usually in the spirit of the "artificial intelligence" tradition.

A majority of students feel that dreams are interesting, exciting, and important. The idea of examining dreams in a formal, highly structured curriculum seems novel, challenging, and possibly of personal value. Some of these students express an interest in dream work and ask if direct experience with dream groups is possible. In one class a few students organized an experiential dream group, but it yielded to "academic pressures" after the fourth meeting. In all three classes there were students who pursued dream sharing, to a limited extent, by the use of the electronic mail and message systems available on the university's computer system. One student explored a complex and obviously troublesome issue arising in a dream, using the dynamic message system in which the student's anonymity was assured. There were a few who thought that dreams had no significance, and a few who thought that one needed professional training in order to deal effectively with dreams. There were a few who were actually embarrassed by the discussion of dreaming. One student told me that she had been working with her dreams for some years and that dream work was far too intimate a matter for classroom treatment.

But aside from these few exceptions most of the students were both interested and enthusiastic about our study of dreams. One girl told me that the course should have begun with the discussion of dreams, so that everyone could appreciate right away the personal dimension of the course material. In the papers submitted by the students there were a number of insights offered.

One paper explored the similarity between the capacity for dreaming and the capacity for language. In each case one uses forms in one category (verbal or visual) to express what is meaningful in a completely different category—the experience of life itself. This paper observed that just as complex grammatical elements are made up of simpler ones, so the complex images in a dream are often composed of much simpler ones. And just as words are constructed from an arbitrary arrangement of letters (there is no reason that any particular arrangement of the letters "a," "d," "n," and "s" should denote the stuff we find at beaches), so a dream image is constructed from simple sensations and complexes of sensations that are not essentially related to the issues dreamed about.

Another student called the dream maker a "communicator between the outer you and the inner you" and described its job as "the least well-understood of all the functions of the human mind." This student went on to describe his own dreams as a means for enriching his life, making available to him experiences and perspectives he would not otherwise have. Whether or not he connects his dreams with his waking life, all his dreams are an "invitation to an open mind."

Another student speculated that the dream maker is at work all day long, collecting raw material for later dreams, sifting the novel from the banal, spotting the individual's unconscious emotional responses to scarcely noticeable intrusions. This fellow described the dream as articulating "the traumas lurking around in our highly adaptive minds" and considered the notion that dreaming is a principal instrument for adapting the organism to emotional realities.

Many of the students were taken by the contrast between the issues of concealment and revelation, and by the obvious fact that a cigar is not always just a cigar. (They also noted that a cigar is not always a lollipop, either!) One student tried to tie this contrast with memory. He observed that although one form of consciousness is held in abeyance during sleep and dreaming, access to the contents of memory seems to be facilitated while dreaming. He saw this as evidence that memory is but one among a number of different "mental organs," one that is accessible by many of the others.

Another student asked why some dreams are so real, so authentic, whereas others are so exotic or fantastic. He speculated that personal difficulties of long standing can be classified by whether they are expressed in a realistic dream, a fantastic dream, or an exotic dream. He said that he had some "boring" dreams but that the boredom itself was part of the dream's message.

Several students commented in depth on the creative capacity that the dream maker uses. Many reached even farther to get a technical notion of creative freedom—the idea that the shape, the physical texture, of the symbol is unrelated to what is represented. The complete freedom with which the dreamer establishes metaphorical relationships was widely noted, for poetry, for fiction, for music, and above all for the dream. Speaking of his dreams, one boy wrote, "The mind is free to act exactly as it pleases." He explained further that during sleep the mind is not preoccupied with the continuous processing of sensory inputs and does not have to organize motor responses. Thus the dream arises effortlessly and spontaneously.

Finally, one girl reported something special about the similarity between our ability to dream and our ability to make music:

> Creativity is the element that is common to both the artist and the dreamer. For example, the poet/composer and the dreamer are both concerned with using imagination to express a feeling or an emotion. These concepts can best be illustrated in quotes from both authors. Ullman and Zimmerman speak of dreamers in general:
>
>> "We have learned, then, to use images the same way a poet has learned to use language: to play with them and recombine them in new ways to express feelings, moods, and stirrings within us that cannot be adequately expressed in any other way."
>
> Sessions document the rolls of the performer and composer in a strikingly similar manner:
>
>> "All the elements of this movement—rhythm, tempo, pitch, accent, dynamic shading, tone quality, . . . are . . . kept under the most exquisite control, by performer and composer alike; . . . By these means a musical gesture gains what we sometimes

call 'musical sense.' It achieves a meaning which can
be conveyed in no other way."

My own response to this teaching experience is that I am now
seeking ways to apply the experience of dreaming to the particular problems that confront a student in computing. These problems arise in the attempt to master unfamiliar and complex
combinatorial structures and to connect them in coherent and
fruitful ways. On the one hand, a problem for computational
treatment may be specified in precise mathematical terms: on
the other hand, algorithms for extracting meaningful results
from these mathematical terms have their own peculiar combinatorial properties. The successful student must learn how to
read, write, and "pair up" these two distinct kinds of structures—the well-defined problem and the correct algorithm.

More generally, the college experience is successful to the extent that it nurtures self-reliance. The teacher is pleased when
the student emerges articulate, disciplined, and curious. We may
use programming as an acquired skill that enhances these desir-
able effects. The complex and rigid character of computer programming offers special advantages in the development of patience, and even compassion. But we know the signs of the onset
of success in learning. The student begins to exhibit the rudi-
ments of style, and even a little finesse. These isues arise in other
classrooms, and the fact that they are germane throughout adult
life suggests that it is appropriate to address them directly. What
Richard Jones has done with creative writing students can be
done and perhaps ought to be done with students in other disciplines. In working with a dream we invest the dreamer with a
certain value not derived from measureable academic performance. What kind of results would we see if students moved
from an experience of this kind of nonjudgmental awareness directly to a demanding combinatorial task? What is the larger-
scale merit of valuing oneself enough to tend to one's relationships with others?

In his study of the recent history of intellectual measurement
Stephen Jay Gould quotes Alfred Binet, speaking of small children with learning difficulties:

What they should learn first is not the subjects ordinarily taught, however important they may be; they should be given lessons of will, of attention, of discipline; before exercises in grammar, they need to be exercised in mental orthopedics; in a word they must learn how to learn.(p. 154)

Binet in fact went on to develop a concrete program of "mental orthopedics," and to implement that program in the classroom. Gould quotes him again:

It is in this practical sense, the only one accessible to us, that we say that the intelligence of these children has been increased. We have increased what constitutes the intelligence of a pupil: the capacity to learn and to assimilate instruction. (p. 154)

One envies Binet the opportunity to invest the student with such respect. One envies him the chance to exclude fear, authority, and the natural capacity for desire, as primary motivating forces in the learning situation. And one admires his appreciation for the fact that precision and clarity in immediate awareness are not only of transcendent importance in learning, but can actually be cultivated and enhanced. How much real distance can there be between Binet's mental orthopedics and the emotional orthopedics of honest, nonmanipulative dream work?

A Course Proposal

There are a number of different ways in which the connection of dreams with computations might be exploited in a college course that centers on the brain-mind issue. One involves the implementation of a "dream bank." Participating individuals would record their dreams into computer files, marking strong content words or phrases. A participant seeking help in understanding a dream might ask to see all those dreams with specified content words or phrases. A dreamer is sometimes stimulated by the way in which another dreamer has made use of a given symbol.

A more ambitious project involves the implementation of an interactive computer system to prompt the dreamer in his attempt to understand the unorthodox symbolism found in the dream. Such a system might take some of its material from the system just mentioned. By this means one can obtain a partial simulation of the contribution of a group. For this system, the dream protocols provided by the first system would be augmented with data obtained from actual dream group activities. These would consist in correspondences between symbols found in the dreams, expressed as words and phrases, and waking life experiences. The computer system functions as a dream oracle, synthesizing its contributions from what is stored in its files.

A third and fairly sophisticated system provides guidance in analyzing the logical form of dreams, their formal structure apart from matters of interpretation. The unfolding of a dream has a skeleton that is expressed as something like a deduction, or a computation. There is, for example, the familiar notion that many dreams are structured as presentations in three acts. These proposals are reasonably well defined, require sophisticated computing technology to implement, and provide natural settings in which one can appraise the end result. They are thus suitable for inclusion in a college course in computing. And they draw the student's attention to the significance of dreams.

Summary

In this chapter I have reviewed my treatment of dreams in an undergraduate course where the perspective is the theory of computation. We saw that dreaming and learning are both concerned with attempting to understand material that is strange and at times threatening, and that they are most deeply involved with the intrinsic worth of the individual. We observed a variety of other similarities between the two experiences.

A number of other "intellectual" activities were reviewed and were seen to be consistent with the assumption that the mind manipulates structures that are specifiable in terms of computation. There was a search for a specific kind of structure—the form of the dream—that might be generated by a capacity that functions in an exact and explicit way, much as Chomsky's grammatical capacity functions to generate syntactic structure.

The content of the reading for the course was summarized,

and the responses of the students were reviewed. We surveyed some basic experimentally determined facts about the central nervous system, its structure and its function. We examined the well-defined structures that Chomsky has postulated to account for the grammar of natural human language, and we considered the existence of musical forms as mental constructs.

My own response to the teaching experience was described— an intuition that the college learning experience may profit from a redirection toward basic mental skills—self-awareness, the management of will, attention, and discipline, and a sense of compassion for and trust in one's own personality. Finally, a programming course was considered that would develop interactive systems to help the dreamer enhance his skill in appreciating and understanding his own dreams.

References

Barr, A., and Feigenbaum, E.A., eds. *The Handbook of Artificial Intelligence.* Los Altos: William Kaufmann, 1981 passim.

Chomsky, N. *Language and Mind.* (enlarged ed.) New York: Harcourt Brace Jovanovich, Inc., 1972.

Davis, M. *Computability and Unsolvability.* New York: McGraw-Hill, 1958.

Ferguson, M. *The Aquarian Conspiracy.* Los Angeles: Jeremy P. Tarcher, Inc., 1980.

Gould, S. J. *The Mismeasure of Man.* New York: W. W. Norton and Company, 1981.

Harth, E. *Windows on the Mind.* New York: Quill, 1982.

Jones, R. M. *The Dream Poet.* Cambridge, Mass.: Schenkman Publishing Co., 1979.

Pierce, J. R. *The Science of Musical Sound.* New York: Scientific American Library, 1983.

Sessions, R. *The Musical Experience of Composer, Performer, Listener.* New York: Atheneum, 1950.

Turing, A. M. "On Computable Numbers, With an Application to the Entscheidungsproblem." *Proceedings of the London Mathematical Society, ser. 2,* 1936, *42,* pp. 230–265; *431,* 544–546.

Ullman, M., and Zimmerman, N. *Working With Dreams.* Los Angeles: Jeremy P. Tarcher, Inc., 1979.

Wolman, B. B., ed. *Handbook of Dreams.* New York: Van Nostrand Reinhold Company, 1979.

·10·

Night Rule:
Dreams as Social Intelligence

JOHN R. WIKSE, Ph.D.

John Wikse is an unusual breed of political scientist. His career was shaped in part by the turmoil and unrest of the sixties. He found himself torn between a way of life linked to academia and an inner drive to seek out a setting more congenial to his scholarly and aesthetic aspirations.

Dr. Wikse takes seriously the often ignored reality that political arrangements have to be understood in terms of their harmful as well as their beneficial impact on human subjectivity. He has brought this view to his interest in and understanding of dreams. Endowed with a rich sense of metaphor, he has used the dream as an instrument to explore some of the critical connections between unsolved problems at the personal level and unresolved issues at the broader social level. In an innovative way he has introduced dream work into his courses in political science.

The chapter that follows is illustrative of his approach.

Here comes my messenger. How now, mad spirit?
What night-rule now about this haunted grove?
Shakespeare, *A Midsummer Night's Dream*

Introduction

Our dreams are our closest counselors. Near to us, like a mirror, they reflect our inmost dialogue with ourselves. Dreams provide our most expansive views of the horizons that are coming into being in us, coming to consciousness. These horizons are various and overlapping, interconnected contexts of significance. Through them, we can identify and recognize ourselves and others.

Recently I was standing in a hallway speaking with a fellow faculty member when a student joined us addressing my colleague: "I had a dream about our class. You were standing at the blackboard, looking over your shoulder at us while trying to hammer a nail into the blackboard. You kept hitting it all around the nail, but not hitting it on the head!" We all laughed, recognizing the pun. The instructor responded that he knew he sometimes talked around a subject, not getting to the point.

This exchange points to one of the most healing aspects of dream sharing, dream humor, which enabled a student to communicate a perception to her teacher that might otherwise have been held back in frustration or expressed as criticism. Because the dream-metaphor was so apt and apparent, clear and playful, the exchange of this perception was direct and friendly. It was facilitated by the humor that bridged the gap between teacher and student.

As the young woman spoke the dream, we discovered the pun and its obvious significance simultaneously. We saw the meaning through the humor. Here is our social intelligence at work.

I place this dream at the introduction to this essay in order to get to the point at the beginning, to exemplify the direct, powerful simplicity of dream communication as a source of social insight. I began studying dreams as social information when I came to understand how limited was my own ability to perceive unresolved tensions and blind spots in myself and others. As I learned to appreciate dream metaphors, I saw that I had come to rely upon and affirm partial self and social images that split people into parts, like jigsaw puzzles.

I first became conscious of this schism when I came face to face with myself in a dream in which I stood pointing a rifle at myself. To see so vividly that I was at war with myself confronted me with a form of doubt, the intuition of a deep-lying ignorance. In our dreams we become aware of the need to bridge the gaps and schisms separating us from others and ourselves.

I once dreamed that I was swimming in the bloodstream of a large organic body, moving from person to person among members of a research group to which I belonged. The feeling has remained with me as a guide. In the dream, it was as if each other with whom I was related was a unique organ functioning within the larger body that composed us. As I approached each member of the group I was sometimes repelled backward through the arteries which connected us; at times I remained in peaceful equilibrium; at times there was the feeling of friction within a fluid medium. I realized that this dream had offered me a vantage point on the patterns of conflict in my exchanges with others in my "social body." This standpoint is accessible through dream appreciation.

In our dreams lie the memories and metaphors of our search for sanity. To learn from the dream work is to feel the metaphors, to appreciate the cultural symbols of the image-making social organism of which we are a part in our dreams. We are a part of this complex, interpersonal organism when we wake as well, though often we do not recognize ourselves. Through appreciating our dreams we can better see the whole of which we are an aspect, the limits that define our possibilities in relationship to particular, contextual, historical conditions. In our dreams we can perceive the interconnectedness of social, individual, and political reality, an insight basic to the development of our sociological imaginations.

The structure of the dream work is timeless. In our dreams we see from the standpoint of a moment that stretches past into future, projecting the history of our emotional associations toward the anticipated horizons of our experience. In the dream space, timebound assumptions are open to scrutiny.

To learn to appreciate this social scrutiny aspect of dreams we must face the contradictions through which we can "identify the collective aspects of individual problems as reflected in dreams" (Ullman, p. 3). Our dreams are pictograms, that is, linguistic and visual representations of our emotions, our social realities. They are composed of our deepest needs and aspirations, our values and interests. They depict the sources of discontent in the relationships we are living, point out possible patterns of adaptation to novel circumstances, provide perspective on our cherished self-images to broaden our understanding of who we are.

When I first started thinking about dreams as social information, I dreamed that I was in a class studying English, my native tongue, as a foreign language, something familiar yet strange. My intent in this essay is to demonstrate the value of appreciating this language. My concern is to help to formulate a psychology that is grounded in a description of the social unconscious, which develops out from the dream toward a fuller awareness of our social selves and which encourages people to learn from their dreams.

Dreams as Social Information

Several years ago I offered a seminar on the political theory of fraternity. Some of the graduate students had worked together and with me before. Toward the end of the term one of the students dreamed that we were all playing a game called "ultimate frisbee." Contrary to the usual practice of the game in which there is no referee, in his dream I was both the referee and a player on one of the competing sides.

This dream depicts a contradiction in the organizational structure of the seminar: While we were a group of people who saw ourselves as friends cooperatively studying the politics of fraternity, nonetheless there were competing sides, and I was formally responsible, by virtue of my position, for evaluating the performance of others. I was both participant and referee.

This is another example of the social information that is present in our dreams. Dream imagery is the result of the personal rearrangement of social metaphors available to us to express aspects of ourselves coming into being and not yet articulated consciously. Dream images arise in dialectical fashion out of contradictory emotional tensions reflecting the gaps between the known and familiar on the one hand and the novel and unknown on the other.

The perspective of this dream is that of critical imagination. It asks us to wonder how our seminar compares to an imaginary game. It presents a metaphoric standard through which to view the dreamer's situation. It is focused along the critical edge of our experience, something familiar but out of kilter, odd. By learning to appreciate this tilted reality, an aspect of the organizational structure of the seminar emerges in sharp relief, juxtaposed with an image that leads us to explore something contradictory about our experience, a dilemma, an ambivalence in the situation.

A dream metaphor brings together at least two assumptions in tension with each other. In the "ultimate frisbee" dream, my student-friend expressed the awareness that he was part of a group that is like another social activity with which he was acquainted. This other activity is characterized by an ethic of equal participation, and the seminar resembles it in this respect. Yet it is also a group in which one individual is distinguished from all the rest by virtue of a position that is like being a referee in a game without a referee. The dream presents the seminar as both this and that, ambivalent, contradictory, novel.

Dreams speak the language of imagination. They do so through images that do not obey the laws of noncontradiction, through metaphors which bring together and focus our emotional ambivalences. Dreams reflect our affective connections with others and the world, placing us in an ever-changing field of exchanges and relationships. In our dream-imaginations we see from the standpoint of the social animal, concerned about our connections, involved in a transpersonal experience, in an emotional, social agitation produced involuntarily within us. As such our dreams can be the source of significant information about the character and quality of our associations.

However, like many things of value, we have privatized our dreams. We tend to view dreams as occurring within the private, separate person, rather than as messages communicating social information. To the degree to which we are unable to recognize our dreams as tools for social insight and analysis, our capacity to act intelligently, our cooperative, communicative competency is impaired. Most of the social information in our dreams goes unacknowledged and unused, is not fed back to the relationships to which it refers, or is done so in certain prescribed ways via professional intermediaries, for example, in therapeutic transactions. We do not usually share our dreams with those with whom we work, though we dream about them. For the most part we are therefore not conscious of the intelligence that we possess about the connections between our feelings and emotions and the social institutions and images that they represent.

Where interaction takes place along a hierarchy of status, power, or wealth, where one is placed "one up" or "one down" with respect to others within a structure of privilege, communication tends not toward open dialogue but is distorted by the tacit necessity to preserve one's position. The relational antinomies of student-teacher, worker-manager, patient-healer, each reflect power-knowledge imbalances in which people learn to say what they mean and need in ways compatible with their perception of danger present. Wherever there are age, class, race, sex, or other invidious divisions among people that correspond to actual power imbalances, there will be distortion of perceptions that could call these assumptions to consciousness, and therefore potentially into question.

It is in this sense that the dream referred to above reflects a kind of danger about the dreamer's situation. On the one hand, the situation seems open and playful, friendly. On the other it is competitive. There are sides and a referee in an ambiguous position, with the power to reward and punish. This sort of danger is the stuff from which the social metaphors of dreams are constructed. Thus our dreams contain potentially subversive information, opening a vantage point beneath assumptions that are coming-to-consciousness, coming to be perceived as contradictory.

Our organism as a whole picks up more information than our consciousness can possess. As sociocultural animals we adapt and survive by producing our environment. If our organizations are open to experimentation in terms of their basic organizing assumptions, then information that focuses the tensions and irritations of the social body, its problems and dilemmas, is of great value. But where association is fearful, coercive, and closed, social information will be factional, partial, and distorted. Wherever we are unable to examine and modify the assumptions of our relationships with others we are confronted with potential information that has no place to go except our dreams.

In Germany before the Second World War many people reported dreaming that the State had abolished dreams (Beradt). This points to the invasion of our dream life by the totalistic State systems of our times. Many people do not remember their dreams. Some believe they do not dream at all. Wherever people are not free to speak and act without fear or arbitrary retaliation, their dreams will pinpoint the source of disturbance of their social selves.

In the watches of the night, our dreams survey, among other concerns, our social situations. A dream is a kind of night watchman, guarding, protecting, and watching over the safety of the city, and checking to be sure that it is safe to sleep. This points us toward the concern for the health of the collective whole that is characteristic of the perspective of the dream work. To the extent to which we view the dream from this standpoint, our dream watches may be said to survey what I will call "night rules": those deep assumptions of our social unconscious, the root metaphors that represent to us the logic of our social identities.

Thus, although we might agree with Freud (1965) that in some sense the dream always points toward the ego, the individual, it is not clear that dreams are as he put it "completely egoistic" (p. 301). Freud himself wrote that he would "reject as a meaningless and unjustifiable piece of speculation the notion that *all* figures that appear in a dream are to be regarded as fragmentations and representations of the dreamer's own ego" (1959, p. 149). The individual is a social organism. In dreams we experience the personal and the social as overlapping transparencies, metaphors that are simultaneously ego- and sociocentric. Social myths, icons, and stereotypes are surveyed by our dream intelligence. To explore the sociocentricity of the dream work is not to deny the existence of dimensions of dream experience that go beyond the immediacy of daily, particular social life. Dream appreciation always remains open-ended, reaching out to the broad periphery of human awareness, to the telepathic and parapsychological and archetypical dimensions of experience. Thus the study of our night rules is a particular practice and discipline of dream work which offers a perspective on dreams that can serve to combat the social ignorance of the dreamer.

In order to fully appreciate the social information in dreams, the dreamer must be able to share a dream in a context in which it is possible to become reflective about the conditions and circumstances of social life, to critically examine assumptions about self and society from the standpoint of the will to therapy which directs the dream. To work with dreams as tools for social investigation entails developing a group process. Ideally, a dream-appreciation research group would be a voluntary association of equals who had a task in common and were committed to using dream information in an understanding of their own group dynamics. Free association works best where the associates are free.

In the sections that follow, I will work with the texts of several dreams, attempting to appreciate them as social information, as pointing out interpersonal, transpersonal, intersubjective, contextual dilemmas. We experience our social selves at many different levels of abstraction. Our most intimate associations and the most remote, mediated images find themselves together in our dreams. Such is the range of our social unconscious.

The Polaroid Camera
and the Nature of Self-consciousness

After a new student joined one of my classes I dreamed the following:

"I am watching a new student in my class trying to take a photograph of himself standing in the front row of a group of his fellow classmates. He is using a polaroid camera, and I see him both standing at the head of this group smiling at me, and simultaneously standing apart from the group trying to take his own picture. He looks at the picture which he takes and sees that he has had his thumb in front of the lens and this has blocked out his own face in the photo. He laughs nervously."

I am struck by the dilemma this dream poses: How can one picture oneself as part of a group of which s/he is a member? The picture the student is taking of himself places him in the front row of the class, grinning toward me and photographing himself at the same time. I see two of him: one facing me, the other trying to view himself as a group member. The split standpoint makes it impossible for him to get a clear view of himself.

Standing in the front row of the group, "at the head of the

class" is a social image, the product of certain rules and relationships—principles of social organization—just as the polaroid camera is a product of a particular technology. The instant camera can provide us with an image of the transpersonal appearance of our lives: here I am with Tom and Andy, or there with Linda on the steps, seen as "others saw us," outside myself in association with others.

In our attempts to get a sense of how we fit in a group we confront objective patterns of membership, structures of status and hierarchy (like "first in the class") that provide a comparative standard by which one's self-image can be judged. In the dream, the student is smiling at me, not at the camera. It is toward me that his pose is directed, for I can determine who is in the front row. His self-image is split into two parts, one performing for me, the other trying to stand back and evaluate himself in terms of the group of his peers. In trying to get a picture of himself he is "all thumbs."

This dream points in-between us to a set of assumptions that structure our relationship. I am involved in his anxiety by virtue of my position in the classroom. The dream points to my own responsibility and emotional involvement, to my participation in the social images that structure self-consciousness in a common social situation. Here the dream can be seen as both ego- and sociocentric, exploring the tensions of status or role anxiety within a social body of which I am a part. Appreciating dreams as social information is like removing the thumb from in front of the camera lens. It opens a fuller picture of our social being.

Contemporaneously with the development of the polaroid camera, we have reached a stage in our group development when we can see that there is need of a technology through which to give a group feedback on itself, so that it may come to reflect upon itself as a whole. In this dream we can see how difficult it is for a member of a hierarchical status-system to face his position, to perceive himself truly. Performance and status anxiety distract and split us, placing on the individual a contradictory demand. This might be called, following Laing and Bateson, the schizophrenogenic aspect of group dynamics, the splitting of the person's attention between the referee-leader-teacher and the rest of the class.

Here we see the sides into which the classroom is drawn, where the two perspectives of the student correspond to the structural separation of the seminar that I discussed in the "ultimate frisbee" dream above. There I, as both teacher and participant, referee in a game without a referee, the only one on my side, directing the discussion and giving the grades, am separated by objective contradictions from the rest of the seminar. The student's experience is split by this structural relationship, focused in two directions and organized so that the possibility of direct and instant feedback with regard to one's place in the group is negated. Where the individuals within a group are split in this way, whatever such a group may accomplish will be distracted by the tensions in its organizational structure which these dreams point out.

Identity, Economy, and Society

Alienation from social information affects both our everyday familial interaction and our relationships with the larger economy in terms of which our familial identities are supported. Family and work are an interconnected web of meanings. Our intimate associations and emotions are matters of economic security. The organization of our workplaces, the division of labor that structures them, and the hierarchical specialization of information and position which defines the patterns of communication within them are all aspects of the context of meaning within which we experience family.

Familial emotions are economic transactions, exchanges within the *oikos* (Gr. for family, household, root of "economics"). Our intimate and extended economic activities are interconnected. How we work is how we live, how we organize the production and the reproduction of life. How we distribute the satisfactions and responsibilities that define us in relationship to our economic identities and our experience of the quality and character of this distribution become apparent in our dreams.

Often it is difficult to distinguish the range of emotions in intimate bonds. Dream-sharing within the family can help to sort out the psychosocial pressures that are released under conditions of intimacy. The following exchange of dreams took place between a couple shortly after the husband had lost his job.

> He dreams that his wife is suffocating him with the bed covers. He throws them off, wakes up lashing out at her next to him, waking her. Frightened, she screams. He realizes he was dreaming and tells her the dream. In the morning when they wake she tells him that she dreamed that he was being suffocated by the god of ecomonic power.

Taken together, these dreams represent perspectives of partners in an intimate association. The problem is suffocation. He dreams that she is suffocating him. She dreams that he is being suffocated by economic power. Here is a dream-communication between them, free association between dreams. The dream information is: There is a connection between his feelings of suffocation by her and the structure of economic power, presented in her dream as a god.

The god of ecomonic power is a metaphor to conjure with. If my anger at you is connected with and mediated by the generalized insecurities and contradictions of the larger economic order, then I must learn to distinguish when my anger at you is a compensation for the weight of a deeper powerlessness.

Viewed from a perspective other than dream-sharing in the family, dream information can clarify the affective connections between individual and work-situation. Here is a dream that depicts the separation of work from social life:
"There is a dinner at my home with people who I think are my work mates. It is an ordinary relaxed dinner. The day after, we go to work. When we get to the work place there is a circus. We talk and change clothes in order to work at the circus."

After working with this dream the dreamer commented:

> The circus is where I work. The dinner is false. It is a way of seeming to have something together, but it is over when the act begins and we have to change clothes. Then we go into an act to please the public, who are the people around me.

The tension involved in not acknowledging that the dreamer works in a circus comes to consciousness through appreciating the manifest content of the dream.

Here is a dream that depicts the pressure of the social neurosis in the workplace:

"I was swimming in a pool. There were lots of people around the pool. I didn't see any faces, only their heads. Suddenly they pressed down my head. Then I was very scared, but said to myself "OK, let them press me to the bottom, then I will fly up again." Then I let them press me. I went to the bottom, then I flew up very quickly, and then I was relieved. I had no clothes on me. I swam like a fish. Children were behind me also swimming like fishes in the water."

They press down my head. They are faceless. Speaking of the work-context which generated this dream the dreamer commented:

> I felt everyone was telling me how to think. They were trying to persuade me to think along what they felt were the right lines. When I deal with them individually they are very nice, but when they become members of an invisible nameless group they can be terrible.

We all belong to this invisible, nameless group which composes the pressure of a diffuse and abstract sense of faceless authority and conformity, the force of normality and social opinion. Imaged in this dream are "heads without faces," hierarchical positional authority (as in "head" of department, class) which depress the individual, submerging her under an impersonal, fearful force that threatens to drown her. There are connections between hierarchy, impersonality, and depression manifest in this dream which suggest that being "pressed down" is a structural consequence of her work life. Here we can see that depression is a pattern of identification both economic and psychological, related to conformity in thinking and the repression of individuality. This pressure weighs down on the dreamer like the spirit of gravity. But her dreams reminds her of her capacity to relieve the pressure. By recognizing her work situation in these metaphors she can identify the social tension, the faceless impersonality that depresses her.

In addition to metaphors which illuminate familial and workplace identifications, dreams can help us to focus the dilemmas of social-sexual role identification, as can be seen in the following:

"I scolded my daughter for spending an exorbitant amount on stationery. My husband asked if I was going to complain. I located the manager, told him I had three daughters and was a longtime customer. He offered me a Barbie Doll. I replied that I was too old for dolls, and asked for my money back."*

This dream depicts a nexus of social-sexual identification, the "Barbie Doll complex," which is coming to consciousness for the dreamer. Scolding her daughter, being perceived by her husband as "complaining," defined by the structural relationship of manager-customer—this complex is a logically interconnected whole. In the dream the resentment of the "longtime customer" who has "bought into" this complex is coming to the surface. The question involves genuine satisfaction and maturation. The dreamer wants her money back; she will no longer be bought off with a Barbie Doll image of herself.

The Barbie Doll is both a personal and a social metaphor. It points to the relationship between a cluster of concerns—anger at one's daughter, recurrent complaining, the passivity of the customer for whom life is managed by others—and the patterns of satisfaction that are expected to compensate for being treated, as an adult woman, like a little girl. This social image integrates a set of tensions around familial, economic, and sexual identity. It illuminates their interconnections. The dream indicates the coming rejection on the dreamer's part of this pattern of identification.

Processes of identification can be more or less conscious. We develop patterns of adaptation in reference to the history of our symbolic identifications. When we become aware of symbols that represent ill-adaptive identifications, we become capable of perceiving what is contradictory and self-defeating. We become more open to the need for genuine satisfactions.

Having explored the psychoeconomic patterns of identity above, we can broaden our lens to include the subject of political metaphors in dreams, searching to uncover contemporary images of political identification.

---

*The above three dreams are courtesy of Montague Ullman's dream appreciation groups.

Spectacle Entertainment

Another dream of mine:

"I enter the department seminar room, but instead of my regular class there is some kind of party going on. I remember that the class is being transformed into a special event. It is combination newsroom and offtrack betting room (a "bookie joint"). News reports fill the room from different radio and TV sets. When a piece of news come in, everyone gets excited and rushes to show it to others. Part of the group is following professional football results. The other is following the presidential election. Someone reads out this information to an old graduate student friend of mine who is typing it all down. Someone reads out a message: 'If the Minnesota Vikings beat Dallas then Powell will win the election.' I enter, several students give reports to me, but I feel unneeded. At one point I announce that if anyone has any questions they can ask me. I sit down for awhile, but nobody asks me anything. I feel very detached from the goings on."

What sort of party is this? The kind of party which is the special event of the dream combines images of two contemporary social activities, football and electoral politics, and connects these activities in a causal statement. If something happens in the Super Bowl, there will be a specifiable consequence in the realm of politics. Both activities seem to be treated similarly as objects of study by the seminar. Electoral politics is like professional football. There are rival and competing organizations, teams that make game plans. In the perspective of the dream, both are spectator events which happen at a distance and are "mediated," encountered as part of that information that is brought to us by the evening news. "Beating Dallas" is like "winning the election," special events which people follow, as fans and partisans: "Party" competition.

The seminar room is a bookie joint. People are placing bets on the basis of predictions. The activities of both football and politics are associated with the activities of professional gambling, and the "if, then" logical form of predictive knowledge of special events which happen at a distance and are experienced as spectacles is the same logic as the calculation of odds. So the sense in which politics is like football in the dream refers us to a way of thinking that is like gambling.

The dream confronts me with my own distance from politics understood in this way and from a dominant research methodology in the study of political behavior based on statistical prediction. When I dreamed this dream I was teaching at a large state university in which I often could not judge whether my political scientist colleagues were discussing sports or politics, particularly when the seasons overlap as they do in the Fall. In the dream I feel unneeded, irrelevant, outside, detached. These feelings of alienation depict my relationship to an academic work environment based on certain assumptions about politics and knowledge.

In Plato's *Republic* (Bk. 7), Socrates presents an allegory by means of which we are to imagine that we are prisoners in a cave, chained together so that we cannot see anything of each other save the shadows of icons that are projected on the wall in front of us. Plato notes that such prisoners might give a prize to those who are "sharpest at making out the things that go by," thereby most able to divine what is going to come. Such knowledge of what is "coming into being" is appropriate to prisoners for whom special events are to be watched, not done. The images on the wall of the cave, like media images, are the iconography of a particular culture, within which it makes sense to think of politics as if it were like football. Imagine a football over which is written: "Campaign '84."

Politics as a special event is the social myth that focuses my dilemma in the classroom. I would like to be useful to those who are studying politics as if it were like football. This would be to talk about the political iconography of detachment, of the consequences, in Ellul's words, of "living in the news." The dream points to a particular political illusion with which I am in tension, to assumptions associated with a conception of politics as spectacle entertainment.

I am no longer identified as a political scientist in my work. In several of the dreams above I have worked with aspects of my own professional identification in the context of exploring those structural contradictions which they revealed to me regarding my work life. The last of these dreams occurred after I had been away from academic life for several years and was getting in touch with deeper contradictions than those of the immediate situation. In the following discussion I wish to point to the ability of dreams to reveal the deep structures of our social unconscious. Here, images of class and racial privilege teach us that despite our most cherished self-images to the contrary, we are objectively, deeply alienated from our fellows, across gaps of privileged, stereotypical identifications.

The View from Across the Aisle

While traveling on a Greyhound bus from Pittsburgh to Chicago I was reading a book on the Haymarket "riots" in Chicago at the end of the nineteenth century. Included were several examples of anarchist posters organizing workers to strike. Across from me was a young black man. I curled into the seat to sleep and dreamed that I was watching myself as I slept from his seat across the aisle. Above me as I saw myself sleeping, in the space reserved for commercial advertising, was a poster. It was composed of a series of columns of figures which computed my lifetime grade point average, from kindergarten through my Ph.D.: 3.9 was the total. Above these numbers was my signature, Jack Wikse. Someone walked over and scribbled "Jack Wis" over the poster.

Here the dream presents me with information about my signature, as seen from a specific perspective, my academic vita viewed as a lifelong, continuous record of my grades. The anarchist posters from my reading have been transformed into a self-advertisment of my academic achievements, a sign or signature for my persona, projected from the perspective of a stranger across the aisle. "I wonder how he sees me?" is the seed of the dream, projected by the social unconscious across the aisle of race and class and privilege. The answer is mediated by the iconography of the lifetime grade point average, simultaneously a personal and a social image (perhaps even an institutional). The dream tells me it is my signature, that is, the way that I am recognized by others. It is an image of privilege and success.

An off-kilter version of this identity is scribbled, across my self-image, a defacing of my poster-signature, "Jack Wis," something strange and feeling unfinished, partial. When I worked with this dream I felt that the transformation of my last name into "Wis" was an ironic way of saying, "You think you're so knowledgeable and 'wise,' studying the history of the working class, such a 'wiz' studying the anarchists, but cut off from the man across the aisle." Several months after having moved to Wisconsin, I saw the abbreviation "Wis." on my address, and thought that this was a perfect metaphor to organize my changing identity in an unexplored environment.

The dream confronted me with my unfinished self-image. It challenged me to integrate this perspective on my social self, pointing me to explore the relationship between race and privilege and academia, those patterns of identification that had made it a dilemma for me to cross the aisle to another part of my divided social body.

Like race and class, deep in our social unconscious are images that probe the larger identification patterns of our collective lives, national and international symbols which allow a broader cultural unconscious to emerge as an object of awareness. In the following I will discuss certain structural characteristics of the social unconscious as they are revealed in a dream that I had in 1980 after traveling from Europe to the United States.

Seriality and Mediation

"We are in a crowd of people, moving along a conveyor belt. Plastic tubes connect our eyes, ears, and mouths. We start up an escalator. "Second floor, France!" says a voice from a loudspeaker, "All French depart here." I see a sign on the wall with a list of the things the French hate, so that people can tell who they are. "Third floor, America, end of the line." I enter a weightless environment, where bags of potato chips and Coke bottles float in space. A young woman grabs a passing bottle, puts it to her groin, has a brief orgasm. It is like an airport lounge, but also like a department store, with goods for sale, and an amusement park, with arcades, and like a prison with separate cells, and a classroom with seats in rows. Everyone is waiting in line.

"Along the sidewalks are slot machines which cough up Ping-Pong balls and pairs of pants, toys, gadgets, and liquor. People are at work feverishly playing these machines, buying another chance, trying to hold Kewpie dolls and glossy magazines in their arms while catching the Ping-Pong balls at the same time. Occasionally short, nervous laughter is heard from the players. Members of the family cheer on their best players as they perform, calling out advice or consolation, threatening retribution against the losers. Someone says:

'It's a real good machine, this one. If you keep playing it, it will go on forever.'"

Let us proceed sequentially through the development of this set of interconnected metaphors. The first image is of being in a crowd on a conveyor belt: mass society. Sensory perception is mediated by plastic tubes which connect our organs of communication: the mass media. The nation-state system is organized around patterns of identification based on hostility and negative reference. We know who we are and where we belong by virtue of what we hate.

America is depicted in this dream as a weightless environment of junk food and consumer-goods orgasms, part department store, amusement park, prison, and school. These overlapping images of contemporary institutions are characterized by seriality, that is, gradation into series of rows. Work and play are mixed together, involve feverish, mechanical performances, compensated for with baubles and prizes. The family offers a range of emotion from consolation to retribution. The tendency of this mechanism is to perpetuate itself.

Seriality and mediation are experiences connected with mechanical organizations (conveyor belts, escalators, slot machines) and networks of communication that integrate patterns of meaning and identification. Performance, compensation, retribution, and negative reference are the dynamics that define particular characteristics of contemporary culture.

To define mass society as the experience of being in a crowd on a conveyor belt (as the dream does) is to treat the image of the conveyor belt as a root metaphor for the mechanical, assembly-line experience and to explore the institutional connections that integrate national identity, mediating our awareness of who we are. Here the dream-definition can be a starting point for the exploration of the overall emotional tone of the dream, the feeling of competition and stress in the midst of apparent enjoyment, the feeling of gorging oneself mechanically.

Seriality, mediation, gradation, depression: these images represent patterns of social organization that provide the background against which we can perceive our dream selves working through the dilemmas of our social unconscious.

Conclusion

There is a richness, a density about dream metaphor, a playful intensity, full of import, pointing to what we need to know. Working with dreams is unfolding, unraveling this density. In group work with dreams there is the interweaving of emotional and metaphoric projections, which build associative connections, back and forth and among the different levels of social awareness. In the dream appreciation group, social intelligence is at home with itself.

Working with dreams in this way opens a vantage point that Trigant Burrow (1984) called "applied anthropology" (p. 137). The man whom anthropology wishes to study stands amidst controversy and contradiction, struggling within himself and with others: he is ourselves.

We develop social intelligence in relation to others through confrontation and controversial involvement, not as detached spectators viewing others, problems or social institutions external to ourselves.

In seeking to overcome social ignorance and neurosis, we are not looking elsewhere. As Burrow (1937) put it:

> The physician occupied with behavior-disorder may say, "Here is a sick or neurotic organism in the midst of a healthy society." Or he may say, "Here is a sick and neurotic organism in the midst of a society of sick and neurotic organisms." Finally he may take the ground: "Here is a sick, neurotic organism, but this organism is really an expression of society itself and I am, myself, of course, necessarily part of this ill behavior-condition affecting society" (p. 247).

As we attempt to evolve more humane social forms, in which the healing wisdom of our dreams can speak more articulately, humorously, and openly to us, we begin to follow the agenda of our dreams, to locate our present dilemmas within a field of potential, through which we may still learn to make our lives more responsive to the logic of free association.

References

Bateson, G. *Toward an Ecology of Mind.* New York: Ballantine Books, 1972.

Beradt, C. *The Third Reich of Dreams.* New York: Times Books, 1972.

Burrow, T. *The Biology of Human Conflict.* New York: Macmillan and Co., 1937.

Ellul, J. *The Political Illusion.* New York: Knopf, 1967.

Freud, S. *The Interpretation of Dreams.* New York: Avon Books, 1965.

_____. "Remarks Upon the Theory and Practice of Dream Interpretation." *Collected Papers.* New York: Basic Books, vol. 5, 1959.

Galt, A.S., ed. *Trigant Burrow: Toward Social Sanity and Human Survival.* New York: Horizon Press, 1984.

Laing, R. D. *Sanity, Madness and the Family.* New York: Penguin Books, 1982.

Ullman, M. Discussion of Dr. Walter Bonime's "The Dream as Human Experience (A Culturalist View)." *Dream Psychology and the New Biology of Dreaming.* Kramer, M., ed. Springfield, Ill.: Chas. C. Thomas, 1969.

Part Three

APPLICATIONS
IN PSYCHOLOGY
AND PSYCHIATRY

·11·

Dream Work and the Psychosomatic Process
A Personal Account
CLAIRE LIMMER, M.S.

Although the basic principles of the experiential dream group process were worked out with Nan Zimmerman before I left to teach in Sweden in 1974, it was while I worked with students in Gothenburg that the process emerged in its present form. On my return to the States in 1976 I was invited to co-lead a course in dreams at the William Alanson White Institute in New York City. It was my first opportunity to try out this newly developed approach in this country. Claire Limmer was a member of that class and has been associated with my work with dreams ever since, as a participant in weekly dream groups, as a member of many leadership training workshops, and as a co-leader with me. She has been developing dream workshops of her own in recent years as well.

Some people are "naturals" in dream work. Claire Limmer is certainly one of them. In this chapter she addresses the healing dimension of dream work in relation to physical illness. Presented in part as a personal narrative she describes her encounter with two life-threatening illnesses and the role she feels that dream work has played in her recovery and in the maintenance of health.

It had not happened before, nor did it happen again that my mother told me a dream. That February morning in 1977, entering the kitchen still visibly moved by the power of the dream fragment that disturbed her sleep, mother described how she had awakened, surprised to find her arms outstretched, as they had been in the dream. All that remained of the dream was the memory of her dream voice, speaking in her native French, calling with tenderness, "Seigneur, Seigneur" ("Lord, Lord").

At the time I was a member of a weekly dream group and was also involved in ongoing psychoanalytic sessions, two types of activity for which mother had little patience. She had been raised strictly in a Calvinistic home in Switzerland where strength of character was valued above all and acquired, it was believed, through deprivation and discipline. She spent most of her adult life married to a Presbyterian minister, never overcoming her natural timidity and need for seclusion, very much valuing the dignity of privacy.

It would be rather an understatement to say I was feeling enthusiastic about my involvement in psychoanalysis and group dream work. More accurately, I was feeling myself coming alive, as I began to share inner thoughts, to allow myself to be known, in both the private and the group settings. I learned, however, not to share that excitement with mother. She had closed the subject abruptly with a statement quite harshly spoken, "We have no right to meddle with dreams." As for psychoanalysis, she wondered after all how anyone could stoop to talk to a man she paid.

My mother's dream has stayed with me all these years, moving in and out of my thoughts, the one small glimpse into her unconscious. What had been on her mind that night as she slept in my home? Had some thought of death sparked a dream vision of life after life? Did the dream reflect not only mother's spiritual nature but a yearning to be relieved of the burdens of her life, to be allowed in final form the dependency long sought? Was the Seigneur she called both her heavenly Lord and her husband, long gone, who had always been very much her lord?

The guessing and the need to guess are lifelong patterns in me, reaching back as far as I can remember to when I was a small child searching my mother's face carefully for some hint of feeling. That morning no more was said about the dream. There was no sharing of inner thoughts in this family. Emotions were controlled and contained, as was any material that might stir up feeling. Mother rarely spoke of her childhood, how many brothers and sisters she had, who her parents were. These were basic facts I never knew. As for the happiness and unhappiness of her adult life, the joys and difficulties of her marriage, these were all concealed by dignity, patience, self-denial, and, I suppose, a fear of what it was she felt.

It is clear to me now, why at forty-two I began writing for my daughters, drawing from dream material of my own gathered over a ten-year period to tell them as much as I could about my struggles to grow and become a person. I suppose some of us live out our lives correcting the past, no doubt overcorrecting at times. It was in that year that I was hospitalized with breast cancer, an event that followed too closely a previous hospitalization with another form of cancer, a melanoma. Both illnesses had been preceded by experiences of loss, the first, a pending divorce after nineteen years of marriage, and the second, an attempt to terminate seven years of analytic work with a most caring therapist. I had viewed the first as a coincidence. The second made it clear to me how my body responded to the threat of separation from a loved one. Now my daughters too were threatened with loss as they feared for my health. I wanted them to know me, as I had not known my mother, to sense how they were like me and how they were not. I felt intuitively that the psychosomatic process, the breakdown of body rather than mind, was connected to a style of relating to loved ones in a fusional form that left one endangered by any threat of abandonment. I hoped that if my daughters knew me better, perhaps their adolescent struggle for separation, threatened by a mother's illness, would be less difficult and protracted than mine.

There was no way of knowing whether or not I would stay well, how I would fit into the cancer statistics I was up against—a 75 percent chance of making it five years, a 50 percent chance of making it ten, taking into account breast cancer alone. In daytime I felt optimistic, but at night my fears took over, filling my mind with apprehension about what would happen to my girls and with questions about what I could leave them. The answer to this grew increasingly clear. What I had to give was my work with dreams. Mine would be a legacy of dreams.*

For four months, on sick leave from my work at a children's psychiatric hospital, I spent four days a week at Memorial Sloane-Kettering Hospital, waiting anywhere from two to five hours a day for the few moments of radiation treatment prescribed as a follow-up to surgery. In waiting rooms I studied the dreams recorded over a ten-year period, eventually choosing sixteen in chronological order to best describe the struggles I underwent and wanted to share with my girls. Upon my return to work, I concentrated all my writing in the summer months when I was on vacation from teaching. I wrote over a five-year period, working on dreams of the past and new dreams generated by the writing itself and by current life issues, completing a final manuscript in the summer of 1983.

During this period there were a number of forces at work. I was systematically reading the current psychoanalytic literature on the psychosomatic process, paying particular attention, as it interested me most, to the writing coming out of the Paris Psychoanalytical Society. I was involved in an experiential dream group, led by Montague Ullman, and had begun to try my hand at leading a group. I was also beginning an important, final phase of therapy marked by a capacity to speak with a new sense of freedom. The process of growth, I've learned, is slow and difficult. It had taken seven years of analytic work and two hospitalizations for me to begin to speak as I did. There was, it seemed, little more to lose. The psychoanalytic literature gave validity, as words and ideas do, to what I was finally beginning to touch, both in dream work and in the analytic setting—that central disturbance which the experience of illness had uncovered. The writing for my daughters on dreams served to begin the process of integration and health.

The dream images I was examining had made me suspicious of a core emptiness, often reflecting, as they did, painful extremes of experience. They helped me see I had not found a comfortable middle ground between an aggrandized sense of

---

*Legacy of Dreams (manuscript).

self and a depleted self. In one dream there was the image of a single peony, a pink flower of delicate beauty that crumbled before my eyes into a heap of petals. In another, the image of an elegant woman, more fashionably dressed than I have ever been, wearing long skirts and boots, that fades to become the figure of a crazy woman, walking on the grounds of a mental hospital in a sacklike dress and socks. There was a dream of a handsomely wallpapered room being painted over in black. There was another of an exquisite mansion facing a river on the other side of which are city streets filled with garbage. I dreamed of small candlelit restaurants, the metaphoric expression of the warmth and intimacy I felt at moments of my life. I also dreamed of barren lunchrooms as I struggled with a sense of meaninglessness and emptiness. Dream color shifted back and forth from white to black in a long dream series of weddings and funerals that suggested I either felt alive and connected or alone and dead.

What this was all about was what I wanted to convey to my daughters in the hope that they would grow to be stronger than I. Putting this into words seemed important, though I did not yet have a full grasp of the urgency I felt. Through dreams I began to write about my primary family and the issues that growing up in this strange home had brought about. There was my father, born in 1883 of Italian aristocracy, who ignored his family's ambitions in the world of finance to enter the Roman Catholic priesthood. At the age of twenty-seven he was brought to trial in a civil court in Rome, a trial involving Pope Pius X himself, to defend himself against accusations of libel. He had publicly stated that the sacred sacrament of the confession had been violated by a cardinal of the Church. The Church, he believed, had wished to bring out into the open the activities of a group of young dissident priests of which father was one. This was my father's final act in a career filled with doubt about Church theology and practice. He left Italy, exiled and excommunicated, arriving in Geneva to study Protestant theology. He came to America just before the Depression, a Protestant minister with many talents but without a church. I grew up frequently reminded of the heroism of my father's actions, the courage he had sustained, above all, in the face of serious personal loss, for he never saw his family again.

Mother was Swiss, a young girl of twenty, when she rode her bike briskly from Geneva to Lausanne one spring day to be interviewed for a position as governess to a well-to-do Connecticut family planning to tour Italy. She arrived, pink-cheeked and excited, and got the job, as well as an offer at the end of that vacation to return with the family to the States. She said quick good-bys to her family and left despite her own mother's foreboding that they would not see each other again. Four years later grandmother's premonition came true. My maternal grandmother died at an early age of a massive heart attack, leaving mother in New York grief stricken, feeling guilty perhaps, certainly depressed and lonely. Two years later she married my father, twenty years her senior, and began her life as a minister's wife and mother of three. She worked hard to supplement her husband's meager income, taking jobs in the clothing district of Manhattan, a much too tough milieu for such a timid woman. She sang in the church choir and polished the floors of the chapellike sanctuary, always remaining shy and remote. Her view of her role as a minister's wife—to be an example for others—set her apart from others, meshing with her own schizoidal tendencies to withdraw into herself. She could not unburden herself to a friend, though I believe she was up against serious problems in the marriage. She grew more and more removed from human connections, relying on spiritual sustenance inside. She kept up correspondence with one sister in Europe whom she did not see for more than thirty years.

It is no wonder that I bound myself too closely to her, that I learned a style of relating where all psychological functioning is dependent on another person, be it mother, husband, or analyst, where there is always fear of abandonment, danger of collapse. Because of my mother's origins, her own psychological damage, and because of life circumstances—the loss of her mother, the distance between her and her primary family, the growing disillusionment in her marriage—she drew me too closely to her. I suppose she found purpose for her life and a sense of identity, not so much in her role as a minister's wife, where she never felt comfortable, but in her role as mother, particularly with her last child and only girl. This child helped to repair a loss, providing a reunion of mother and daughter. She applied all her Swiss discipline to the act of mothering, exerting control over her child's bodily functions and proudly depriving the child of gratifications she felt might cause me to be spoiled. In terms of physical caretaking she was not just a "good-enough mother" (Winnicott, 1966) but an "over-good mother" (McDougall, 1980a), responding to me almost as an extension of herself, leaving little psychological space where an independent self might develop. There is no question in my mind that my mother's relationship to my father took second place to the mother-child unit, that the mother-baby relationship replaced the husband as the primary source of love and comfort. There was in the relationship to me that strange blend of "deprivation" and "impingement" (Guntrip), of too much or too little emotional space which is written about in so much of the psychoanalytic literature. These words describe both a quality of overdiligence in a mother's caretaking, as she fulfills an intense need to be a good mother, and a strange unresponsiveness to the child's own particular needs and moods. In the home in which I grew up there was much dedication, zealous caretaking, much worry over all three children, and too much control. We were told what to do and how to feel. There was a dulling of all inner life.

At twenty-eight I was only vaguely aware of a strange possessiveness I felt guilty about when my first daughter was born, as I watched my mother hold her grandchild and feared she would not let me be mother to my own child. In later years I felt the same possessiveness about my house, as each of my mother's visits left me fearing her overpowering presence. There was a danger of fragmentation as I felt my physical and emotional boundaries invaded. If I was aware of any anger, I did not know what to do with resentment toward a much loved mother with soft green eyes who had never hurt me deliberately, who had lived a hard life of considerable self-sacrifice. If there was discomfort, it was the sense that I could never be as selfless, as patient as she, or as Christian as my parents.

At thirty-five, with my marriage bankrupt, I began therapy, speaking of love for my mother to an analyst who eyed me a bit skeptically but responded to me patiently. There was surprise in the dreams that followed over the next few years. In one a child is vomiting, made sick by the pounds of Swiss chocolate she had consumed. In another an infant is crying because the milk in its bottle is too hot.

The analytic relationship was, of course, fertile ground for the development of a similar connection, the difference being that this one was evolving before our eyes and could be examined with care. Each separation from therapist made clear how attached to him I had become and how difficult it was for me to sustain a sense of connection on my own. Dreams before even a week-long vacation contained numerals denoting in precise countdown fashion how many days were left before separation would occur . . . four . . . three . . . two . . . one. How fragile I was in terms of ego development was not clear, however, until it came time to say good-by, to terminate seven years of analytic work that had given me many insights, made me feel alive, and altered the quality of my life. I had known for a long time that the analytic work would have to end. I tried to look at this positively; the ability to end would be proof of the success of our efforts. I was training to become a psychotherapist myself, so there was some need to test my mental health. I was most of all eager to please a loving therapist who had given me a second chance to grow up, and I hid from him what strain I was feeling in the months before our last scheduled session. I did not pay attention to several dreams that were predicting illness, dreams in which my breasts appeared strangely beautiful but vulnerable. Within days of that last session I was hospitalized for surgery and began the treatment for breast cancer described earlier.

This was a period of considerable crisis. The psychoanalytic work I had prized so highly seemed to have played a strange trick on me, for I had exchanged emotional illness for physical illness. I was disturbed by the anger I felt toward a much loved therapist, rage I would not have survived had I not had an analyst with much courage who assured me we would both get through this.

The psychoanalyst, Joyce McDougall (1974), has written:

> In the attempt to maintain some form of psychic equilibrium under all circumstances, every human being is capable of creating a neurosis, a psychosis, a pathological character pattern, a sexual perversion, a work of art, a dream, or a psycho-

somatic malady. In spite of our human tendency to maintain a relatively stable psychic economy and thus guarantee a more-or-less enduring personality pattern, we are liable to produce any or all of these diverse creations at different periods in our lives. Although the results of our psychic productions do not have the same psychological, nor indeed the same social value, they all have something in common in that they are the product of man's mind and their form is determined by the way his psyche had been structured. They all have inherent meaning in relation to his wish to live and to get along as best he can with what life has dealt out to him. From this point of view it is evident that the psychosomatic creations appear the most mysterious since they are the least appropriate to the overall desire to live (p.438).

My own psychosomatic "creations" were evident to me, though most of my friends argued with the notion of emotionally induced cancer. I knew I had had a physical crisis in my life instead of a mental break brought on by a level of conflict I had not been able to identify in time, a struggle clearly connected to separation and loss.

During this period the image of a Christmas tree figured in at least a dozen dreams, a dream image borrowed from an actual photo of my daughters, taken when they were five and eight, looking at a Christmas tree that had been moved from the living room to the backyard. The ornaments had been put away in boxes and replaced with orange hulls filled with peanut butter and bird seed, a post-holiday feast for the neighborhood birds. I had used this photo in a visualization exercise to help me fall asleep at night when my level of anxiety was heightened, the image of all three of us, hand-in-hand, forming a circle around that small tree, a circle I was now determined to keep unbroken. The tree of my dreams, the Christian symbol of birth and celebration, expressed the dilemma I was in. Therapy had filled me with a dazzling sense of rebirth, perhaps, I know now, still all too new. Like the holiday tree filled with splendid ornaments, I too looked good, but I felt cut off from what all trees and people need to survive—a source of nurturance. Like the tree without roots, I could not stand on my own and I might die. This long dream series produced interesting variations. The Christmas tree of one dream is threatened by a smoldering fire, just as the anger in me threatened to destroy me. In another, a small fir tree that I embrace is found to have a great hole in its center, just as I was becoming aware of a core emptiness within me.

Lawrence LeShan 1977, who has been a therapist to terminally ill patients, has written that the basic emotional pattern of the cancer patient appears to have three major parts. The first "involves a childhood or adolescence marked by feelings of isolation" such as I had known. "There is a sense that intense and meaningful relationships are dangerous and bring pain and rejection. The second part of the pattern is centered upon the period during which a meaningful relationship is discovered, allowing the individual to enjoy a sense of acceptance by others (at least in one particular role) and to find meaning to his life." The analytic relationship had been this to me. "The third aspect of the pattern comes to the fore when the loss of that central relationship occurs. Now there is a sense of utter despair, connected to but going beyond the childhood sense of isolation. In this third phase, the conviction that life holds no more hope becomes paramount. And sometime after the onset of the third phase the first symptoms of cancer are noted" (p.70).

For me the loss of a central relationship was postponed for a few more years. The decision to end therapy was undone, more than a secondary gain to illness. As my analytic work continued, I began to speak with much less restraint, relying on dreams above all, for I had learned to value their honesty. I was determined to get to the bottom of this, for I was fighting to stay well. In the dream group, I presented dreams as often as I could, unafraid to go public with any issue the dream might reveal. The group gave me new thoughts to bring back to the individual therapy setting. The writing for my daughters kept me thinking about the past and sparked new dreams that shed light on my beginnings as well as my present situation.

But it was the research I was doing on the psychosomatic process that excited me most, helping me see that in an intuitive way, through the dream processes with which I was involved— my own psychoanalysis, the group dream work, my own writing about dreams—I had stumbled upon a path of healing. It provided a link, offering me understanding of what I was feeling inside. I tempered my excitement, a bit apprehensive of challenging the gods with hubris. Yet over the months and years that passed I was surprised by my capacity to sustain a new sense of peace. I sensed that an inner change had occurred which would help me stay well.

On the Psychosomatic Process

Before I can explain this further, it seems necessary to try to summarize the writings on the psychosomatic process that were important to me, as complex as they are. Joyce McDougall, a New Zealander who trained as a psychoanalyst in Paris where she practices, writes that our psychic processes are on the side of life, that we create whatever psychic structures we do in order to manage as best we can whatever life has to offer. "The structure of the psyche is a creative process destined to give each individual his unique identity. It provides a bulwark against psychic loss in traumatic circumstances, and in the long run in man's psychic creativity may well lie an essential element of protection against his biological destruction" (1974, p.438).

It is for this reason that the psychosomatic process is so curious. It may well serve to deflect an impending sense of psychic loss, but it certainly does not protect us from biological destruction. It can leave us, as it did me, a patient in a hospital, facing serious illness. It seems to pop into use when we lack some capacity to manage the pain life brings using mental processes. There may also be a limit to the intensity of pain any individual can manage, "a threshold beyond which his psychic defense-work can no longer cope, at which moment the body bears the brunt" (p.445).

There are, however, individuals who seem less well equipped in general to encounter emotional pain, who are incapable of tolerating the suffering that comes with that pain and of working it through. This working through of pain is an important concept that needs elaboration. Federn makes a subtle distinction between "feeling pain" and "suffering pain." Suffering is the active inner experience of the pain, pain that we allow ourselves to take in, to feel as present, and to endure. It involves a full realization of whatever event caused the pain, such that the next time thought or memory of the event occurs, that pain will no longer be felt to quite the same degree. This is what is involved in normal grief and mourning—the repeated realization of the loss incurred and the gradual lessening of pain connected to it. "The acceptance of pain", Federn writes, "is the tribute we pay to normality" (p.268).

In the case of "feeling pain," the individual doesn't work it through but takes flight from it, short-circuiting psychic activity, much as someone who uses alcohol or drugs, to flee from his problems. Some developmental failure leaves this individual unable to tolerate or endure pain. It is viewed as an existential threat that has to be warded off at once, for what is feared is psychic disintegration. Afraid that he will fall apart, this individual protects himself with what McDougall (1980a) calls "psychic armour plating," by a refusal to yield to anguish or depression. He does not allow painful feelings to come into awareness and is often quite unaware of the level of conflict he is experiencing. To his friends he appears remarkably hardy. He looks as if he copes with difficult situations amazingly well. In an important sense, however, this type of individual is left passively exposed, always in danger, for no inner change has occurred. Thought of the painful event, when it is permitted, produces feelings similar in impact to their original intensity, or with anger connected to them.

What we are talking about is a fragile self, a psyche that has not emerged into maturity, one that is not strong enough to process the knocks that life brings, particularly ones connected to loss. We are also describing a type of individual who finds his sense of identity not within himself, but externally—in activities and relationships sought out because they enhance his sense of self. Because he needs another person to feel like somebody, he clings symbiotically, seeking merger with another, losing a sense of separateness. He remains sensitive to any threat of loss that would leave him feeling once again like nobody. McDougall (1974) writes, "What should be an internal conviction—of narcissistic integrity and individual identity—has constantly to be confirmed externally" (p.452).

Related to this are two phenomena noticed in the psychosomatic individual. One is a characteristic mode of thinking, first termed "operational thinking" by Marty, M'Uzan, & David. It consists of a preoccupation with the minute details of daily life, an attachment to facts and things in external reality with thoughts that are pragmatic in aspect rather than a reflection of one's inner life. The second phenomenon, termed "alexithymia" by Sifneos, involves an inability on the part of the psychosomatic patient to speak about his feelings. When asked to try, as in the analytic setting, he seems to have little or no vocabulary available, frequently responding with such statements as "I can't find the words." When pressed to try, he often responds with a description of the external events of his life—what's going on— rather than how events or individuals in his life touch him inside. He has difficulty getting in touch with his fantasy life, often denying that he has any fantasies. He may also say he never dreams.

It was this material that interested me, especially as I was so much involved in dream work and in writing about dreams, finding words for feelings and fantasies, drawing from material coming from within me for the first time in my life. The importance of dreaming and fantasies in maintaining emotional equilibrium has been noted by many writers. I was experiencing a kind of equilibrium previously unknown to me.

What makes someone feel so fragile? When does an individual learn a style of relating to others adhesively, remaining so vulnerable to loss? How and when are the types of mental processes described above, that is, being in touch with one's inner life, enduring pain, learned? It is difficult, of course, to speculate about the origins of any type of emotional disturbance, especially when it seems rooted, as this does, in the early relationship of infant to mother. It is in that first dependency, at the beginning of life that *psyche* evolves out of *soma*. It is then, as infants, that we experience life in such extremes, with either a sense of well-being when our needs are responded to, or with the threat of annihilation when they are not. To understand this we have only to picture the panic-filled infant, suddenly hungry, who cries as though he had truly been abandoned.

What the growing baby seems to need to learn from his mother is a dependency that does not compromise autonomy but nourishes it and sustains it. The empathic mother who responds sensitively to the infant's nonverbal expression of need, giving validation to what the baby is experiencing, is allowing both dependency and separateness, helping a young self grow with increasing autonomy and self-esteem.

A mother's ability to respond empathically to her child originates, however, in the experiences of her own infancy that are reanimated when she herself becomes a mother. A mother who has herself been deprived, whose own hunger and need for love are reactivated in mothering her child, may respond with overprotection and possession of the infant, exaggerating the normal functions of mothering, doing things *to* a baby out of her own need. What the child seems to need is a mother who provides protection against the stimuli in the world that would overwhelm the unprotected infant but who is not overindulgent in her function out of her own need to find a "good-mother self" (Benedek), that is, a sense of identity in this function. It is the careful modulation of care, not being too close or too far away, being there to respond to the baby's needs yet not impinging on the baby, which appears to aid the growing individual in the development, as well, of certain mental capacities. The baby can permit herself to feel whatever is there to be experienced because she is neither overwhelmed nor ignored but is supported. She is helped to know what she feels because her own feelings have been responded to. Perhaps she has learned through the mother the verbal representations of feelings, as the mother expresses her own emotions or mirrors those of the child. The baby begins to attach some meaning to what she experiences.

In 1971 Fain described a study of infants so overprotected by their mothers that they were unable to fall asleep unless they were rocked continuously in their mother's arms. The mother's overprotection had left the infant unable to conjure up some image of mother that would connect him to her, soothe him, and allow him to sleep—the beginning of a self-sustaining self. Commenting on this study, McDougall (1974) writes, "Instead of the development of a primitive form of psychic activity akin to dreaming which permits most babies to sleep peacefully after feeding these babies require the mother herself to be the guardian of sleep" (p.446). Anxiety that touches this infant is experienced as a global threat, involving a sense of annihilation and disintegration. "The baby who cannot create within himself his mother's image to deal with his pain is a lonely island. One way out is to turn oneself into a rock. Thus many psychosomatic patients continue on their unwavering tight-rope, ignoring the body's signs and their mind's distress signals" (p.458).

Is it this capacity for symbolization, for making connections, for creating links, that is damaged in the psychosomatic adult, so out of touch with his inner experience, unable to distinguish feelings, to find the verbal representations for emotions, who is fearful of relationships that leave him in a vulnerable position, yet who knows no way of relating other than symbiotically? Ammon writes of a "hole in the ego" which the psychosomatic symptom serves to fill. He portrays psychosomatic illness as the expression of a structural ego illness that leaves the individual unable to move beyond a symbiotic dependency to a demarcation of his own identity. His efforts to relate to others break down because he uses relationships to repair a psychic gap. When loss does occur, the psychosomatic process takes over. As McDougall has noted, pain bypasses the psyche, unequipped to deal with it, and affects the body (1974).

Perhaps in some pitiful way even the psychosomatic process is on the side of life. For me, a lifelong fear of emotional fragmentation was replaced by a fear of death. As I was on the edge of psychic annihilation, illness occurred to push out all concerns but the wish to live. At Memorial Sloane-Kettering Hospital I pleaded to be allowed the privilege of using an outside terrace, basking in a sun that felt warmer and more wonderful than I have ever known, looking thoughtfully at the blueness of the city sky and the changing shapes of the clouds I felt connected to.

The Healing Aspects of Dream Work

In the early weeks after discharge from the hospital I dreamed of a serious fire rising up through a wooden fire tower perched high on a lookout. I was standing at the top of the tower very much in danger of being enveloped by smoke. The dream image of a fire tower, itself on fire, a structure designed to alert people to danger, itself in danger, trouble at that lookout, was a poignant metaphor for the analytic situation which had expanded my view, very much protected me over the years, but where I was now in serious danger. The fire was the anger I was feeling; the smoke was the confusion I could not see beyond in the rage I felt toward someone who had cared so consistently for me.

McDougall (1974) speaks of the psychosomatic patient as one who "tends to react with either psychosomatic maladies or increased sensitivity to infection and a tendency to bodily accidents, when faced with traumatic events and conflictual situations arising from the past or the present *including the psychoanalytical situation*" (p.450, italics mine, C.L.). I had responded to the prospect of ending treatment that had given meaning to my life with a life-threatening illness no one could have predicted. The illness brought perspective to the crisis of completing my analysis. If I was torn about the pending separation from my therapist, I found myself far more torn about the threat to my children. I was determined to stay well, just as in the dream I was determined to climb down the tower and find my way out of the smoke.

In the analytic situation the way "out of the smoke," paradoxically, was in allowing a deeper transference to occur, permitting myself to feel and express for the first time the full depth of my dependency on another person and to begin to understand the anger that is bound to occur whenever anyone's psychic existence is so dependent on another. I was beginning to see reflected in that transference the symbiotic quality of my need for mother, a relationship where independence had not been encouraged.

In a 7:30 A.M. session, an extra session I had worked up to for days, I talked nonstop for an hour, amazed at how easily and clearly words came, packing in one illustration after another to make certain I conveyed fully the urgent quality of my caring, the great need I felt, the anger it contained, and the fright of expected loss.

Feeling embarrassed or humiliated by such admission no longer got in the way. I could feel the power of my words to heal. The more accurately and honestly I spoke, the more relief I felt. What seemed to matter was a new integrity I felt in presenting myself *exactly as I was*.

Looking back on this point, I know now that my involvement in dream work—in private therapy, in group dream work that complemented that therapy, and in writing about dreams—had helped me work up to that day, gradually creating structural changes, giving me new ego strengths to work through the transference, and in so doing, to stay well. It is my hope that in the remainder of this paper I will be able to describe what I mean—a growth that cannot, of course, be proven but which is deeply felt.

I have been a participant in an experiential dream group since 1976, a regular member of a Monday night group. Men and women have joined the group, learned dream skills, and left while I stayed on year after year. I wondered sometimes why I continued. I only knew the work was important to me.

The process, outlined in Chapter 1 of this volume, did not come easily to me. In Stage IIA (p.6), when members of the group begin working on the presented dream, making it their own, trying to identify the feelings it evoked, I was often silent, unable to do this, just as I had sat in analytic sessions, unable to begin, feeling the panic of silence mounting with the minutes that passed. I would long for a question about what had been going on in the days since my last session, so I could begin to narrate events or describe a set of circumstances. It was talking about what I was feeling at the moment that I couldn't do. In the dream group, if I had difficulty responding to the dream and even more difficulty finding words for my responses, I could be silent and listen to the responses of others and begin to acquire a richer vocabulary for emotions. The process, as it is structured, gives us an hour and a half to work on a handful of images in a single, brief dream. The slowness of this exquisite process was always on my side, permitting me to move deeper and deeper into a level of consciousness somewhere between waking consciousness and the dreaming state, eventually allowing some feeling, however vague, to float to the surface and be felt.

If the initial stage of the process left me feeling inadequate, Stage IIB (p.6) left me excited and deeply moved. At this point each member of the group is asked to draw upon his own imagination and unconscious to consider what possible metaphoric meaning the dream images conveyed. In dream work it was always the creative metaphor in dream imagery that stirred me. I was touched by the force and beauty of the dream metaphor just as, many years ago, as a literature major, I had been moved by the felt connection of thought and feeling in a literary metaphor. This should have been a clue to me. I know now that I have always been affected by such moments of connection, experiencing in them an aspect of healing.

Whether it involved work on a dream of my own, or work on another person's dream, the gentle pace of group dream work and the nonintrusive approach of the process, a combination that succeeds in lowering defenses, had offered me long-term practice at feeling my emotional response to a dream and at staying with that response until I could give it some verbal form. From the first words group members used, as they made the dream their own and responded to the feelings evoked by the dream, to the play with the visual images of the dream, to the final integration offered by the leader—throughout this long process I was gaining experience at tapping into the resources of my psyche to identify emotions and to stay with them. I was learning not to short-circuit psychic activity but to develop whatever capacities for mental creativity I could, getting practice in managing whatever emotions were evoked, however painful they might be.

Joyce McDougall (1974) has written that the "psychoanalytic processes are the antithesis of psychosomatic processes" in that they "re-establish separated links and also forge new ones" (p. 439). I encountered this concept with excitement, for I was beginning to understand the need and importance of such links and the power of such connection to heal, and to appreciate the many connecting forces available in dreams and in dream work.

If I had been overly cerebral, a bit "operational," functioning impressively in all aspects of my day-to-day life but out of touch with my inner world, I was now connecting to the naturally creative part of myself, to the strange beauty of the visual images we all produce at night. If I had been somewhat "alexithymic," I was learning to find meaning for these images at an emotional and informational level and to give that meaning some verbal form. Writers on alexithymia have questioned whether an alexithymic patient can acquire a vocabulary for feelings. I certainly had. As I began writing about my dreams for my girls, I was astonished at how much I could draw from within myself, a self I had long experienced as shadowy and empty, in need of reliance on what others had written, certainly lacking in fantasy and creativity.

I felt the power of the dream to make many connections—to bring together past and present, thought and feeling, visual and verbal, to compare the myths we hold about ourselves and reality, to perceive our commonality to others and the ways in which unique sets of life circumstances have made us different. Finally, in the exquisite moment when the dream comes together at all levels of our being, when we experience the "feeling of fit that goes beyond linguistic categories and defies analytic approaches" (Ullman, p.123), I felt a beginning connection of mind and body, of psyche and soma.

Out of moments such as this, repeated again and again, as I had made a commitment to dream work, something new and important was evolving that I would begin to use in the psychoanalytic setting as in every aspect of my life. In waiting for the "fit" to occur, I learned to rely on something within myself as the measure of the accuracy of that fit. The group was there to help, each member tapping his own unconscious, his own imagination and life experiences, making an offering that might give the dream richness. The leader was there with his resources of intuition and intellect to help pull together the threads of the dream, but only the dreamer herself could know when the "fit" was accomplished. The knowing was felt inside, as a gentle release, like the relief of being able to take a deeper breath, a quietly felt truth, spiritual and aesthetic in impact, that is felt in the mind and in all of one's tissues.

For me this was no small achievement. There was a beginning sense of internal connection such as I had never known, a budding appreciation of my own authority after a lifetime of looking to others for authority. The pattern had begun in childhood with the formidable figure of my father in his pulpit and with my mother who loved me as herself, which was the problem. I strove to please her by being like her at a cost to my own individuality. The pattern had extended into the present and was readily apparent in the transference to analyst, another major figure in my life whom I tried to please. The change, when it came, was a subtle shift, strangely quiet and undramatic. It was the sense of peacefulness connected to it that made me take notice. It had, however, the power to alter the quality of all my relationships, leaving me less needy of approval, less defensive, less apt to try to prove my point, less threatened by the authoritarian stances of others, more understanding of the struggle with which any individual is involved when he takes such a stance. Most importantly, in the analytic setting, it offered a new independence with which to confront the core of my dependency. I could begin to approach the very needy quality of the connection to my analyst because I was also feeling the beginnings of separateness.

"The freedom to let oneself be known," Ullman has written, "is also the freedom to be oneself." I was feeling a new freedom to let myself be known and to be my own self—in the dream group where I had been given "privileged glimpses deep into the souls of other people" and had seen there "the same mix of vulnerability and strength" that I came to see in myself, where I had "the rare experience of human beings who come together as healers for each other" (Ullman, p.124). I felt that freedom in the writing for my daughters which culminated in a decision to publish. I felt it as well in the private analytic setting where I was looking at my most ancient and most current struggles with new honesty and clarity. In the struggle around dependency I began to acknowledge the anger toward a dearly loved therapist, anger long familiar to me from my past. It was the anger that occurs when we are fragile and needy, when we remain bound to others emotionally. As *that* connection was made, the anger could be relinquished—not quickly or entirely but eventually and sufficiently, leaving me stronger in the years that followed, more peaceful than I have ever been, and well.

References

Ammon, G. *Psychoanalysis and Psychosomatics*. New York: Springer Publishing Co., 1979.

Benedek, T. "Parenthood as a Developmental Phase: A Contribution to the Libido Theory." *Journal of the American Psychoanalytic Association*, 1959, 7, 389–417.

Fain, M. "Prélude à la vie fantasmatique." *Rev. franc. psychanal.*, 1971, 35, 291–364.

Fain, M., and David, C. "Aspects fonctionels de la vie onirique." *Rev. franc. psychanal.*, 1963, *27*, 241–343.

Federn, P. *Ego Psychology and the Psychoses.* New York: Basic Books, 1952.

Guntrip, H. *Schizoid Phenomena, Object Relations and the Self.* New York: International Universities Press, Inc., 1969.

LeShan, L. *You Can Fight for Your Life: Emotional Factors in the Causation of Cancer.* New York: Harcourt Brace Jovanovich, 1977.

McDougall, J. "The Psychosoma and the Psychoanalytic Process." *International Review of Psychoanalysis*, 1974, *1*, 437–459.

––––––. "A child is Being Eaten." *Contemporary Psychoanalysis*, 1980a, *16*, 417–459.

––––––. *Plea for a Measure of Abnormality.* New York: International Universities Press, Inc., 1980b.

Marty, P., M'Uzan, M. de, and David, C. *L'investigation psychosomatique.* Paris: Presses Univ. de France, 1963.

Nemiah, J., and Sifneos, P. "Affect and Fantasy in Patients with Psychosomatic Disorders." *Modern trends in psychosomatic medicine*, vol. 2. Hill, O., ed. London: Butterworths, 1970.

Nemiah, J., Freyberger, H., and Sifneos, P. "Alexithymia: A View of the Psychosomatic Process." *Modern Trends in Psychosomatic Medicine*, vol. 3. Hill, O., ed. London: Butterworths, 1976.

Sifneos, P. *Short-term Psychotherapy and Emotional Crises.* Cambridge: Harvard University Press, 1972.

Ullman, M. "Group Dream Work and Healing." *Contemporary Psychoanalysis*, 1984, *20*, 120–130.

Winnicott, D. "Psychosomatic Illness in its Positive and Negative Aspects." *International Journal of Psychoanalysis*, 1966, *47*, 510–516.

·12·

Teaching the Use of the Dream in Clinical Practice

SUSAN KNAPP, Ph.D.

In this chapter Susan Knapp writes about the dream course she teaches to psychoanalytic candidates. As an innovative teacher, she has integrated classical and newer ideas about dreams. She has tackled the difficult task of demystifying the whole subject of dreams and the way dreams are worked with in therapy.

It has been my experience that, in the course of their training, therapists are given a heavy dose of theory but are left stranded when it comes to firsthand knowledge of dealing with a dream in the actual therapeutic situation. To some extent the command of theory stands in the way and has the effect of making dream work seem far more formidable than it is. What is needed and, for some reason, never fully addressed, is for the beginning therapist to have a "hands-on" approach to dream work. Through the group techniques she works with, Dr. Knapp succeeds in developing both a sense of competence and an appreciation of the wonder of dream imagery. Dr. Knapp also points to other possible uses of group dream work in the setting of a training institute.

In my work as a supervisor and in the courses of dreams that I have taught to students at various levels in their training, I have found that the dream is all too intimidating to the average student therapist. Therapists in training have told me that they shy away from dealing with dreams because they feel that they do not know what to do with them. When questioned further they say that on first hearing the dream they can make no sense of it. They seem to assume that a more experienced therapist would immediately know what the dream meant and indeed that the dream has a specific meaning. Moreover, they have read or been told that work with dreams belongs only in some form of extensive psychoanalytic treatment, and finally, that it is unwise to attempt to work with dreams of more disturbed patients because mishandling can be dangerous. Therefore, they avoid dealing with dreams and, gradually, as with any kind of communication that does not elicit a response, they find that the patient's report of dreams diminishes and even disappears.

I believe that the dream is a very vivid, immediate communication that encompasses the momentary state of the dreamer as he or she is attempting to deal with his or her most pressing issues. The act of constructing the dream represents the first attempt to deal with these issues; telling it to another is the means to beginning the process of apprehending and owning these issues as well as determining the potential resolutions that the dream suggests. Many of us have had the experience of having had a dream and not understanding it, yet on telling it to another, suddenly grasping its meaning. The other's response can, of course, be invaluable, but even when that person just listens, there is something about being heard and feeling that one is being understood that seems to greatly increase our capacity for self-understanding. Indeed this point of view has achieved considerable appreciation due to Heinz Kohut's emphasis on the crucial role that empathy plays in the treatment process as well as the recent research which describes the infant as a skilled communicator who seeks contact with his environment almost from the moment of birth.

Therefore, I suggest that the *content* of a response to a dream may be, at times, less important than that the response, either verbal or nonverbal, communicates a receptivity and willingness to try to understand. The listener must convey the conviction that through a collaborative effort you and the other will be able to reach some degree of understanding even if much of a particular dream may be unclear for some time or even forever. For example, a patient of mine told me, early in treatment, that it was pointless to discuss her dreams because they were so ordinary and concrete. She then gave me an example of a dream that consisted of nothing more than a jar of Gulden's mustard. Being a very young therapist at the time, I silently agreed that discussion of her dreams would be pointless and moved on to another issue. Several years later we spent three sessions discussing this dream when the patient, for the first time, described how her schizophrenic mother destroyed everything that she touched. The only way that the patient and her brother could get through their mother's revolting meals was to coat everything in Gulden's mustard. The image of the mustard reflected both the patient's need to protect herself against the mother and the bond that she had developed with her beloved brother. It was an image that came up each time the patient needed to reassure herself that she had the necessary resources to deal with the destructiveness of others. Along with a delayed understanding of the patient's dream there was an awareness that a fear of inadequacy had prompted me to neglect to respond to the dream as an attempted communication whether or not I understood it. No matter how hard any of us try, some aspects of dreams—because they recreate nonverbal idiosyncratic experiences—can never be comprehended with words. I agree with the many theoretical approaches that stress the value of the therapist's response to the dream as being as important as, if not more important than, interpretation.

Students of the dream have always attributed immense value to dreams. Prior to Freud, divine intervention was the most popular explanation for the power of the dream. Then in 1900 Freud, quite early in his development of psychoanalysis, published *The Interpretation of Dreams,* in which he outlined both his invaluable technique for the analysis of dreams and his theory of dreams, that is, dreams are formed as a means of expressing instinctual impulses that would be routinely repressed during waking life. Reactions to his emphasis on the notion of instincts led other writers such as Jung, Horney, Fromm, and the like to shift their focus to seeing the dream as expressing heretofore unconscious meanings and experiences of self and others. These unconscious meanings and experiences become more available in dreams because the state of sleeping frees the dreamer, as Fromm suggests, from external distraction; and he has more time to organize and express his internal state, albeit through symbolic and metaphorical means. Horney described the symbols expressed in dreams as being "like metaphors and analogies in our speaking and writing, which exemplify our creative efforts to capture the essence of previously unspoken or unexpressible aspects of ourselves at a specific point in time" (Knapp, p.345).

Montague Ullman offers an exciting and provocative description of the dream in his paper, "Dreaming as Metaphor in Motion." Based on his own extensive laboratory research and on that of others, Ullman sees dreaming as a process that occurs in all mammals. He, like other researchers, believes that dreaming is a means by which the organism is kept at an optimal level of arousal so that it can act immediately on being awakened if his survival becomes endangered. Because of the limitations of the physiologically altered brain milieu that exists during sleep, this biologically determined state of vigilance takes the form of manipulation of concrete visual images. Ullman describes the rapidly changing sequences of visual images as combining in such a way as to form what he calls "metaphors in motion." He quotes the modern philosopher Suzanne Langer, who describes the metaphor as "an instrument of abstraction . . . which comes into play in situations where an idea is genuinely new." It has no name, and there is no word to express it. It is an effort at conceptualization, an abstract process that paradoxically uses concrete imagery as a means for arriving at this conceptual abstraction. Combining vigilance theory and Langer's notions of the metaphor, Ullman extends the concept of vigilance by describing the dream as representing the dreamer's effort to deal with psychological threats to his intrapsychic and interpersonal equilibrium by sorting through the intrusive data from his waking life and developing potentially new relationships to this intrusive data through a montage of visual metaphors.

Freud suggested a similar tack both by his description of the dream as being expressed in the language of primary process, which is also the language of artistic creation, and by his concept of the visual means of representation of the dream. Roland states this well: The "manifest content had to represent underlying thoughts and meanings in a basically pictorial manner which was far more metaphorical and symbolically expressive in nature than more rational, scientific, secondary process thinking" (p. 437).

Many so-called "naive laymen" respond to dreams as if they were somewhat whimsical but highly informative little stories that cannot be taken literally but must be treated like a poem or a piece of art. Moreover, these "naive laymen" often make quite insightful and productive responses to the dreams that they are told. Take, for example, a patient described by Fromm (1951) who constantly ridiculed her analyst's assertions that her dreams were meaningful. The patient with her usual disdain for her analyst's efforts told her husband what she described as a mundane, meaningless dream in which she was serving him, her husband, strawberries. Her husband responded with a burst of laughter and then said, "You only seem to forget that strawberries are the one fruit that I do not eat" (p. 149).

Given that dreams are potentially available for discussion and understanding, why were my students and supervisees so constricted and fearful when they were told a dream? Based on my own memories of being in their position, the very fact that they were now undertaking a lengthy stint of psychoanalytic training, it is conceivable that they might have felt that they would have to respond to the dream the way "an analyst" would. Forget the fact that Leon Altman, who wrote the book *The Dream in Psychoanalysis,* cheerfully states that there are many dreams that completely elude him, student therapists feel that they must have answers. Moreover, they have just gotten their first whiff of classical Freudian metapsychology in Chapter 7 of Freud's 1900 *Interpretation of Dreams.* So who can blame them for not wanting to touch dreams with a ten-foot pole?

Gedo and Goldberg in their book *Models of the Mind* point out that during each major stage of his work Freud developed a conceptual model that captured the essence of his thinking about a specific facet of mental functioning. They go on to say, "Because they [the various models] were chosen on an ad hoc basis to meet differing didactic needs, no single guiding principle runs through these varied concepts, and there is no simple way of organizing the relationships among them" (p. 22).

Freud's theory of dreams is part of one of his earliest models —the topographical model of psychic organization. According to this model, Freud states:

> We were only able to explain the formation of dreams by venturing upon the hypothesis of there being two psychical agencies, one of which submitted the activity of the other to a criticism which involved its exclusion from consciousness. The critical agency, we concluded, stands in closer relation to consciousness than the agency criticized: it stands like a screen between the latter and consciousness. Further we found reasons for identifying the critical agency with the agency which directs our waking life and determines our voluntary conscious actions (p. 540).

Freud is here presenting his famous picture of the mind divided into three topographic regions or systems: the Conscious, the Preconscious, and the Unconscious. Dreams, like other neurotic symptoms, represent a compromise solution. Unacceptable impulses can only traverse the repression barrier between Unconscious and Conscious by "outwitting" the censor, whose job is to protect the dreamer from the potential unpleasure of the unacceptable unconscious impulse.

Many people have quarreled with this formulation for various reasons. Indeed, in referring to this model Freud states:

> Analogies of this kind are only intended to assist us in our attempt to make complications of mental functioning intelligible. . . . We are justified, in our view, in giving free rein to our speculations so long as we retain the coolness of our judgement and do not mistake the scaffolding for the building (p. 536).

At this point my students are likely to say, "Well and good, but what about the fact that this marvelous source of information —the dream—is more often than not so confusing and hard to understand?" My response is to invite them back once again to *The Interpretation of Dreams*. Freud's brilliant description of dream interpretation contains all the answers, but he presents them in such a way that for many years I felt myself in some kind of straightjacket with regard to dream work. Let me attempt to make my point by means of a caricature of the student therapist's first encounter with Freud's principles of dream interpretation.

First of all, in this caricature, the student must immediately discard any interest in what the patient *says* is the dream. The dream story that the patient tells is only the manifest content, an elaborate disguise designed to throw both patient and analyst off the track. (As I have pointed out before, Freud freely broke his own rule and often made interpretations based on the manifest.) At any rate, this notion of the manifest as a disguise immediately puts both the patient and the analyst in an adversary position in relation to the dream. I mean someone (the ego) is trying to hoodwink us, but we are not going to be outsmarted. Moreover, this seemingly innocuous story which we know is a facade is not all that is afoot. (The paradox here is that the dream does involve a form of duplicity in that we often must disavow truths about ourselves. Conflictual material in the dream will be presented cryptically. However, at the same time there is much in the dream that is not so much disguised as it is expressed through symbols and at times, actually stated quite directly.)

As easy as it is to describe dream work as hopelessly confusing, it is equally easy to show how simple it can be by describing the "Knapp Family Favorite Television Shows in Disguise" game. This game, which is a snap to play, will instantly demonstrate how seemingly confusing and even contradictory rules actually pose no problem at all. If I tell you that I love this year's big television hit *Mountainroad Reds,* all of you familiar with television will readily know that I am referring to *Hill Street Blues* without my having to tell you that the rules of the game allow you to use both opposites and similarities to construct your title. At other times rhymes, clang associations, puns, and the like can also be used and not render the game unplayable, because our minds are capable of holding onto various complex rules with little difficulty. So now I am saying that although the notion of dream work and secondary elaboration seem problematic, they really aren't at all once you and the dreamer begin to play together.

Moreover, if you get stuck on the notion of uncovering infantile wishes without some kind of way to creatively fit them into everyday discourse, you can't get anywhere with teaching students how to work with dreams. What students do have to learn to be able to do is to quickly make the kinds of playful, intuitive leaps that good clinicians make all the time without even thinking about it. The student must learn to view the dream in the total context of the dreamer's present situation. This means working with the dream not just in terms of infantile wishes per se but in terms of the particular problem presented and the overall pattern of organization, defenses, and creative capacities, and so on.

But now, given all that I and "my mentors" have said, I feel that I have to admit that I am actually putting much more rather than less pressure on the therapist as he or she listens to a patient's dream. Gone is the somewhat laborious but more single-minded pursuit of unconscious infantile wishes of yesteryear. Now I am asking the therapist to deal with a happening, a holistic event chock full of here-and-now readouts and confrontations of self states, past conflicts and repressed infantile wishes, and future growth-enhancing possibilities. Gone, too, in most instances, is the several times a week analysis. The therapist cannot leisurely come to his or her formulations as the well-trained patient painstakingly associates to all the elements of the dream in a relatively orderly fashion, although this is the way it is described in the books from which most dream courses are taught. Indeed, many of our patients tell dreams as if they were alien events, handing them to the therapist in the desperate hope that the therapist will make something of them.

In order to deal with this pressure I propose the following guidelines:

First, the dream is an important communication to which the therapist must respond.

Second, I do not routinely ask for dreams. I prefer to let patients spontaneously offer them, taking note of where in the therapeutic process they occur. There are, of course, a few exceptions to this practice. With some patients who have considerable difficulty in talking to me directly I find dreams can act as an intermediary about which we can both talk. When I am at a loss with a patient, I may also ask for a dream in the hope that it will clarify what is going on in the treatment. Or with a new patient whom I am having a hard time assessing, I may ask about dreams as a way of orienting myself. For the most part, however, I like to allow dreams, which are such private communications, to emerge spontaneously in the therapy.

Third, no dream can be understood or responded to out of context. Over and over in case conferences, seminars, and so forth I have heard therapists fill the room with associations and theoretical formulations and then clam up in a panicky silence when someone says, "Well and good. Now what do you say to the patient?" Upon hearing the dream, wait for the patient's initial spontaneous responses, which will guide you in choosing yours. Under the most ideal conditions, your response will be an affirming silence because the patient is able to find his or her own meanings. However, more often than not, the patient's spontaneous responses are inconclusive or nonexistent. In some instances, it may be helpful for the therapist to consider the aftereffects of the previous session. She may detect evidence of possible empathic failures or reactions to the countertransference of the therapist. The therapist is concerned with such questions as: "Is this a dream indicating acute psychic distress and possible dissolution to which I must respond with supportive, tension-relieving aids and pull out any evidence of strengths that I can detect, or is there potentially conflictual material with which the patient is ready to deal, and if so, which elements shall I pick up as points of departure? Is this dream (as is often the case with dreams early in treatment) for my information but only minimally available for work? Is this dream being used by the patient to avoid contact with me, and if so, shall I accept or contest this effort? Where is the growing edge in this dream, the point that offers hope to both me and the patient, to show us what is to come even if it is 'rough sledding' in terms of greater pain and disorganization for the patient as old forms break down? Does it point to transferential struggles and therapeutic battles between me and the patient? What does this dream have to tell me about the overall therapeutic process and the patient's relationship to me and the process?"

The following dream is a beautiful example. My patient, Maria, was becoming increasingly angry as she experienced more and more difficulty denying her growing feelings of dependency on me. I was to be nothing more than a reference book that would offer her useful advise. During this period she reported the following dream: "I go to my exercise class. I lie on a mat to do the exercises but instead of being firm, the mat is soft like a bed that can rock back and forth. I leap up upset and outraged saying, 'What's the matter with this?' A girl with a scarf wrapped up like a mummy says it's supposed to help you experience the kinds of feelings that you had as a baby. I say, 'Oh, no, I am not going to do that because I will get hysterical!' and I got up and left." Fortunately, I saw the dream as predicting a premature termination of therapy. Therefore, I was able to engage the patient in looking at the terror and shame connected to her need for human contact before these emotions drove her out of treatment.

Fourth, begin the process of making tentative hypotheses out loud with the patient. Use his or her *response* as feedback, which will enable you to discard those of your responses that do not "fit" and to develop a more comprehensive and useful *response*. There are, however, always those dreams requiring nothing more from the therapist than that she or he serve as a witness while the patient tells a dream that needs no interpretation. A patient of mine has for many years maintained a successful facade of self-assurance while consistently working below her potential, terrified that failure would make her crazy. Recently she began preparing for the Graduate Record Examination, a first step toward a new career. Both she and her husband had questioned the wisdom of risking what might happen if she failed to get into graduate school. After a session in which the patient talked about her struggle against her husband's attempts to persuade her not to pursue the exam and her own fear that he might be right about her fragility, she reported the following dream: "I dreamed that my teeth were falling out. Then the support system beneath them, which was made out of toothpicks, also fell out. But then underneath both the old teeth and the toothpicks was a perfectly good set of new teeth."

The material that I have presented represents guidelines and didactic material that should be included in a course on the use of the dream in clinical practice, material best presented to the student through lectures and readings. It is, however, not enough to teach students metapsychology and clinical theory. A comprehensive course on the clinical use of dreams involves much more than the teaching of theory. It must also enable the student to develop the clinical skills necessary for the implementation of theory. It is all too easy for the student to remain in awe of the "expert" without finding the courage to work freely on developing his or her own responses. In order to overcome the student's difficulties with mastering this process, I have found that dream group work is an excellent way to introduce students to the skills involved in dream exploration and interpretation while allowing him or her to practice these skills within the kind of group setting that facilitates optimal learning.

I have found that the experiential dream group as described by Ullman and Zimmerman is quite adaptable to the training of psychotherapists. All that is required is that each student therapist presents one of his or her patient's dreams to the class as if it were his or her own. The class then works with the dream in exactly the same way outlined for an experiential dream group. The effect of the use of the dream group technique is quite dramatic.

Above all, the dream becomes alive for everyone in the class. It is no longer something to be talked about in the abstract. Each student is able to engage actively in both experiencing and understanding the dream. Suddenly Freud's notion of dream work ceases to be intimidating as the layers of the dream fall into place. The wealth of material that emerges and is validated by the therapist who presented the dream lessens individual group members' anxiety about what can be learned from the dream. The emotional richness derived from the first stage of the dream group and the variety of meanings derived from the second stage present the student with an altogether new dilemma. The student no longer complains about not being able to get a feel for the dream or not knowing what the dream is about. Now he or she must choose from a multitude of responses, those responses which are most appropriate to where he or she is in relation to the work with the patient. This then places the instructor in a much better position. In the traditional classroom situation the student presents completed clinical work with a dream for comment and criticism. Ideally the student will find this effort helpful, but often he or she becomes defensive or compliant. When, however, a dream is presented to a class for group work, the instructor, the student therapist, and the class can examine and evaluate the possibilities in a collaborative effort that leaves no one feeling wrong or inadequate.

As the multitude of perspectives introduced by the group work illustrate the complexity and richness of the dream material, the instructor can link these responses to the theoretical positions that have been presented in the didactic portion of the class. Thus at a point when the class has been aroused by the excitement of the dream group work, I am able to more effectively illustrate theoretical and technical issues regarding diagnosis, therapeutic process, resistance, and transference, drawing upon the live material that we as a group have generated. I am able to demonstrate how the emotional responsiveness of the therapist backed up by skilled clinical work can be integrated into a succinct therapeutic intervention. This enables the patient to see the defensive strategies that he or she has erected to avoid the truths that the dream embodies.

In addition to the powerful effect that dream group work has on the gathering and organizing of dream material, I have also found that the work affects the emotional growth of each individual participant as well as that of the group as a whole. In classroom situations where one student's work is "supervised" by the group, there often evolves a powerful undercurrent of competition and defensiveness which inhibits individual growth and learning and paralyzes the group's effort to act as a creative unit. Indeed, each time that I conduct a dream group I am impressed by the power of this mode of work because of both what it does and does not do. Even though in this instance the group is working with the dream of a patient rather than of one of the group members, the associations that arise reflect the participants' own inner world as well as their understanding of the patient. Experiential dream work frees every member of the group to get in touch with his or her own feelings and symbols while constantly being reminded that these are his or her own. At the same time, it fosters a greater sense of community with others and creates a sense of hopefulness about one's clinical skills as individual and group capacities for empathy and understanding emerge during the work. Out of a sense of mutual sharing generated by this experience, a positive spirit is generalized for the group in all their activities.

What the dream group does not do, precisely because of the very clear guidelines, is to violate the individual therapist's privacy beyond what is comfortable for him or her. Each student is able to go at his or her own pace, to offer and test hypotheses without feeling that what he or she says will be held against him or her. It is important that student therapists be challenged, but I feel that the classroom should represent a more neutral, nonjudgmental atmosphere and that criticism should be reserved for the individual supervisory session.

Finally, I have found that the use of dream group work creates an exciting and stimulating atmosphere in the classroom. While lectures and discussion of readings can be informative and intellectually challenging, they represent a departure from what is more relevant to the therapist in training. Training centers are like an apprenticeship in that students are working with their patients at the same time that they are studying. Dream group work provides an experience'that more closely approximates the therapy situation. It offers the students a "hands-on" experience in a controlled environment in which to explore concepts which up until this point have only been intellectually interesting. Moreover, the experience of the dream group work tends to be so satisfying that it generates an enthusiasm in relation to dreams that enhances the students' work with patients.

In a training institute, dream group work has potential uses beyond the classroom. For example, the dream group could be used as a means to create more positive working relations among various members of the training community. In the past, sensitivity training modeled along the lines of group therapy has been used for this purpose. It seems to me, however, that dream group work in which members of the community present their own dreams is far less likely to promote the kinds of conflict and anxiety that may be fostered in a more open-ended group and which can often be more disruptive than productive. The dream group resembles a task-oriented group with an incredibly curious mixture of intimacy, privacy, and productivity. Therefore, as a technique for building staff relations and therapeutic skills, it is the technique of choice.

Prior to my analytic training I was very much involved in the encounter movement. Therefore, I feel that I can fairly accurately assess the power and impact (negative and positive) of various kinds of groups generated during this period. Although group experiences were not without value, I was often left with a sense of their potential for destructiveness precisely because the goals of the group were wide open. The potential for individual violation was high, as there were no boundaries regarding intimacy and aggression. In a situation so potentially explosive, I found that the healthier individuals (cognizant of the reality that they would have to work with the other members of the group on a day-to-day basis for some time to come) established their own boundaries, resorting to a form of pseudointimacy and openness. More vulnerable members, on the other hand, failed to draw boundaries or limits. Their defenses broke down, and they were left open and exposed in a situation that could never meet their needs.

Dream group work may also be valuable in situations where a particular group has to deal with a crisis such as an illness or accident involving a classmate. Other instances in which dream group work might prove to be valuable include helping an entering class to become a working unit, facilitating the termination process of a graduating class, enabling the staff as a whole to deal with major changes in the institution, and so forth.

In summary, all clinical material presents complex problems for the student therapist. The dream, because of its unusual density and its multiple determinants, can be particularly difficult to work with. Therefore, I have presented and discussed three major problem areas:

First, students must be shown that dreams are unusually intense and comprehensive communications of the present state of the patient vis-à-vis himself and his world. Moreover, these communications require a response. The form of the response will, however, vary according to the patient, the session, and the like.

Second, students must be taught a clear but expanded understanding of Freud's metapsychology, his psychology of dreams, and his technique of dream interpretation, as well as the body of literature that psychoanalysts have created in order to deal with what Freud did not address.

Third, no matter how good the material or how well it is taught, nothing will happen until the student makes it his or her own. I have proposed that the most effective way of ensuring this ownership is dream group work. The classroom must be a stimulating and a safe atmosphere in which students can actively participate in the creative process of dream understanding and interpretation rather than just passively taking in the "wisdom of the expert." Dream group work provides just this kind of experience. Students are able to actively engage the dream in such a way as to promote their own personal growth and their skill in working with the dream as well.

References

Freud, S. *The Interpretation of Dreams.* Standard edition, vols. 4 and 5, 1900. J. Strachey, ed., London, Hogarth Press, 1953.

Fromm, E. *The Forgotten Language.* New York: Grove Press, 1951.

Gedo, J., and Goldberg, A. *Models of the Mind: A Psychoanalytic Theory.* Chicago: The University of Chicago Press, 1973.

Knapp, S. "Dreaming: Horney, Kelman, and Shainberg." In B. B. Wolman, ed., *Handbook of Dreams: Research, Theory, and Applications.* New York: Van Nostrand, 1979, pp. 340–359.

Roland, A. "The Context and Unique Function of Dreams in Psychoanalytic Therapy: A Clinical Approach." *International Journal of Psychoanalysis,* 1971, *52,* 431–439.

Sharpe, E. *Dream Analysis.* New York: Brunner Mazel, 1978.

Ullman, M. "Dreaming as Metaphor in Motion." *Archives of General Psychiatry,* 1969, *21,* 696–703.

Ullman, M., and Zimmerman, N. *Working With Dreams.* Los Angeles: Jeremy P. Tarcher, Inc., 1979.

·13·

Psychohistorical Dreamwork
A New Methodology Applied to a
Dream of Sir Humphry Davy
PAUL H. ELOVITZ, Ph.D.

Paul H. Elovitz and Donald Hughes are both leaders in the field of psychohistory. Dr. Hughes is a historian, and Dr. Elovitz is both a historian and a psychoanalyst. They are responsible for introducing the experiential dream group into their specialty as a tool for the exploration of the dreams of the historical personalities that engaged their interest at the time. While the historical figure was no longer around to speak for him or herself, the process did prove stimulating enough to open new avenues for their research efforts, thus adding a new dimension to their work. In this chapter examples are offered that illustrate their approach.

Introduction

Psychohistorical dreamwork is an exciting new field of endeavor that allows the researcher to explore the meaning of the extant dreams of historical personages as well as to gain additional insights into the personalities and motivations of the dreamers. Dreams of premodern man were held in a much higher regard than is the case in our modern, "rational" society. Important events would not be commenced without probing the unconscious through exploration of the dreams of leaders. Consequently, despite the ravages of time and the indifference and even contempt of many historians, a good deal of dream material exists for our analysis. We are fortunate to have a large number of diverse dreams of such celebrated figures as Alexander the Great, Alexander Graham Bell, Sir Humphry Davy, Charles Darwin, Charles Dickens, Otto Von Bismarck, René Descartes, Sigmund Freud, Leon Trotsky, and Xenophon. In the cases of Sigmund Freud, Peter the Great, Tippu Sultan, Emanuel Swedenborg, and others, we even have dream sequences that we can correlate with the day-to-day events of their lives.

Role-playing the Dreams of Historical Personages

My desire to apply the techniques of experiential dream groups to the dreams of historical personages led me to conceive, organize, and direct the first historical dream workshop on March 30–31, 1985. My plan for the first day was to have Montague Ullman model the experiential dream process using several recent dreams of participants. On the second day we also began with a contemporary dream and then moved on to a historical dream. I modified the experiential dream technique so that the biographer would role-play the historical dreamer and would subsequently explain his actions to the group. J. Donald Hughes brought Alexander the Great to life before our very eyes. Montague Ullman ran the group in his normal fashion without any special concessions to Alexander's grandiosity. I modeled the deferential attitudes that I recollected from my studies of ancient history. The group enthusiastically joined the process. The results of the workshop will subsequently be described by Professor Hughes.

For the historical dream group process you need a dream of a historical personage, preferably with day residue and a biographer who is willing to role-play his subject. There must be an experienced dream group leader and six to twelve dream group members. It is helpful for the members of the dream group to be familiar with experiential dream group techniques. It is also helpful, though again not essential, for the dream group members to be expert in or familiar with the historical period.

To effectively role-play a historical personage in a dream

workshop, the biographer should be thoroughly immersed in the figure's writings and life. He should read everything available, concentrating on the primary sources. Emphasis should be on what was going through the dreamer's mind in the period as close to the night of the dream as possible. Artifacts from the dreamer's life should be examined in detail. The biographer should examine his own day or night dreams about the subject to help him understand his own emotional relationship to the dreamer. The night before a historical dream workshop, he should get a good night's sleep and then reread the dream to be discussed in the morning. He should also think a great deal about the physical appearance and mannerisms of his dream subject as if he were an actor who was preparing to play the role of a well-known person.

Reconstructing the Life of Sir Humphry Davy

Let us turn our attention to my problem as a biographer of Sir Humphry Davy. Biographical research is very much like detective work. You have bits and pieces of evidence that you piece together to solve the mystery of just what motivated your subject and what he or she was like. Sir Humphry Davy (1778–1829) was a boy wonder of science and philosophy. He experimented with laughing gas as an anesthetic; isolated barium, chlorine, magnesium, potassium, sodium, and strontium; invented the Davy safety lantern for miners; traveled widely in Europe, and wrote extensively on science and philosophy (Forgan).

And yet the man who was heralded as a culture hero of science in his twenties was lambasted in his forties as one of the "Humbugs of the Age" (Anonymous). In his fourth and final decade his productivity declined, his presidency of the Royal Society was flawed (Miller), his marriage was unhappy (Treneer, p. 215), and his "death wish" became obvious (Fullmer 1960, p. 124). His biographers have been as ambivalent as his contemporaries. Dr. John Aryton Paris published a "Life" shortly after Humphry's death depicting him as a brilliant, superstitious charlatan and social climber (Fullmer 1967, p. 287). Humphry's adoring younger brother, John Davy (1836, 1839–40, 1858), presented a Victorian caricature of the man in three extensive studies. Though

Davy attracted numerous additional biographers, none has been able to provide a fully satisfactory explanation of the man.

I became fascinated with Davy when I came across some of his letters at the Science Museum in London in January 1983. Before long I was giving papers (Elovitz 1984, 1986) on Davy's childhood and attitudes toward science, magic, travel, and death as I sought to make some sense out of his life. It was apparent that this great scientist worshipped nature "as poet, as philosopher, and as sage." How could I reconcile this belief in magic with his passionate commitment to science, his scientific fearlessness with his subsequent fear of going out after dark, his zest for life with his death wish? For the answers to the puzzle I turned to the evidence of Sir Humphry's dreams. One moonlit night in 1819, while walking in the Colosseum, Davy had a daydream that was connected to a nightdream of April 1821. It was the latter that I presented on June 16, 1985 to the attendees of the Dream Group Experience: Clinical, Personal and Psychohistorical Applications.

The Davy Dream Workshop

Let us look at Davy's dream, and at this unique historical workshop itself, and discuss how it helped me as Davy's biographer. In the guise of Sir Humphry, with messed hair, shirttail out, and a squeaky voice (Paris), I announced that on the night of April 7, 1821, at the age of forty-two, I had the following dream:

"I imagined myself in a place partially illuminated with a hazy reddish light. Within it was dark & obscure but without & opening upon the sky very bright, I experienced a new kind of sensation which it is impossible to describe: it seemed as if I became diffused in the atmosphere & had a general sense of a balmy warmth:—a sort of agreeable (   )* with my whole body. Floating for a little while in this atmosphere, I found that I had wings & slowly & with some difficulty I rose in the air & gradually ascending above the cave or recess in which was the red light, I

---

*Blank in the original Davy manuscript at The Royal Institution.

found myself in the (unclear) sky amidst bright clouds or galaxies of light. It seemed as if I was altogether entering into a new
state of existence. I for some time reposed upon the brightest of
these galaxies & saw as it were in the immensity of space systems
of suns & worlds forming a sort of Abyss of light into which I
seemed doubtful whether I should plunge. At this moment I
seemed in communication with some intelligent being to (   )*
I stated that I had always been of opinion that the spirit was external & in a stage of progression from one form of existence to
another more perfect; that I had just left a world where all was
dark & cold and gross & heavy; that I now knew what it was to
have a purer & better existence, but that I hoped for something
still more perfect; that I was now in natural warmth & light &
ether & that I hoped to be ultimately in a world of intellectual
light where the causes of all things were developed & where the
sources of pleasure would be unbounded knowledge.

"After this my dream became confused; my fields of light
changed to a sort of luminous wood filled with paths & the
bright vision degenerated into a common dream."

Upon the completion of the telling of the dream Montague
Ullman, as the leader, explained that the group would be bor-
rowing the dream in a sense, provided that this was acceptable to
Sir Humphry. Following are some of the projections generated
by the process:

I feel tranquil, jubilant. I feel great.

Like I met my master and guide.

Like I've been given a marvelous gift of insight.

I feel energized and radiant. My main feeling is one of new
vistas—almost without limit. . . . Knowledge is a mystical
experience.

I feel privileged to have had this marvelous opportunity. I also
feel unified with it.

I feel I am experiencing what Kübler-Ross has described as
the light near the moment of death experience. Light is very
meaningful.

I have entered into a state of undifferentiated oneness.

---

*Blank in the original Davy manuscript.

I think of Henry Bond's poem, "I saw eternity the other night.
. . ."

I am very disappointed to wake up. I don't want to wake. I
don't want my body. I feel very heavy.

I feel like I have risen out of Plato's cave. I saw his shadow and
I've been given a brief glimpse of truth.

As I listened and took notes, I felt a sense of oneness with
Davy and with most of the group. I also found myself mentally
going beyond some of their statements so that when someone offered, "I have whatever feeling I would have if I were personally
involved with infinity," I thought, "I am infinity!"

When one dream group member responded in an unsympa-
thetic, intellectualized manner I felt an extreme intolerance and
was reminded of Davy's irritability. At references to space travel
my mind raced to flying images which abound in his notebooks
and poetry. Did he fantasize himself as having flown to earth
from another planet when at age fifteen he wrote in "The Sons
of Genius" of "The immortal children of another age" (J. Davy
1839, I, p. 36) who are associated with the heavens? Since his final work that he wrote at age fifty was specifically about immor-
tality and space travel, perhaps this was a lifelong preoccupation.
The process of listening was intellectually stimulating and enormously exciting.

The group moved on to discuss metaphors in the dream. Let
us look at a number of these:

I feel in the dark . . . get me out of that cave, that darkness.
This is scientific spiritualism. Science is unbounded. It is the
light.

In my dream the woods represent growth.

In my dream the paths represent different theories which represent different explanations.

Coming out of the cave is a metaphor for somehow resolving
separateness and discord.

The reddish light reminds me of being in the embryonic sac.
Light comes. . . .

I feel like I am being born again.

There are three different states of experience. It begins and

ends in a dream. It is an out of body experience. An altered
state. I want to be a spirit.

As the biographer I found the metaphor of Plato's cave, which
I had not previously considered, to be apropos to Sir Humphry's
attitude toward knowledge. He indeed saw himself as having
seen the light of true knowledge, which he passionately wished
to share with others. But he was also plagued by his fear of the
dark which haunted him in childhood and during the last few
years of his life. The light as birth is a related idea which made
sense to me especially since there is considerable birth imagery in
Davy's notebooks, most especially during his nitrous oxide experiments (J. Davy 1836, I, p. 102). The woods as growth was
also worth considering. He was often traveling to the countryside for rest and rejuvenation. The notion of "an out of body experience" was also quite relevant to the great scientist. The one
short story he wrote involves a king whose body is transformed
and who is condemned to eternity in the spirit world (J. Davy
1836, II, pp. 329–330). He had a "horror of being buried alive
before animation was completely extinct," since he apparently
thought that his spirit might return to the interred flesh. His instructions, which were not followed, were that he should not be
buried until ten days after he appeared to have died. His desire
that there be no autopsy was honored (J. Davy, 1836, II, p.368).
The idea that he could step out of his body may help to explain
why one friend described him at age twenty-one during his nitrous oxide experiments as acting as if he had two or three spare
lives in reserve (Cottle, pp. 198–203).

As a biographer I was finding the input from the dream group
to be extremely helpful. Next came my chance to give the group
a clear view of Sir Humphry's character and history and to share
some of the associations that I was making between their projections and his life. This was one of those cases where "thinking
on my feet" was productive. Using the first person singular, I
spelled out an explanation for his scientific mission which incorporated some psychoanalytic theories and the known facts of
his childhood. It is based on the evidence that when he felt
abandoned by his mother and family at age six, he fantasized
"Mother Nature" and some extraterrestrial beings who had ap-

peared among the Romans as his "true" parents. The desire to gain a closer knowledge of these imaginary parents is what prompted his search into the mysteries of science. My portrayal of Sir Humphry was that of a driven, self-centered and disillusioned man. I sought to present an accurate picture of his frustration with his wife from whom he was usually separated (Fullmer 1960, p. 114). Sir Walter Scott said they both had tempers and fought publicly like "cat and dog" (Treneer, p. 199) and another contemporary called him "a martyr to matrimony" (Edgeworth in Fullmer 1960, p. 124). The group seemed rather struck by the transformation of Paul Elovitz into the boyish, brilliant, grandiose, and irascible Sir Humphry, and they listened attentively. It was then time for them to ask information eliciting questions. I think it would be most helpful if I give some examples of the dialogue that ensued:

> *Group Leader*: Sir Humphry, we're so happy that you felt willing to share so openly with us your feelings. And we want you to know that we listen with great appreciation and not with the attitude that perhaps your own contemporaries have. Rather we are willing to hear your ideas, different from our own, but we accept them and we would like to hear more about how your experience ties into the dream you have given to us and that we've taken as our own for awhile. And I'd like to begin by asking on behalf of the group, do you recall the day before your dream, the evening before? What were your feelings? Are there any particular remembrances that you have of that time?

> *Davy*: Would I could. But it seems as if the dream were not last night, but as if I had it 164 years ago. I just cannot remember.

> *Group Member*: I'd like to hear what you remember of your childhood and mother. You used a phrase "scolded like a baby" and I wonder if you could elaborate on that and tell us a bit about your mother.

> *Davy*: My mother is a marvelous woman. My mother is really the finest woman I've ever known.

> *Group Member*: She never scolded you?

Davy: I can't remember my mother doing anything that was not perfect. Even in the cares of the day, I can't remember her scolding me. I seldom see her; I've never introduced my wife, Jane, to her these seven years we've been married. But I write, and my mother is in my thoughts constantly. . . .

Group Member: Can I ask Sir Humphry to speak less about his life in general and more about the dream.

Group Leader: Perhaps we ought to remind Sir Humphry and the group to stay focused on the dream.

Group Member: Do you see some relationship between images of the dream and what you have told us?

Davy: Yes (responding irritably), but you like me to be bounded, and I don't want to be bounded. I'm a boundless man. Yet I'm stuck in a world in which people are restricted by schedules and . . .

Group Member: Sir Humphry, may we speak about the red, hazy light in that segment of the dream? Can you tell us more about that segment? Can you identify the intelligent being? Is it someone that you know?

Davy: No, the being is from another planet. My senses were so keen in the dream that it was amazing.

Group Member: Can you tell us anything else about the "intelligent being" in the dream?

Davy: It was a visitor from the Milky Way (laughter and snickering in the room).

Davy: (with hurt and outrage) Do you see what I face? Do you see why I don't even try and talk to many narrow-minded people who claim to be educated?

Group Member: I didn't laugh, I asked a question. I was very interested in what you mentioned about reincarnation and also in your being upset that your wife has head knowledge, but that she is not nature knowledgeable. And I was wondering if the intelligent being that you met was knowledgeable in nature, man, and science, in all things?

My lack of knowledge regarding the day residue and the events in the weeks prior to the dream meant that I had to frustrate the dream group. I sought to make the point emphatically that Davy idealized his mother. This was based on a lot of evidence, especially the fact that his "death wish" (Fullmer 1960, p.124) emerged strongly after her death, after which he declared, "What I regard most tenderly, was in the grave" (J. Davy 1840, IX p. 315). I was rather amazed at how strongly I reacted to being questioned unsympathetically by several group members and how stung I was by their laughter, because there was lots of evidence to support the view of Sir Humphry as thin-skinned, self-absorbed, and pompous. I chose to reveal these characteristics in my answers. Since his belief in extraterrestrial beings and reincarnation were lifelong, the ridicule was all the harder to endure. Unlike a real-life dreamer, I could not remember additional materials in relationship to the dream. However, I could bring the materials on Sir Humphry into clear focus.

At this stage of the process I was free to remove the cloak of the great early-nineteenth-century scientist and resume the normal garb of Paul Elovitz. As a biographer I was elated by the process that I had just been through and presented to the dream group a fuller view of my reconstruction of Sir Humphry's life and character. I began with his belief in magic, which I related to his childhood, and ended with a discussion of the breakdown of his defenses. In addition I shared a dilemma I faced. The Davy research is part of a much larger project in which I am testing the hypothesis that the ninety-two leading innovators of the Industrial Revolution were psychologically healthier than the general population. Yet the image that I was presenting was that of a troubled individual who in the face of frustration was retreating into his own private world. Toward the end of his life he simply could not tolerate scrutiny or even serious work. He was incessantly traveling to his "old haunts" (J. Davy 1836, II, p. 308; Tobin, p. 51) in a highly manic fashion.

The solution that was emerging to the question of Davy's mental health or the lack thereof was complex. He was an unusually intelligent, well-cared-for young child. At age six he used his exquisite creativity to solve the problem of fearful loneliness. Separated from his family, he imagined extraterrestrial parents who were associated with Mother Nature (Elovitz 1986). When at age fifteen he suffered the additional trauma of the death of his father, he translated his love of nature into a lifelong mission as a scientist. He would know nature as no one had before. Though there is considerable evidence to support this thesis in his highly autobiographical letters, notebooks, poetry, prose, and scientific writings, it is most explicit in his dreams. I knew that Sir Humphry's final work was based upon several of his dreams (1840). However, due to the enormous corpus of his writings, I had not yet read it. During the dream workshop I realized that the dreams were key to my understanding of Davy. I would at least be able to break loose from the Victorian caricature created by the adoring younger brother. Dr. John Davy's superficial portrayal was being replaced by the much more flamboyant, self-centered, and poetical image that I had just shared. The dream workshop in June generated so many possibilities that by August I went to the Davy archives at the Royal Institution in London to check my new hypotheses with the evidence. The outcome of this was the paper, "Sir Humphry Davy's Creation in His Dreams of Extraterrestrial Imaginary Parents as Benevolent Supporters of His Scientific Career: The Evidence from *Consolations in Travel, Or the Last Days of a Philosopher*," that I presented in December at the International Psychohistorical Association's Long Island University Convention.

In the London archives I found the accurate manuscripts for the 1819 daydream and 1821 dream and day residue. There were additional dreams in the manuscript along with new materials on his life. My work as a Davy biographer was enriched by the use of these dreams.

Conclusion

Dream work has had an enormous impact on my teaching. When I returned from the dream workshop, I shared with my students my enthusiasm and the main outlines of what had happened. They liked what I described. They were especially interested in the process of verbalizing the feelings and images of the dream and in role-playing. They have joined in the process to probe the dreams of Darwin, Davy, and others. Don Hughes and I had adapted the method to political cartoons, various texts, works of art, and, most notably, to historical re-creations. The enrollment in my history classes has increased. It is most fortunate that this new historical methodology enlivens the classroom while it aids our biographical research.*

References

[Anonymous]. "The Humbug of the Age: No. 111: Sir Humphry Davy," *The John Bull Magazine and Literary Review.* 1824, 1, 89–92.

Brook, S. *The Oxford Book of Dreams.* New York: Oxford University Press, 1983.

Cottle, J. *Reminiscences of Samuel Taylor Coleridge and Robert Southey.* New York: Wiley and Putnam, 1847.

Davy, H. Notebook M.S., box 21d, Archives of the Royal Institution, 7 April 1821, 178–181.

Davy, J., ed. *The Collected Works of Humphry Davy.* 9 vols. London: Smith, Elder, 1839–40.

Davy, J. *Fragmentary Remains, Literary and Scientific of Sir Humphry Davy of London:* John Churchill, 1858.

Davy, J. *Memoirs of the Life of Sir Humphry Davy.* 2 vols., London: Rees, Orme, Brown, Green & Londman, 1836.

Eberwein, R. T. *Film and the Dream Screen.* Princeton: University Press, 1984.

Elovitz, P. H. "The Childhood Origins of Sir Humphry Davy's Preoccupation with Science, Magic and Death." Presented 1984. In the 1986 proceedings of the International Psychohistorical Association.

――――. "Scientific Genius and Innovation in the English Industrial Revolution: Sir Humphry Davy (1778–1829)." In Joseph Dorinson and Jerrold Atlas, eds., *The Many Faces of Psychohistory.* New York: International Psychohistorical Association, 1984.

Forgan, S., ed. *Science and the Sons of Genius: Studies on Humphry Davy.* London: Science Reviews, 1980.

Fraiberg, S. *The Magic Years.* New York: Scribner's, 1959.

Freud, S., *The Interpretation of Dreams.* New York: Avon, 1969.

Fullmer, J. Z. "Davy's Biographers: Notes on Scientific Biography." *Science,* 1967, *155*, 285–291.

Fullmer, J. Z. "Humphry Davy's Adversaries." *Chymia,* 1962, 8, 147–164.

Fullmer, J. Z. "The Poetry of Sir Humphry Davy." *Chymia,* 1960, 6, 102–126.

---

*There are special difficulties in attempting to locate dreams of historical figures. With the exception of the psychoanalytic literature indexers almost always ignore dreams. *The Oxford Book of Dreams* (Brook) is a valuable source; however, its selection is limited and it does not give any of the context of the dreams. This historical dreams in the *Dream Network Bulletin* appear to come from Brook. Readers who know of dreams of historical personages that are not referred to in Brook or my paper are asked to contact me at The Psychohistory Forum/246 Highwood Avenue/Ridgewood, New Jersey 07450 or at Ramapo College/505 Ramapo Valley Road/Mahwah, New Jersey 07430/U.S.A.

Miller, D. P. "Between Hostile Camps: Sir Humphry Davy's Presidency of the Royal Society of London: 1820–1827." *The British Journal of Science,* 1983, 16, 1–47.

Nagera, Humberto. "The Imaginary Companion." *The Psychoanalytic Study of the Child,* 1969, 24, 165–196.

Paris, J. A. *The Life of Sir Humphry Davy.* 2 vols., London: Colburn & Bently, 1831.

Sandford, M. *Thomas Poole and His Friends.* vol 2., London: Macmillan, 1883.

Tobin, J. J. *Journal of a Tour Made in the Years 1828–1829 Through Styria, Carniolia and Italy Whilst Accompanying the Late Sir Humphry Davy.* London: W. S. Orr, 1832.

Treneer, Anne. *The Mercurial Chemist: A Life of Sir Humphry Davy.* London: Methuen, 1963.

Ullman, M., Krippner, S., and Vaughan, A. *Dream Telepathy.* New York: Macmillan, 1973.

Ullman, M., and Zimmerman, N. *Working With Dreams.* Los Angeles: Jeremy P. Tarcher, 1979.

Psychohistorical Dreamwork
Dreams from the Ancient World
J. DONALD HUGHES, Ph.D.

Alexander

My interest in the dreams of Alexander the Great comes from two areas in which I have worked. For about ten years I have taught a biographical course on Alexander and have noticed that the personality of the famed conqueror fascinates many students. For eight years I have also been involved in dream groups as participant and leader. Through the groups I became familiar with the writings of Montague Ullman and began to use his method in working with dreams. As I read the ancient writings on Alexander, I saw that his dreams were frequently reported, and that they included images of striking clarity. It occurred to me that these dreams might represent a way of studying the enigma of Alexander's personality, so I scanned the scholarly literature for studies of his dreams. I found none. Commentaries mentioned individual dreams, but no one had tried to assemble them all and subject them to psychohistorical inquiry. So I combed the ancient sources. Some dreams ascribed to Alexander have to be rejected for textual reasons, and because dreams are private, it can never be asserted that an account represents what the dreamer actually saw. But I was able to collect six dreams that have a defensible claim to be ones that Alexander saw and reported to those who were with him. I commented on these in "The Dreams of Alexander the Great," *The Journal of Psychohistory*, vol. 12, no. 2 (Fall 1984), pp. 168–192. Anyone who wishes to know what my thoughts were on the subject before the psychohistorical dream workshop described here may consult that article.

For the workshop, I selected the dream in which the principal image was least culture-bound, therefore most amenable to associations by a modern group. That was clearly the dream of the snake, last of the six in historical order, and the one reported by the greatest number of ancient sources; Diodorus (17. 103), Cicero (*De Divinatione* 2. 66), Strabo (15. 2. 7), Curtius (9. 8. 25-27), and Justin (12. 10). With five texts, differing in detail, I had to concoct a version of the dream to present to the group. I decided to play the role of Alexander. While role-playing is not essential in work with historical dreams, it makes the historical character more vivid for the group. It also enables the biographer to act out his/her projections, making them conscious in a way that intellectual reflection often cannot. I gave the dream as follows:

"I had a dream. In the dream a snake appeared to me. The snake was carrying in its mouth a plant: root, branch, leaves, and all. And as the snake approached with the plant, it said, 'Look at this. Notice the color of this plant. It grows in a place not far from here, which you can find. Take this plant; administer it as a poultice to the wound of Ptolemy. Steep its leaves in boiling water and make a tea. Give the tea to Ptolemy. He will recover.' The snake departed. The dream ended."

Following my narrating the dream, the group was invited to ask factual questions about it. I was pleased to find that my colleague, Paul Elovitz, entered into the spirit of the personification and addressed me as a deferential Greek courtier might have addressed Alexander. We enjoyed the exchange, and it encouraged the group to attempt to bridge the historical and cultural chasm that separates us from the world of Alexander. In this stage of the work, the biographer must provide historical background. No one in the group, with the exception of Dr. Elovitz, had read my article, and most were aware of no more than the most rudimentary facts about Alexander. The information that the questions elicited was, briefly, as follows: The color of the plant was gold. Ptolemy, a commander under Alexander, had been his boyhood friend. He was wounded by a poisoned arrow during a siege in India. The remedy suggested by the dream was tried and it worked. The snake was Alexander's mother's pet snake. Alexander regarded his mother as a goddess. He had sex with his wife, but also possibly had sex with Ptolemy when they were younger, and still loved him. Alexander had a lover named Hephaestion. The dream took place in 325 B.C., when Alexander was about thirty-one years old. These are not all known facts, but are inferences drawn from ancient accounts of Alexander.

The projections on the dream offered by group members were of potential use to me as psychohistorian. I expected that some would be wide of the mark, but suspected that, because of the nature of the unconscious, some of them would confirm my own impressions and those of other scholars. Beyond that, I hoped for insights that would expand my understanding of Alexander's personality. All this happened during the time that the group members took on the dream as their own and made 152 projections. Among the feelings expressed by group members that seemed to confirm my own associations between the dream and statements by ancient authors about Alexander were the following:

I need Ptolemy. I am in a strange land far from Macedonia, far from home. I need men I can trust.
The thought of losing a friend is very painful to me. If I ever lost my current lover, I think I would kill.
I subdue other countries. They're like women to me, because my mother is so powerful.

The first comment coincided with my intuition that Alexander's seeing a means of healing Ptolemy in the dream revealed an unconscious desire to tap the "Ptolemy" element in his own personality: a steady part, unlike his usual volatility, that could be trusted; the ruler rather than the conqueror. The second comment reminded me of Alexander's overreaction after the death of Hephaestion, when he massacred a hill tribe to assuage his raging grief. The third underlined my judgment about Alexander's Oedipal need to conquer "Mother Earth" as surrogate for his inaccessible mother.

A surprisingly large proportion of the projections offered new perspectives on the dream or on Alexander, or stimulated me to reflections I had not made before. One saw the snake's plant as the Tree of Life. Others thought of the serpent and tree of the Garden of Eden, a connection I rejected as impossible for Alexander, who presumably had never heard of Genesis. An association between plants and nature or the earth was offered. I connected that with Alexander's need for "grounding." Snakes, the tongue, and wisdom were coordinated by another. I was intrigued by the attempts of several to equate Ptolemy with Alexander's mother, Olympias. One went so far as to say, as if Alexander were speaking, "I am alive and strong when Ptolemy is in my mouth," equating an oral homosexual act with suckling at the maternal nipple. Other creative associations were offered, enough to keep a psychohistorian busy.

But I had no time to evaluate all those leads. I had to respond as Alexander, making clear the way in which I judged he would have responded to the dream. So I had him say that dreams are from the gods, and that this one in particular was from Asclepius, the god of healing, whose sacred animal is the snake. Several members of the group had expressed a feeling of gratefulness for the dream, and "Alexander" said he felt himself to be Alexander the Grateful! He admitted the importance of his mother in the dream, something he had not noted. He emphasized his love and need for Ptolemy as friend rather than lover.

Then the members of the group were able to ask "Alexander" questions to elucidate the life situation of the dream and psychological factors connected with it. Questions about Dionysos, the god of wine, brought out Alexander's drinking problem, which led to tragedies like the killing of his friend Cleitus while he was drunk. Cleitus, also in his cups, had accused Alexander of illegitimacy, and this issue also emerged in answer to questions. The "day residue" of the dream was readily determined, since it is stated in the sources. Ptolemy had been wounded by a poisoned arrow in battle, and Alexander, who desperately wanted him to recover, had asked for a cot so he could sleep next to him. When Alexander fell asleep, he had the dream.

A major line of questioning related to the snake, the central image of the dream. There were snakes everywhere in Alexander's life; a snake in his mother's bed at his conception, his mother's pet snake as he grew up, snake poison in the arrows, a snake that heals, and the snake in the garden of Eden, of which "Alexander" would not admit knowing. "Alexander" pointed out that snakes are sent by the gods and that he had outgrown a youthful fear of snakes.

When asked if not only Ptolemy, but also he himself had been healed by the dream, "Alexander" replied, "That is a very wonderful thought. I believe that must be true." I was not sure how much I should let "Alexander" learn of what he would not have known. This problem I mentioned to the group in the last phase of the process, when I dropped the persona of Alexander and spoke as a psychohistorian. Someone asked me if Alexander was a person who learned, and I had to admit that I thought he learned a lot as he traveled and observed the customs of countries through which he passed. Perhaps I worried too much about letting him have realizations in the course of the questioning. Another factor that bothered me before the group process was that some of the associations that "Alexander" might have with snakes, plants, and so forth would be so culture-bound to ancient Macedonian or Indian history that it would be hard for a group that had not studied those subjects to come up with valid associations. But they put their fingers on almost everything that I was able to get from the sources.

The group pushed me on Alexander's possible knowledge of the Garden of Eden myth. While I still think it improbable, I had to admit that Josephus says Alexander visited Jerusalem, talked to the High Priest, and was shown the Book of Daniel. Since he was interested in the stories of many peoples, he could have known about the snake and tree in Eden. Another mythological association that the group brought me to see was that of the Golden Fleece, which was hung in a tree and guarded by a dragon (the Greek word *drakon* means "snake"). Jason made a long trip to the east (like Alexander) to get the fleece, and his name means "healer." Alexander saw "wool trees" (cotton) in India. Remembering that Alexander's dream was of healing, and that the plant was golden, I became excited about multiple connections of the images with a myth that Alexander certainly knew.

Another question to which I would have to give more attention after the group work on this dream is the close personal relationship between Ptolemy and Alexander. When I was asked as "Alexander" about that, I just intuitively said they had a homosexual relationship when they were boys, but it is not at all unlikely given the place of homosexuality in Greek society. Whether it continued in later years or not, the lifelong relationship between the two men was very close, if never imbued with the kind of passion Alexander felt for Hephaestion. After Alexander's untimely death, Ptolemy seized his body and gave it a magnificent burial in the Egyptian Alexandria.

Alexander was my first excursion into psychohistorical group dream work, and I found it stimulating from scholarly and psychological standpoints. Whether from practice or because of the nature of the material, the work with Xenophon's dream was, however, more instructive.

Xenophon

I became aware of Xenophon's dreams while searching for dreams reported by ancient Greek historians. In this project I had the assistance of the *Thesaurus Linguae Graecae,* a computerized text of all important Greek authors before A.D. 600. The able director, Dr. Theodore Brunner, helped me key in various Greek words for "dream." The computer searched for these morphemes and in each instance printed three lines of text. I found that Xenophon was unique in that his work, the *Anabasis,* is an eyewitness narrative containing two dreams of his own in detailed settings. For both (*Anabasis* 3.1.11-13; 6.1.22 and 4.3.8-9, 13) Xenophon tells what happened in the hours before the dream, its content, his interpretation, and what action he took as a consequence. I judged that either dream might have served as a good exercise for a psychohistorical dream group, but chose the first as more crucial and dramatic. Although I had completed an article on this subject, it had not been published and no members of the group had access to it. Here is the dream as I told it:

"In the dream I saw a thunderstorm. And a bolt of lightning came from the sky and struck my father's house and set it on fire. The flames raged all around. I was trapped within, and had no idea how I might escape. I awoke with a start. That is the dream."

The few factual questions from the group established that Xenophon saw himself alone inside the burning house. The group then took the dream as its own and offered about eighty projections involving feelings and metaphors. Some of these caught and expanded the sense of the dream as I judge from historical sources Xenophon would have experienced it. Among these were feelings of fear, ominous foreboding, being caught by sudden disaster, being abandoned and alone, impotent, and the victim of divine punishment. Among the metaphorical projections that bore out insights that I had already formed and included in my article were the following:

> I'm angry at my father. Fathers should protect their sons.
> In my dream being trapped in my father's house is a metaphor. The influence he has over me is binding. It does not allow me to be free.

A surprising number of contributions by group members suggested connections new to me, or whose implications I had not worked out fully. Here is a selection:

> Where is my mother, where are my sisters, where are the women? We Greeks keep women in the house. The houses are always full of women. But in my father's house, I see no women. It's sad. I like being with women.
> Maybe my saying I'm in my father's house may not so much be a reference to a former time, a childhood time, but in some way to my usurping, my moving into his role now, displacing some other power. And it might bring Zeus' thunderbolt down on me.
> I'm glad I woke up because now I know what I need to take seriously.

I then responded to the projections as Xenophon, offering the response which we know from his account to have been his own:

> At first I said to myself, "What a propitious dream! I have seen a great light from Zeus." But when I reflected on it further, the interpretation that came to me was not such a happy one. For I recalled that Zeus is king. The god to whom my expedition was devoted is Zeus the king. And I was in the mid-

dle of the king's country, the king of Persia who is King of Kings. So the dream may have been saying to me, "The king has me surrounded, has me trapped in his own country. For the king's house is the king's land." And so when I awoke I thought, "What must I do? I must find a way out of the troubles which encompass me on every side." And though I was young and not experienced as generals are supposed to be, I volunteered myself to be general, to lead us out of the trap formed by the Persian army. It was indeed a dream that changed my life, and I think I may judge what it means by what happened afterward.

Then I gave Xenophon's response to the comments of group members as I judged he might have done, confirming the feelings of sudden danger and being overwhelmed by an enemy army. "Xenophon" came to the realization that the dream had been saying he was in his father's house then, at the time of the dream, not so much as in a former time. That is, he was moving into his father's "house," taking over his role in life. Xenophon's father was a great general, and the dream called on the son to do things his father could do: take command; be a man. "Xenophon" said he almost laughed at the suggestion that he was happy to awaken from the dream, since his waking life situation was worse than the dream; he was threatened not only with death but by dishonor in Persian hands. Since he considered himself to be not only a soldier but a philosopher as well, "Xenophon" was willing to speculate along lines suggested by one group member, that all four elements (fire, air, earth, and water) were represented symbolically in the dream. He did not, however, get very far in this realm of abstract thought, a failing that is present in Xenophon's writings. "Xenophon" concluded by saying that upon his return to Greek shores he had offered a sacrifice of thanksgiving to Zeus the king, who sent the dream that had taught him to deliver himself and his companions from danger.

"Xenophon" was so sure that he understood his own dream that it took a bit of explanation by the group leader to make him aware that he might learn more about it by responding to questions. But the ancient soldier was soon willing to proceed. The line of questioning centered, astutely, on Xenophon's assurance that the dream had told him to take action. Just what in the dream indicated that? His assumption that it had been a warning, an omen, was not enough to satisfy the group. General questions intended to draw forth associations from "Xenophon" seemed to work better than directive questions aimed at possible interpretations of dream images. Here is an example of the former:

Group Member: Do you recollect what you were thinking about before you went to bed?

Xenophon: Very much so. We were all thinking of the same thing. What could we do? The same fate awaited us as the commanders before. They would take us and with every sort of insult put us to death. It would be worse than death in the time before we died. When we retired for the evening, few of us ate anything. Almost no men started fires. We could hardly sleep. I, particularly, felt the same way. My very best friend Proxenus had been killed by the Persians, for he was one of the commanders, and I grieved his death very much.

Group Leader: Now, that was a very fruitful question. It's probably the first time in dream work history that we got a context that's 2,385 years old.

Before the group could close in on the meaning of the dream, it was necessary to elicit more of the context, and this was done adroitly. It was established that on the previous day, Xenophon had been elected as one of three representatives chosen to carry word of the Greek army's refusal to accede to the Persian demand for surrender. Then questions focused on Xenophon's associations to images in the dream. He remembered that when he was a child, his father's house near Athens had indeed been burnt by Spartans. Asked to say more about his father, "Xenophon" said he was a man whom he always admired. "Truly, there could be no Athenian citizen more worth emulating than my father." Knowing that the historical Xenophon had subscribed to the traditional values of the conservative Athenian aristocracy represented by his father, I refused to let him accept the implications of questions aimed at having him realize that he had an unconscious desire to kill his father by burning down his house, a wish apparently fulfilled in the dream. Such a thought was impossible for Xenophon, a conventional Greek who believed that dreams were sent by the gods, not "made" by the individual psyche. The group leader remarked, "At this point we have a very evasive dreamer. He won't explain this to you because it came from the gods. He has the world's greatest dodge. It's not his dream; it was given to him by Zeus."

The group returned to the first enigma of the question period: Xenophon felt the dream left him with the conviction that he had to take action, but the image in the dream seemed to say only that he is surrounded by flames. As "Xenophon" I could find no way out of the ring of fire, so the conversation continued:

Xenophon: I have been several times in places where there seemed to be no escape at all, and then a way opened. The dream was like that. I saw no way out, but even so one must continue to try and find a way.

Group Leader: Now that's a very interesting response. Because the fact is that there was a way out of that fire. There was a way out of what was emotionally experienced as a totally entrapping, hopeless situation. The way out was waking up. That's where he's getting the feeling—"Well, all right, my dream is confronting me with this reality; there is a way out, and I have to find it." He's intuitively saying that.

Xenophon: Good point, because then when I was awake, I could wake up in another sense and take a positive action instead of letting myself get killed through despair.

Waking up, then, was itself a dream image which could have meaning. The paradox was resolved. A final exchange uncovered the fact that Xenophon's father had died when he was young, and that Socrates had been a surrogate father figure. Finally, I took the opportunity as "Xenophon" to reply to the comment that those who are concerned with dreams are foolish:

"I might say that Socrates, my teacher, also paid great attention to his dreams. He guided his life by them. So I was taught both by our traditions to believe in dreams, and by Socrates the philosopher to take them with great care and to try to listen to them with wisdom. So it is my idea that only a fool would not listen to his own dreams."

Ullman replied in good humor, "Socrates spoke of all my ideas 2,410 years ago." It was then time for me to step out of my role as Xenophon and to become the psychohistorian-biographer again. There were observations I felt compelled to make on the interaction between psychohistorian and group, and the perspectives that had been offered on possible meanings of Xenophon's dream. The psychohistorian working with Xenophon is faced with a richness and paucity of information. We have abundant details of the context surrounding the dream and the day residue that contributed to it. We know how he interpreted it, and what he did afterward. One seldom finds that much for a dream so long ago. But we know little about his childhood, other than the fact that he followed his parents as closely as any man can. Almost nothing is known about his mother, which is why "Xenophon" ignored the remark about the lack of women in the dream. However, he might have done well to comment on that. Xenophon was unusual among ancient Greek men by being exclusively heterosexual. There is evidence that he related well to women. He fell in love with his wife, which was considered so strange as to be laughable. He didn't exhibit the social-educational homosexuality which was the norm for the Greek upper class. But women for him are subordinate, instruments of the man in taking care of house, family, slaves, and budget. He could resent women who rise above their station and try to rule men like a mother. This may explain why, when on the advice of Socrates he went to the Delphic Oracle, a woman, to ask about his forthcoming expedition to Persia, he framed the question so as to prevent her from giving him a negative response.

How useful is it to me as a historian to try to put myself in the place of a historical figure in interaction with a group? It should be evident that it opens up many possible explanations, particularly in the area of motivation. These are hypotheses that must be rigorously tested by reference to historical sources. But developing a creative hypothesis is half the battle. Thus I am grateful for several important suggestions that I received in the workshop.

Paul Elovitz and I were asked a question in this workshop which I have had to answer several times before. Role-playing works well for us, but we seem to have a knack for it. What about scholars who don't feel they have the ability? While there is a difference in the talent of individual historians in role-playing, I think there is a much greater difference in willingness to try it, or emotional thresholds against it. I believe that this ability lies untapped in many who would get much more out of it than they think, if they would try it. We need more workshops for historians to learn it.

I see this method as offering a tremendously enriching way to approach historical figures of any period. Many of my colleagues who are not familiar with dream work would reject it through fear of being misled by emotion, of being carried too far into this unfathomable realm of motivation. Yet dreams have been a real force in the lives of people throughout history. Historical dreamwork offers us another tool in reaching explanations for human actions in the past. Part of the difficulty with many historians is a distrust of imagination and the unconscious. After all, they are trained to depend on the thinking function in their work. They know that their colleagues expect historical ideas to be presented in purely intellectual dress, which is why so much historical writing is so dull. But most historians are in touch with the creative area of the unconscious, even if many of them do not realize it much of the time. They use the imagination, but they hide it behind a facade of intellectualization. Herein lies the danger that they may fall victim to the very dangers that they perceive in dream work and role-playing, namely, that their own psychological hang-ups may be projected back on historical figures. Psychohistorians try to be conscious of this process; we know that it happens. Thus we may be able to avoid getting tied up in a complex with a man, woman, or movement in the past without being aware of it. As in the dream group method, projections can be helpful when they are recognized for what they are, so that in historical research, we can use our projections as tools instead of mistaking them for self-evident truth.

References

Anderson, J. K. *Xenophon*. London: Duckworth, 1974.

Artemidorus. *The Interpretation of Dreams*. Ed. and trans. Robert J. White. Park Ridge, N. J.: Noyes Press, 1975.

Cicero, M. T. *De Divinatione*. Ed. and trans. W. A. Falconer. Cambridge, Mass.: Harvard University Press (Loeb Classical Library), 1964.

Curtius Rufus, Q. *History of Alexander*. Ed. and trans. John C. Rolfe. Cambridge, Mass.: Harvard University Press (Loeb Classical Library), 1946.

Diodorus Siculus. *Library (World History)*. Ed. and trans. C. B. Welles. Vol. 8. Cambridge, Mass.: Harvard University Press (Loeb Classical Library), 1963.

Hughes, J. Donald. "The Dreams of Alexander the Great." *The Journal of Psychohistory*, 1984, *12*(2), 166–192.

Justin. "Epitome of Trogus Pompeius," *Philippic Histories*. In John S. Watson, ed. and trans., *Justin, Cornelius Nepos, and Eutropius*. London: G. Bell and Sons, 1910.

Strabo. *Geography*. Ed. and trans. Horace L. Jones. Cambridge, Mass.: Harvard University Press (Loeb Classical Library), 1933.

Xenophon. *Anabasis*. Ed. and trans. Carleton L. Brownson. Cambridge, Mass.: Harvard University Press (Loeb Classical Library), 1922.

·14·

Dreams and Society

MONTAGUE ULLMAN, M.D.

The relationship between the private lives of individual members of a society as revealed in their dreams and the overt and covert nature of that society is an intriguing subject. Cultural anthropologists have had a go at it in their studies of primitive and preliterate societies but have hardly gone very far in exploring how the fallout from modern industrial societies shapes the dream images of their citizens. This chapter suggests one possible approach through noting and understanding the appearance in dreams of images that betray the existence of social stereotypes characteristic of a particular society. Were greater attention paid to imagery of this kind, the individual dreamer might gain a deeper awareness of the role such stereotypes play in his or her life. Through dreams we get at what the individual sweeps under the rug. Dreams may someday make us more sensitive to how societies do this as well.

The images that appear in our dreams speak to us of our most private concerns. They have much to tell us of the true nature of our encounters with others and with ourselves. They are particularly adept at pointing up distortions and deceits while being equally concerned with uncovering dormant resources and strengths. They derive from two sources, the natural world and the man-made world. We are familiar with the way these images are fashioned idiosyncratically to say something significant about the dreamer. Do they have something significant to say about the historically fashioned world in which we live?

Dreaming Consciousness

Dreaming consciousness can be looked upon as analogous to waking consciousness, but it uses metaphorical rather than discursive language. Using a different language, we are also saying different things. Awake, consciousness is influenced by an external reality and helps us find our way through that reality. Asleep and dreaming, we are temporarily disconnected from the world and begin to experience ourselves from a profoundly altered perspective. We forsake the logic of time and space that frames our waking life, replacing it with a historical view based on the emotional contiguity of past events. Asleep and dreaming, we move into the feeling dimension of our existence. The emotional residues that linger with us at the end of the day do so because of their connection to still unresolved issues in our life. Our feelings act as a kind of fluid matrix that connects present concerns to their roots in the past.

Dreaming consciousness may be looked upon as a steering mechanism that orients us to the future by offering both a wider and a more honest perspective on the current scene. Awake, our passions often chart a devious course for themselves. Far from being devious our dreams reflect this deviousness honestly. While dreaming we are not concerned with deceiving ourselves. We are concerned with showing, in no uncertain terms, that we are deceiving ourselves, if that be the case. The dream is a kind of emotional range finder that locates our deeply felt and true position amidst those influences, good and bad, known and unknown, that impinge on us from within and without. This is what makes their pursuit more than a game and more meaningful than fantasy.

To understand the essence of dreaming we have to consider the unique and versatile role of metaphor. While dreaming we seem to have turned all our resources into a metaphor-making operation. Whenever we find ourselves in the REM* stage of sleep, we come upon a spontaneously generated flow of visual

*Rapid eye movement or dreaming phase of sleep.

metaphor. In some way we have transformed a primitive imaging capacity, that ability to reproduce pictures inside our heads, into an emotionally expressive language. Metaphor is more than a figure of speech. It goes right to the heart of whatever it is we mean when we speak of creativity. It seems to be a way of moving into new and unexplored areas, cloaking them with analogous, original, and sometimes fantastic creations. It is a vehicle that helps us absorb the emotional thrust of new experience. An original metaphor (live, as contrasted to a dead one) is a leap into the mysterious.

The Dream and Society

Cultural anthropologists have long viewed dreams as useful instruments for studying the mores and value systems of exotic cultures. Logically, they should be as useful in the examination of our own society. Social in origin, our dream imagery has an intrinsic bidirectionality that points inwardly to the innermost and often hidden aspects of our personal being and outwardly to the source of their origin and to their possible connection to prevailing social realities that otherwise tend to be obscured from view. Just as dream work in the ordinary sense brings into consciousness what has not been understood or truly felt, so something analogous may be occurring in connection with what has in other contexts been referred to as our social unconscious (Fromm). I use the term to refer to all what we do not let ourselves see of the emotional fallout from the social arrangements and institutions about us.

There is no simple way to relate social issues to dreaming consciousness. As socially and culturally conditioned beings, we have to a large extent created our own environment. The pictures that appear in our dreams arise from the infinite wealth of material available to us because of our historical past. We refashion them to suit our personal needs, but they are there for us because we exist as social beings. Borrowed, as it were, from society, do the images maintain significant connections to society? Can the dream be looked upon as a societal as well as a self-confrontation? What can the images reveal of our social support systems and the social dangers linked to that system?

Dreams provide an admirable instrument for unmasking personal myth, that is, the self-deceptive processes that operate to blind or distort the individual's view of himself as an actor in society. When understood, the result is an enhanced consciousness of one's self. The question we are exploring begins where that process leaves off. Can we go back to the dream and get beyond the personal micromyth to the social or macromyth? Can the dream's capacity for truth help us identify those aspects of society that interfere with our connections to significant others, as well as to ourselves, and our potential for self-realization?

The bidirectionality of dream imagery is best illustrated by the appearance in the dream of social stereotypes such as portraying a black man as a rapist or a female as a cow playing out a domesticated role. Images of this sort have a dynamic aspect in their meaning both for the dreamer and for the society that gave rise to the image. Exploited by the dream in attempting to resolve a conflict the stereotype is further enhanced. A mutually reinforcing influence is at work. Through the use of metaphor such imagery tells us something about the unsolved problems both of the dreamer and of society. By clarifying the role that social stereotypes play in our dreams and by seeing the way that socially derived biases and prejudices influence our lives, we shift some aspects of our social unconscious into the realm of social consciousness. Where we go from there will be determined by many factors. The point is that, through dream work, we have the opportunity to position ourselves more honestly vis-à-vis some of the social realities we face.

The other indication of this bidirectionality is the appearance in dreams of images that reduce natural human attributes to the status of objects that can be manipulated and made available in the marketplace much as any ordinary commodity. Often this takes the form of depicting sexual organs as objects, hollow or pointed and dissociated from any truly human context. Appearances, that is, the beauty of women and the macho look of men, sell everything from cars to cigarettes. Dream images that are derived in this way reflect forces at work in the larger social scene that are both subtle and strident in their dehumanizing impact.

Example: A woman in her late thirties is about to embark on a new relationship with a man. She senses some hesitancy on her part and has a dream that displays the roots of her ambivalence. At one point in the dream she sees her father sitting on a swing with four female relatives in their heyday, dressed like cancan girls. What emerged from the work on the dream were two powerful images that surfaced from childhood to influence the dreamer's approach to a new relationship. One was that of the male, derived from the image of her father as privileged to flirt and become involved with other women. The other, that of the female victimized by the profligate male, was her mother. These are images the dreamer still struggles with but, in a larger sense, they relate to the residues of sexism, a social issue not yet disposed of. The privileged male and the victimized female are still available social stereotypes.

Our dreams usually focus on the psychological dimension of our lives. In the following dream of a professional woman living in the north of Sweden there is an interesting interplay of the biological, the psychological, and the social.

"There is a man in my dream who seems to be a combination of my husband, Bengt, and Per, a man I was with as an activist in the sixties. He is lecturing to a group of medical students. He is talking in a spontaneous and vivid way as well as demonstrating by very simple movements of his thumb what he means. He holds both hands up and keeps flexing and unflexing his thumbs. Then he makes all the students stand up and do this exercise. When they stop different things begin to happen in the group. He then explains the physiology of what is happening.

"Then the lecture ends, and I am alone in the room but the exercise stays with me. I write down the entire lecture. It is as if, by doing that, it acquires a whole new dimension. It is transformed from being a medical phenomenon illustrating bodily reactions to a more generalized kind of understanding of the nature of fascism. I have acquired a new understanding of why fascism spreads and have learned something more about the oppression of women, the existence of self-destructive impulses, and why they have such vitality.

"The lecturer had indicated that the more you move your body in the way he indicated the more kinetic energy is developed, this being a form of aggressiveness in a positive sense. The exercise he had given the students resulted in the kinetic energy being handled in different ways. Some of the students expressed it directly by engaging in small playful fights. Others made only a slight gesture by touching their right shoulder with their left hand. These students were suppressing the energy so that only traces of it appeared in their gesture. The lecturer had then asked the students about the way they experienced the exercise. They were to rate their reactions on a scale of 1 to 5. A systematic difference emerged from this. Those students who were concerned about the social context and who felt that letting out the impulses would not be constructive for that context suppressed this energy. They rated the experience very low. Those who let it out without concern for the social context rated the experience very high.

"As I wrote the lecture down and began to think about it, it suddenly occurred to me that this experiment explains the victory of fascism. Those who live out these aggressive impulses without concern for the social fabric feel better and grow stronger. Fascism is simply the system under which these impulses can be acted out legitimately and freely. On the other hand those with a sense of responsibility for the social context are more discontent, become weaker, and are finally swept aside as the others inevitably win control. The society they strive for is not able to survive.

"In the dream I also felt I understood more about the male-female problem. Women, being suppressed, are made unfit for life. I became aware of the self-destructiveness that results when the aggressive impulses are turned against the self. At the end, however, I realize that, in spite of this happening, it will be better in the end and will ultimately bring me more strength and power when I no longer need to hold them back."

This dream was presented in a group and the process described in Chapter 1 then unfolded. After the group had offered their projections and the dream was returned to the dreamer she then responded:

"I awoke from this dream feeling both relieved, as if I had discovered something, and also very sad. In the dream I had the very strong feeling of coming close to the way things are in the world—how something like the murder of Olaf Palme could occur. That filled me with a sadness and anger I felt in my body. Per and I were lovers in the sixties, and we had worked together in the movement. We were very much against the signs of American aggression. Per's reappearance in my dream is connected with my thoughts about the murder of Olaf Palme. Was the CIA involved? Were they trying to create unrest? Palme was a very powerful spokesman for the oppressed and for that reason may have been thought of as a threat. Why is it that those responsible for world affairs create situations that are so disastrous for the common people? In the dream I realize this is the nature of the way mankind has developed and it has come to the point where it may no longer survive. Why is it that what is constructive is not viable and what is viable is not constructive? Psychiatry teaches us to let our impulses out, which is the reverse of what I say will make for survival in the dream.

"When I awoke from this dream I felt it was important to remember it. What was strange about it was that it seemed more like a lecture than a dream. In thinking about the context I had this dream the night of the last day of a one-week stay at a convalescent home. Being there made me even more sick. The food didn't agree with me and I lost 4½ kilos in weight. I had headaches, insomnia, and nightmares and discovered that my blood pressure became very high. It was only on the last day that I began to feel better. I had gone there because I had been so sick all winter.

"I felt very isolated and miserable at this home. I had forgotten my eyeglasses and couldn't read, and reading to me is like an addiction.

"A research project that I have been on for a year was also on my mind. I had been given time from my job to do this project, and where I work time is a very scarce commodity. I was too ill to make any progress with the research. It was at a standstill. I felt I wasn't using the time properly.

"Then I suddenly thought of where that strange movement of the thumb came from. I had been to many doctors but none took my symptoms seriously until I came to Dr. K. He was sympathetic and investigated all my complaints thoroughly. For the first time I felt someone was really listening to me in an understanding and respectful way. One of the tests he had me do was exactly the thumb movement shown in my dream.

"The way the man in the dream lectured was also very much

like the vivid and dramatic style of Bengt, which I admire very much. I would like to say important things to people in such a vital way. I have worked with these men in the movement against the war in Vietnam, and I have also been active in the struggle against the abuse of women.

"What brought me to this convalescent home was the self-destructiveness I refer to in the dream. Yet, as in the dream, it comes out of something healthy and this represents a contradiction for me that is hard to resolve. The problem is how to mold destructive impulses so as to put them to good use, to allow them to gain expression without harming the social context so that, as they come out, they would be good for both society and the individual. In the dream it was a kind of insight that this was not possible but that the realization of this impossibility might be the useful beginning of some kind of process. Listening to the lecture, taking part in what was going on, was a good feeling. I also liked my writing it down and working on it. That was very important to me. It was my way of doing things. It was different from the way Bengt and Per did things but it was no less effective. The dream is telling me that different kinds of contributions are necessary and that I can be satisfied with mine. Bengt and Per are both nourishing men and both gave me a lot and now I have the feeling I am putting it to good use. I don't have to create out of nothing. I can use the good things I have gotten from others.

"On awakening I had the feeling of having made an important discovery. It almost made me feel embarrassed. I had feelings of both satisfaction and guilt. I even felt afraid to present this dream to the group for fear something would be harmed, that in some way it would be turned into its opposite."

At the end of this rather moving and lengthy response the dreamer expressed the need for more help with the dream and invited the group to engage in the dialogue.

Before any questions could be asked the dreamer herself began to talk more about her feelings around the time of the dream.

"The time at the convalescent home was a kind of breathing space. We had canceled a family trip because I wasn't feeling well. For the week I was away I had no contact with the outside world. The dream group was on my mind. We were very in-volved in making the arrangements for it. While I was at the home it was such a relief being among simple, common, working people. It was so different from the usual academic atmosphere around me. It felt good. There was a kind of natural warmth and a genuine, alive interest in each other. It made me aware of how worn out I felt by the limited contact that exists among my colleagues. The people I was with that week were content just be-ing and living day to day. Being with them was like being in a healing atmosphere.

"Not being able to read, of course, was a problem. Reading is a kind of passion with me. I was touched by the atmosphere of the place as well as relieved at getting rid of the usual poisons I take into my body—coffee, sweets, and the like. The sudden change in my life-style produced an abstinence syndrome. I felt stressed and my blood pressure shot up. When that was discovered I was 'sick-written,'* and that relieved my conscience about taking time off.

"I thought about your (M.U.) coming back for this dream group work. I usually have a dream when I'm preparing for the workshop. But this time I didn't want to have one. I had been working too hard and felt worn out. And the problem with my research was stressing me.

"My dream seems to be pointing out how strong are the self-destructive forces in myself. The dream also seems to be saying that, although they win in the short run, they lose in the long run."

The dreamer was then asked if she could say more about the double image represented by the man.

"They are people I love and have loved. Both have touched my heart. Per is always connected to my concern with the condi-tion of the world. It may also refer to Monte who touched my heart. It was the combination of the lecture, the phenomena manifesting themselves, and my pondering about them after-ward that seemed so important. I liked what Monte said last night. In dream work we work not only for ourselves but also for our species."

---

*Permission given to remain away from work for medical reasons.

The dreamer was asked about the arm-to-shoulder gesture.

"I wouldn't have noticed the gesture until the lecturer pointed it out. It had no meaning for me."

She was asked if there was anything more she could say about the thumb movement.

"I was so touched by Dr. K. taking me seriously. I have been to many other doctors who hadn't taken me seriously. He made a thorough investigation and found a basis for further diagnostic exploration."

The following orchestrating projection evolved out of the dream work:

"At the time you entered the convalescent home you were in a state of despair, both physically and emotionally. It was only on the last day of your stay at the home, a time when you were beginning to feel better, when hope was again entering your life, that you were able to create a dream in which you searched out the root causes of your despair. The result was a heroic effort on your part to explore the connections between what you were going through personally, physically, and psychologically and the way you were experiencing what was going on in the world around you. The clarification of these connections comes through the words you put into the mouth of the lecturer and your pondering over them. They seemed to provide you with an answer that was very important to you, namely, how bodily distress and psychological despair derive from choices made with regard to concern over the social context. When that concern is absent the anarchic play of the energies released moves in the direction of fascism and the ultimate dissolution of the social fabric. For those with a concern for the social context the energies have gained expression in self-destructive ways. Just as you felt yourself moving to a state of paralysis physically, as you felt stalemated in your research work, the recent events in the world, specifically the bombing of Libya and the atomic explosion in the USSR, conveyed a message of hopelessness about the world at large. Your dream places this despair in its proper context. There is cause for despair in the short run, but there is hope in the long run. Your physical recovery and the regeneration of your faith in the common man provided the basis for this hope.

That hope was also sparked by the respectful concern shown you by the one doctor who really listened to you. This validation of your worth as an individual is the most powerful weapon you can have in the struggle against destructive forces that are coming at you from without and within. This is even more important when it seems as though the external destructive forces are on the move and are invincible. Perhaps that strange little movement of the thumb can take on added significance in this connection. It is a very small movement but it is movement and that is the important thing. It is movement out of the state of paralysis."

The dream plays out a counterpoint between social hopelessness and personal hopelessness on the one hand and social and personal hope on the other. As long as there is a sense of personal paralysis there is a sense of social paralysis. An important point in the dream is the scene where the dreamer has written down the lecture and is pondering about it. This is her style, her way, and she is satisfied with it. It is not the same as Bengt or Per, but it is her own. The sense of insight this gives her, although it recognizes the "impossibility" of changing the social context in any immediate way, provides her, at the same time, with a basis of hope for the future. Contributing to this hope, even laying the groundwork for it, was her physical improvement and her interaction with the people about her at the home that revived her faith in the goodness and strength of the ordinary person.

The context for this dream has to be understood. It occurred at the time of the Soviet nuclear mishap and the murder of Olaf Palme, and when the U.S. invasion of Libya was still a live issue. These events have to be looked at from the point of view of the Swedes who, despite their very strong negative reactions, felt helpless and frustrated in the face of all three events.

She awoke with a feeling of discovery and relief. It was as if an oppressive weight had lifted. In part it had to do with the realization that it was not up to her alone to come up with a solution, but that she could take what was valuable from others in her effort to keep alive her hope for a better world. She was feeling the support she was receiving at the physical, psychological, and social levels. Just as the body could get rid of the poisons that harmed it, so could the social organism—even in the face of what seemed most impossible. Reparative mechanisms were set in motion, undermining the congruence between personal and social despair.

Social and Personal Disorder

We are not only individuals—we also are part of a vast continuum held together by mutual needs, by feelings, and by biological necessities. We live and move as part of the whole of our society, our culture, our species. All our lives we are subject to complex social forces which, at best, are only partially understood. We all possess social blinders that screen out or distort those aspects of the social scene which we prefer to dismiss or separate from ourselves. Consider Nazi Germany where so many people kept their distance from what was going on. The fact is, of course, that these forces leave their mark on each of us despite our limited or distorted vision. That mark is often at odds with the aspirations and potential inherent in human nature.

To the extent that social arrangements foster biased or distorted views they are inevitably internalized by its members in the course of their development. We incorporate the resultant disorder within our own psychological-biological processes. However, to make contact with the disorder and to recognize the social myths that envelop us in so camouflaged a manner, we must somehow adopt a position from which our customary milieu can be viewed against a different background. From such an altered frame of reference we may sense the existence of a social aberration or impediment which, under ordinary circumstances, feels natural and "right" and goes unrecognized. The dream is one resource that can offer this different perspective. If there exists within each of us and within society as a whole, as I believe there does, an uncorrupted core of being, there is an opportunity in the private, penetratingly honest world of the dream for this innate, basic mode to assert itself. For this to take on meaning in our lives requires some understanding of how personal and social disorders interweave and interpenetrate.

When emotional problems endure they do so because of their congruence with prevailing social values and because of the absence of countervailing social influences. A neurotic trend to endure must be experienced as reinforced, implicitly or explicitly, by the social field surrounding the individual. When a social field offers resistance to its operation it creates the opportunity for the emergence and strengthening of healthy trends. In our striving for wholeness and self-realization our perceptual apparatus constantly registers, whether we are conscious of it or not, the neurosis-reinforcing or health-evoking aspects of our social milieu.

Our dream images are self-confrontational constructs. They call attention to hidden assumptions about ourselves that some recent event capriciously uncovers. The image selected or created to serve this purpose is often one which, in exposing the personal dynamics involved, also provides us with clues as to the neurosis-reinforcing and health-evoking qualities of the social field related to the particular predicament we are dreaming about. To investigate this involves the shift from a concern with the vicissitudes of an individual's struggle with the strictures imposed by the socializing process itself to a concern with the individual vis-à-vis a historically determined but currently existing and specifically identifiable social structure. Fromm is one of the few analysts who has taken this route, but he has had few followers, and certainly the implications for our concept of dreaming have not yet been spelled out.

The private myth or micromyth highlighted in the dream often gains expression by attracting to itself images drawn from experience that carry a congruent social or macromythic valence. This fact generally escapes notice because we are not in the habit of extrapolating from the dream image to the social reality that lies beyond. Both forms of myth are highly resistive to change. In the case of the individual micromyth the distortions and limitations of the waking ego have to be overcome. The personal myth embodied in the dream does not respond to interpretation but to the socializing practice of dream appreciation wherein the emotional thrust of the dream becomes recognized by the waking or social self. It is this process of engagement with one's feelings in a supportive and cooperative milieu that makes for change. While the personal myth doesn't vanish, it is restructured so as to encompass the newly recognized aspects of the self more accurately.

Dream work involves the transformation of an experience felt under conditions of temporary suspension of the social self into a communication meaningful to the social self. The process is difficult, uneven, troublesome, but infinitely rewarding. It is more than the negative process of ferreting out personal foibles and hypocrisies. It becomes a treasure hunt where one can discover an unsuspected quarry of human virtues. Our capacities for concern, courage, tenderness, and so forth confront us in our dreams, waiting to be recognized and validated by our social self. Paradoxically, it is often our obtuseness to the existence and strength of these virtues that serves to perpetuate the very myths that get us into psychological and emotional difficulty.

When the dream image points to problem areas at a more broadly social level, dream work takes a different turn. When individual meaning is pursued the dreamer moves closer to the resolution of the issue. When the focus shifts to the social meaning of the image, we are faced with a somewhat more complex task than if we were to concern ourselves only with the personal meaning. Our dreams then take us beyond the personal unconscious and into the realm of the social unconscious. A two-step process takes shape. First, the particular predicament can be seen with greater objectivity once the broader social perspective comes into view. There results greater responsibility for whatever the issue may be. This approach highlights what Bastide describes as the use of the dream as a disposal system for social garbage. He is referring to the way certain tension-generating issues that are primarily social in origin are experienced as personal and private. This privatization of what may be regarded as social waste products serves society. In Sweden, for example, the economic pressure on young women to pursue dual careers as working mothers is greater than in the United States. This is reflected in dreams by feelings of personal guilt associated with the necessity to leave very young children in day-care centers and going off to work.

This is not to say that the dream confronts us with social issues explicitly but, rather, that the emotional fallout registers subjectively, and this is what the dream image objectifies. This pertains to both the good and bad impact of social arrangements, although it is the latter that gives us trouble. Allowing ourselves to be confronted not only by the personal but also by the social referents of the dream can lead us to a deeper understanding of society.

The second step referred to above concerns the course of action once social insight occurs. Dream work in the ordinary sense helps people to modulate their behavior. In the framework of this added social dimension the element of social concern comes into the picture, and here effective action takes a collective form and is directed toward modulating the behavior of others as well as ourselves. We become involved in issues that go beyond what the individual can do as an individual. Solutions to social problems require concerted social action. Dream work helps us to see and feel the constraints and pain that come from trying to fit human needs into somewhat less than human containers. It can set the stage for some form of action. What then follows depends on the interest and degree of social concern of the dreamer. It is important to bear in mind that, just as personal insight is a consequence of work done against defensive resistance, social insight also requires work against resistance. Not everyone will find it easy to relate to this dimension of dream work. For those who do there are many possible paths into this territory, so that anyone who is interested can find one that is congenial to his or her own style and interests. We can move into the realm of the social unconscious through social science, politics, psychology, the arts, and so on. The important thing is the awareness that there is territory to be explored.

We come now to a rather interesting question of why it is that society as we know it, so-called civilized society, has been so neglectful of dreams. Attesting to the truth of Bastide's thesis is the generally derogatory attitude toward dreams that exists in civilized societies. I have referred to this bias as "dreamism" (Ullman & Zimmerman), and like all "isms" of that kind it connotes a prejudicial attitude. It serves as a defensive maneuver that protects society against the social truths that are apt to emerge if the social relevance were to be given its just due. The only socially sanctioned use of dreams is its use in formal therapy or in laboratory research, neither of which touches more than a small part of the dreamer's world. Neglecting this most honest, reliable, and available way of monitoring our subjectivity, we have gone somewhat astray. Were we more attentive through our dreams to the negative emotional fallout from some of the social arrangements we have been heir to, we might move to greater unity instead of tolerating and fostering the level of divisiveness that now characterizes the nations of the world. In our dreams we share similar basic concerns. If dream work developed on a large scale, might we then become more tolerant and more accepting of differences?

From my experience in group dream work I am convinced of the high price we pay for this neglect. Dream work is a natural avenue for unloading personal secrets and moving toward greater personal freedom. This universal need is not met in our society except in a limited fashion in the client-therapist situation. The need is not only not met but is generally not even recognized as a need. This might also be said of society as a whole. Society has not recognized the need to have a view of itself from outside its usual perspective. This is what the dream does for the individual and, because of the bidirectionality of the dream metaphors, what it can do for society as well.

Summary

The images we make use of in our dreams are social in origin even though they are idiosyncratically transformed for our personal use. Some of these images are bidirectional; that is, they have something to say about the unsolved problems of society just as they do about the unsolved problems of the individual. Looked at in this way they are pointers toward some of the negative or limiting aspects of society and indicate the way that social arrangements support and sustain the individual. Dreams have a connection to the social scene that is worth exploring. Social insight derived from dream work can deepen social concern and provide an impetus in the struggle against constraining social influences.

References

Bastide, R. "The Sociology of the Dream," in Von Grunebaum, G. E., and Caillois, R., eds., *The Dream and Human Societies*. Los Angeles: University of California Press, 1966.

Fromm, E. *The Sane Society*. New York: Holt, Rinehart and Winston, 1955.

Ullman, M., and Zimmerman, N. *Working With Dreams*. Los Angeles: Jeremy P. Tarcher, Inc., 1979.

Contributing Authors

JOHN BRIGGS, PH.D., teaches on the faculties of The New School for Social Research and Mercy College. He is co-author of *Looking Glass Universe* (Simon and Schuster, 1984) and *The Logic of Poetry* (McGraw-Hill, 1974). He has a book forthcoming with St. Martin's Press on creative genius and is co-authoring a book on chaos for Harper & Row. His poems, stories, articles, and criticism have appeared in *New American Poetry* (McGraw-Hill, 1972); *The Craft of Poetry* (Doubleday, 1974); *Science Digest; Northwest Review; The Iowa Review; Prairie Schooner; The Hartford Courant; Artnews,* and others. He has been managing editor of *New York Quarterly* and *The Academy* (American Academy of Psychoanalysis). He was host of the WNYC-FM radio show, "The Logic of Poetry."

JENNY DODD was born in Kent, England. Her grandmother was a psychoanalyst, and her mother is a psychotherapist. Ever since she can remember, dreams and the psyche have been an integral part of her life. She was graduated from Edinburgh University with a Bachelor in Music degree and subsequently spent several years training and working in the field of music therapy and music teaching. Since 1981 she has lived in Long Island, New York. Apart from the full-time job of raising three children, she has developed an enthusiastic interest in dream work and is currently leading two experiential dream groups.

PAUL H. ELOVITZ, PH.D., a psychohistorian and psychotherapist, is the Founder and Director of the Psychohistory Forum, a Research Associate of the Institute for Psychohistory, and an active member of the International Psychohistorical Association. After teaching at Temple, Rutgers, and Fairleigh Dickinson universities, in 1971 he became a founding faculty member at Ramapo College, an innovative, interdisciplinary four-year liberal-arts school in northern New Jersey. Aside from dreams his primary research interest is in the process of creativity and innovation. He is a contributing editor of *The Journal of Psychohistory* and author of "Science, Magic and Death in the Thought of Sir Humphry Davy," "Teaching Psychohistory," "Three Days in Plains," "On Doing Fantasy Analysis" (with Lawton and Luhrmann), etc. Currently, he is writing *Historical and Experiential Dreamwork: A New Methodology Applied to the Dreams of Alexander Graham Bell, Alexander the Great, Bismarck, Darwin, Davy, Freud, Trotsky and Xenophon*. He conducts dream groups in New Jersey, New York, and Philadelphia.

HELENE FAGIN, PH.D., is a psychiatric social worker and psychoanalyst in private practice in Westchester County, New York. She earned her doctorate in psychology from the Union Graduate School, exploring the relationship between dreams and the creative process. Her research project focused on an experiential dream group of artists with whom she worked over a period of a year, recording their subjective evaluations of the experience and any changes in their work. She has given courses and workshops on dreams privately in the community in which she lives as well as for the Mental Health Association and the State University of New York at Purchase. She has also conducted workshops for professionals throughout the United States and in Canada for the American Group Psychotherapy Association.

DEBORAH JAY HILLMAN, M.A., is completing her doctorate in anthropology from the Graduate Faculty of the New School for Social Research. Her interests include transpersonal anthropology, gender, dreams, and aging. In addition to the field study described in her article, she has conducted ethnographic research on an urban program using older volunteers as caregivers to their isolated and homebound peers. Active in the movement to make the American public more aware of dreams, she has served as a contributing editor of *The Dream Network Bulletin*. She has kept a dream journal for many years and particularly enjoys paying attention to the playful, artistic, and spiritual dimensions of dreams.

J. DONALD HUGHES, PH.D., is Professor of History at the University of Denver and Visiting Professor of History at the University of Colorado, Boulder. He teaches ancient history, environmental history, and psychohistory. He is the author of books and articles including "The Dreams of Alexander the Great" in the *Journal of Psychohistory* (vol. 12, Fall 1984). He is presently writing a book on ancient dreams. A graduate of the University of California at Los Angeles, he received a Ph.D. in history from Boston University. He was the recipient of the Burlington Northern Award as outstanding faculty scholar at the University of Denver in 1985, based in large part on his work in psychohistory. He is a trustee of the Carl G. Jung Society of Colorado and a member of the International Psychohistorical Association.

RICHARD M. JONES, PH.D., received his B.A. from Stanford University in 1950 and his Ph.D. from Harvard University in 1956. He has served on the faculties of Brandeis University, the University of California at Santa Cruz, and Harvard University. In 1970 he joined the planning faculty of The Evergreen State College in Olympia, Washington, where he now serves as Professor of Psychology. He is the author of *Ego Synthesis in Dreams, The New Psychology of Dreaming,* and *The Dream Poet.* He is currently working on a manuscript, *Dream and Metaphor.*

SUSAN KNAPP, PH.D., is a faculty member and supervisor at the Postgraduate Center for Mental Health and at the National Institute for the Psychotherapies. She has a private practice in psychoanalysis and psychoanalytically oriented psychotherapy. Her publications include "Dreaming: Horney, Kelman and Shainberg" in *Handbook of Dreams: Research, Theories and Applications,* Benjamin B. Wolman, Wilse B. Webb, and Montague Ullman, eds. (Van Nostrand Reinhold Company, 1979), and *Contemporary Theories and Systems in Psychology,* Benjamin B. Wolman in collaboration with Susan Knapp, eds. (Plenum Publishing Corporation, 1981).

CLAIRE LIMMER, M.S., teaches at a children's psychiatric hospital in New York City and is a psychotherapist in private practice. Over the years she has worked with dreams from several viewpoints—as a member of an ongoing dream group, as an analytic patient bringing the fruits of group dream work to her own training analysis, as a therapist working with the dreams of patients, and as the leader of experiential dream groups in her home community and at conference centers. Most recently, her interest has focused on the role of dream work in the psychosomatic process. She is a member-in-training at the National Psychological Association for Psychoanalysis and an associate member of the National Association for the Advancement of Psychoanalysis. She has recently completed a manuscript, *Legacy of Dreams.*

EDWARD F. STORM, PH.D., is Professor of Computer and Information Science at Syracuse University. He took his undergraduate degree in mathematics and physics at the University of Delaware and received his

Ph.D. in applied mathematics from Harvard University. His technical research interests include programming languages, the foundations of computation, and the teaching of computer science. His general research interests are in the nature of computation, the possibility of naturally occurring computations in physical, biological, and mental systems, and in the formal structures underlying human capacities for language, for music, and for dreaming. He is a member of the Association for Computing Machinery and the American Society for Psychical Research.

MONTAGUE ULLMAN, M.D., is a psychiatrist and psychoanalyst who founded the Dream Laboratory at the Maimonides Medical Center, Brooklyn, New York. In the course of his career he has been interested in dreams from physiological, psychological, sociological, and parapsychological perspectives. These various aspects came together in shaping the group work he has done with dreams over the past decade, both in this country and in Scandinavia. He is currently Clinical Professor of Psychiatry Emeritus at Albert Einstein College of Medicine, a Life Fellow of the American Psychiatric Association, and a Life Member of the Society of Medical Psychoanalysts. With Nan Zimmerman he is co-author of *Working With Dreams* (Jeremy P. Tarcher, Inc., 1979) and the author of numerous other publications on the subject.

JOHN A. WALSH, D. MIN. is currently a staff psychotherapist at the House of Affirmation, Clearwater, Florida. His doctoral studies are in the area of the relationship between psychology and religion, and specifically in the understanding and interpretation of dream experiences as a ministerial focus. He is a graduate of Aquinas Institute, St. Louis, Missouri, with a doctorate in ministry, and a graduate of Marywood College, Scranton, Pennsylvania, with a master of arts degree in psychology. He is an ordained Catholic priest of the Diocese of Scranton, Pennsylvania.

JOHN R. WIKSE, PH.D., is currently Associate Academic Dean of Shimer College, Waukegan, Illinois. He first became interested in dreams in the late 1960s while a graduate student at the University of California at Berkeley, where he was studying political theory and psychology. Influenced by Perls, R. D. Laing, Gandhi, and Marx, he started thinking about the relationship between therapy and revolution in order to evaluate the civil rebellion occurring around him. Influenced by the Reichian renaissance, the beginnings of men's and women's liberation groups during the end of the antiwar movement, and the increasing complexity and self-consciousness of "relationships" of that time, he began to perceive that dreams were useful counsel. He left California in 1971 to teach at Pennsylvania State University and published *About Possession: The Self as Private Property* (Pennsylvania State University Press, 1977). During these years he became acquainted with the work of Trigant Burrow, and, under the auspices of the Lifwynn Foundation, met and worked with Montague Ullman, who encouraged him to appreciate his dreams and understand them as social information.

NAN ZIMMERMAN is a writer, musician, and teacher. Her interest in dreams became focused in 1960 when she began keeping a journal. This journal became the seedbed for later work with Montague Ullman with whom she collaborated to write *Working With Dreams* (Jeremy P. Tarcher, Inc., 1979), now published in seven foreign countries. Through her association with Dr. Ullman, she recognized that understanding dreams was a natural, organic process. She has led many workshops based on the premise that anyone can learn to work creatively with their own dreams if given certain skills and support. She is a graduate of The College of William and Mary. In addition to teaching piano and dream work, she is currently writing two books. One is a children's novel, and the other is a book on the contributions of literature and related resources to the healing process of working with dreams.

Copyright Acknowledgements

The authors are grateful for permission to quote from the following previously published works:

Excerpt from *The Emerging Goddess* by A. Rothenberg. Reprinted by permission of The University of Chicago Press.

Excerpt from *Imagination* by Harold Rugg. Copyright © 1963 by Elizabeth Rugg. Reprinted by permission of Harper & Row, Publishers, Inc.

Excerpt from *Memories, Dreams, Reflections* by C.G. Jung. Copyright © 1961, 1962, 1963 Random House, Inc. Recorded by Aniela Jaffe and translated by Richard and Clara Winston. Reprinted by permission of Random House, Inc.

From pages 24–25 in *Wishful Thinking: A Theological ABC* by Frederick Buechner. Copyright © 1973 by Frederick Buechner. Reprinted by permission of Harper & Row, Publishers, Inc.

Reprinted with permission of Macmillan Publishing Company from *The Way of All the Earth* by John Dunne. Copyright © 1972 by John F. Dunne, C.S.C.; and Society for Promoting Christian Knowledge.

From *The Poetry of Robert Frost* edited by Edward Connery Latham, 1916, Copyright © 1969 by Holt Rinehart & Winston. Copyright 1944 by Robert Frost. Reprinted by permission of Henry Holt and Company, and the Estate of Robert Frost.

Excerpt from *Metaphysics in Midwestern America* by Melina Bollar Wagner (Columbus: Ohio State University Press, 1983), p. iv.

Excerpt from *Welcome to the Magic Theater* by Dick McLeester. Reprinted by permission of the author.

Excerpt from *Dream Work* by Jeremy Taylor. Copyright © 1983 by Jeremy Taylor. Used by permission of Paulist Press.